CULTURAL DIMENSIONS OF PLAY, GAMES, AND SPORT

Editor

Bernard Mergen, PhD
George Washington University

Human Kinetics Publishers, Inc.
Champaign, Illinois

Proceedings of the 10th annual meeting of The Association for
the Anthropological Study of Play (TAASP) held March 28-31,
1984, at Clemson University, Clemson, South Carolina.

Library of Congress Cataloging-in-Publication Data

Cultural dimensions of play, games, and sport.

  (The Association for the Anthropological Study
of Play, ISSN 0885-8764; v. 10)
  Papers presented at the 10th annual meeting of
The Association for the Anthropological Study of
Play held in Clemson, South Carolina.
  Bibliography: p.
  1. Play—Congresses.   2. Games—Congresses.
3. Sports—Congresses.   I. Mergen, Bernard.
II. Association for the Anthropological Study of
Play. III. Series: Association for the Anthropological
Study of Play (Series); v. 10.
GN454.C85 1986   306′ .48   86-10563

Developmental Editor: Patricia Sammann
Copy Editor: Alison Ransdell
Production Director: Ernie Noa
Assistant Production Director: Lezli Harris
Typesetter: Yvonne Winsor
Text Layout: Janet Davenport
Cover Design and Layout: Jack Davis
Printed by: Braun-Brumfield

ISBN: 0-87322-078-1
ISSN: 0885-8764

Copyright © 1986 by Human Kinetics Publishers, Inc.

Printed in the United States of America

10 9 8 7 6 5 4 3 2 1

Human Kinetics Publishers, Inc.
Box 5076, Champaign, IL 61820

Contents

Preface

The papers in this volume illustrate once again the wide range of interests represented in the membership of The Association for the Anthropological Study of Play (TAASP). The Association is clearly a source of strength and creativity. For 10 years we have met, presented papers, and discussed the meanings of play. For a decade we have published the best of these papers and other essays submitted to the annual. Ten times we have identified themes to organize the miscellany of our study.

The theme of the 10th annual meeting, held in Clemson, South Carolina, in cooperation with the Clemson University Conference on Sport and Society and The North American Society for the Sociology of Sport, was "Cultural Dimensions of Play, Games, and Sport." The essays in this volume address this theme in various ways and from the perspectives of several disciplines. Many patterns of thought on play emerge in these papers, but each author expresses something of the pleasure of his or her discovery that play lurks in unsuspected corners of daily life. It is this discovery that will sustain TAASP in its next decade of exploration of play.

For their help in the preparation of this volume, I want to thank Linda Brandt, Bob Humphrey, Wid Washburn, Rainer Martens, and the staff of Human Kinetics Publishers. It has been a privilege to work with them and the contributors to *Cultural Dimensions of Play, Games, and Sport*.

Bernard Mergen

Descriptions of Play

Taken at face value, the papers in this section are, as the title of part I states, "descriptions" of play, but in each case the author's analysis has led to conceptual possibilities that go far beyond mere description. There is a sense in all the papers that social scientists can learn a great deal more about the behavior of our species from the play of children and adults than has been generally assumed until recently. The papers explore what Alyce Cheska (1981) calls "play's potential interpretive significance of self and society" (p. 7).

The thrust of the first paper, by Roberts and Enerstvedt, is methodological. Using a computer program to reveal hierarchical clustering and multidimensional scaling, the authors have attempted to gain meaningful insights into the categorizations of middle-childhood play in Norway from the viewpoint of children of both sexes. Apart from being an important addition to the growing literature on children's play in different cultural contexts, the study suggests that there are much broader uses for the data than the basically ethnographic.

The descriptions of Norwegian games and the attitudes of children toward them provide some fascinating cross-cultural material from a strictly ethnographic viewpoint, but it is the insightful approach to the boys' and girls' own perceptions of similarities and differences in the games that begins to reveal the deeper significance of the study. By using attributes assigned to the games by children of both sexes it becomes possible to better perceive the underlying cognitive and value systems in play, and the authors stress the importance of understanding cognition in children's games in order to use games for educational and even therapeutic purposes. Roberts and Enerstvedt seem to be aware of many of the problems inherent in this quantitative kind of approach. The fact that the differences perceived between attitudes of boys and girls are both interpretable and culturally meaningful, however, supports the use of their methodology. The success of the methodology rests in large part on the use of children as informants and, as the authors suggest, it would be desirable in future studies to elicit not only attitudes but also labels, names, and behaviors from the children themselves rather than using those arbitrarily assigned by social scientists.

The second paper in this section, by Stuart Reifel, takes a more impressionistic approach to the study of children's play. In this case the setting is the elementary school cafeteria, which turns out to be a marvelous place to look at the noninstitutionalized aspects of play within an institutional environment. Reifel's observations were made in three public school cafeterias in middle- and upper-middle-class neighborhoods among children in Grades K through 6. In this environment of high academic expectation and tight regimentation, there seemed to be little time for play. Indeed, the teachers, monitors, and other adults present perceived no play activity occurring until it was pointed out to them.

Like Roberts and Enerstvedt in the preceding article, Reifel makes a strong case for using children as informants. If those adults who are in contact with the children every day can overlook play behavior, one suspects that trained social scientists can also miss important examples of play unless they gain rapport with the participants. Reifel presents several examples of the children learning to use the unknowing adult cafeteria monitors as pawns in their games, working within the set rules in ways that were deliberately confusing to the adults.

The paper also raises some interesting questions. Although Reifel begins by suggesting that we might expect to find "a good deal of description of food" as in Opie and Opie's (1959) study of British children, he found that this was not the case. In my own early school experience, foods such as hot dogs, hamburgers, eggs of various consistencies, Jell-O, and so forth were discussed at great length and often in very colorful terms. I wonder if this kind of information, perhaps because of the forbidden vocabulary used to discuss it, is shared *only* by children with other children and is therefore not to be overheard by adult monitors, teachers, or visitors. It would also be fascinating to compare Reifel's observations of middle-class public schools with similar studies of upper-class private schools, lower-class inner-city schools, rural schools, and parochial schools. At any rate, the author ends with the encouraging observation that children's play can survive even the most drab and regimented setting adults can devise.

The third paper in part I, by Robert Horan, deals with play fighting at a state-operated residential treatment center for emotionally disturbed male adolescents. The author entered this community as an employee and found himself in that chronically difficult dual anthropological role of participant-observer, in which it often seems impossible to do justice to both. Horan gives an especially clear description of play fighting at Boys' Home, which at face value does not seem very different from the same kind of activity among "normal" adolescents. In this institutional setting, however, many of the functional aspects of play fighting become much more strikingly clear.

As the author points out, play fighting clearly functions as social as well as physical training. The activity seems closely tied to the establishment and maintenance of a status heirarchy that is particularly important in a circumscribed society like that of Boys' Home. Importantly, play fighting is also a *public* activity for a number of good, socially functional reasons: to ensure the safety of the players when an audible blow may turn play fighting into *real* fighting; to shock adult spectators, especially if they are strangers; and to downplay any sexual connotations the activity may have. As Horan points out, however, the most important function of play fighting seems to be to make the rank-ordering of society generally known and to train participants and spectators alike in the importance of knowing and understanding both the dominant and the submissive roles in this closed society.

Horan's analysis suggests that the network of dominance and submission behaviors is much more complicated and fluid than ordinarily thought and that play fighting operates as a learning process for the participants. In this aspect, Horan's study is reminiscent of some of the anthropological studies of nonhuman primate groups and of prison societies, where such equilibrating behaviors are an absolute necessity for survival. The necessity to establish and maintain relationships, to respond correctly in the status hierarchy, and to anticipate the needs of others is perhaps more keenly felt and more easily observed in a closed society like Boys' Home, but it reflects on a smaller scale the function of such behaviors in society as a whole. As the author points out, echoing similar feelings from the two preceding articles, it seems extraordinary that not one single staff member at Boys' Home had considered play fight behavior as anything more structured than "acting out" or "nuisance" behavior.

The final article in part I, by John R. Bowman, considers various forms of spontaneous speech play among adults. Bowman studies speech play in terms of its social setting, recognition, and context but is especially interested in its communication ingredients. In his particularly clear and concise discussion of the sociolinguistic aspects of play talk, Bowman gives humorous examples of how playfulness can occur at all four organizational levels of language, including phonology, morphology, syntax, and semantics.

Although this paper is set at the adult level, many of the word games described share the same social functions noted for play activity among children and adolescents in the previous articles. As in the school cafeteria or Boys' Home, play is introduced by the disruption or suspension of ordinary rules, in this case linguistic rules. The word games recounted by Bowman also have many of the social aspects of play fighting, but at the adult level. They establish and maintain certain social and emotional ties among a network of friends or a social class, and they can also function to reinforce a system of intellectual dominance and submission; dominance may be asserted by talking in more or better accents, being more linguistically innovative, having a more extensive vocabulary, or being faster on the uptake. Bowman suggests that the epitome of playful speech competition among adults is the dreaded pun, of which he gives several delightfully dreadful examples.

Although they encompass the whole human age range from child to adult, these papers strike a common chord. They are all concerned, through a study of the activities that we categorize as play, with achieving a better understanding of the processes of creativity, cognition, learning, and other complex facets of human culture that are difficult to perceive using the traditional ethnographic approach. It is clear that play can no longer be relegated to a minor chapter on the enculturation of children. The cognitive and perceptual abilities developed in play activity enable us to begin to relate to the ideas and feelings of other human beings and to conceptualize our relationships to society as an institution. As the papers in this chapter amply demonstrate, to relegate play to a minor role simply because it does not fit within the ordinary framework of cultural expression as perceived by social science is to ignore one of the most important human tools for learning and communication.

The papers in part I are all examples from contemporary Western societies, and as such most likely include a bias toward separating "play" from "learning," "communication," or "work" that may be less discernible in tribal societies. Nevertheless, the similarities in the form and function of children's play in the two worlds are striking, and it would be interesting to contrast, for example, the highly competitive categories of play identified by Norwegian children with those of a similar age group in a non-Western-European-oriented group.

Another theme that unites these papers is the clear understanding that children must be considered as reliable informants and that to examine the underlying behavioral ramifications of play we must consider them as such and elicit their cognitive input. As difficult as it can be to study directly, childhood is a critical time of life for the formation of adult values, and play is the major activity of that time period. We clearly need more controlled experimentation and rigorous methodology of the kind represented by the first paper in this part, but there is an equally vital need for naturalistic, impressionistic observation and consideration of the subjective cognition of the participants themselves.

One final element is common to these papers for which we should all be thankful. A streak of playfulness runs through all four papers that removes them from the realm of dry academic parlance and makes them *fun* to read. One of the beauties of the study of play is that nearly all of us have played, and when we did, it was *fun*. Papers like these make it much easier to identify the common, cross-cultural bond that ultimately defines the human community.

Robert L. Humphrey

References

Cheska, A.T. (Ed.). (1981). *Play as context*. West Point, NY: Leisure Press.

Opie, I., & Opie, P. (1959). *The lore and language of school children*. London: Oxford University Press.

CHAPTER 1

Categorizations of Play Activities by Norwegian Children

John M. Roberts
University of Pittsburgh

Åse Enerstvedt
Hordamuseet, Bergen, Norway

Children's play activities, particularly games, have often been categorized by adults, usually on the basis of some set of formal characteristic such as the game classification developed by Roberts, Arth, and Bush (1959). Such categorizations, however, have seldom been derived from the views of children. The few authors who have described classifications based on data elicited from children (e.g., von Glascoe, 1976) have dealt with smaller arrays than the 53 Norwegian play activities considered here. This paper represents a large-scale consideration of children's categorization.

This research offers an insight into the play categorizations of middle childhood in Norway. At the same time it permits an examination of the similarities and differences between the perspectives of girls and those of boys.

By now a discussion of the importance of studying children's play in different cultural contexts can be waived. Schwartzman's discussion, for example, of the work of Brewster, Howard, I. Opie, P. Opie, Sutton-Smith, and other scholarly pioneers attests to the significance of such research (Schwartzman, 1978). This limited case study from Norway will only add to the growing corpus of comparative material.

This study has its place within a larger, ongoing investigation of games and allied phenomena that began in 1959 (Roberts et al., 1959; Roberts & Chick, 1984). Similar quantitative techniques have been used in other studies of such games as pool (Roberts & Chick, 1979), trapshooting (Roberts & Nattrass, 1980), tennis (Roberts, Chick, Stephenson, & Hyde, 1981), and soccer (Roberts & Luxbacher, 1982). Unfortunately, the full scope of the general inquiry cannot be reviewed here, but Chick has discussed important aspects of it in his comprehensive review of the cross-cultural study of games (Chick, 1984).

This research also has its place in a long-term study of the play activities of Norwegian children. The junior author, Åse Enerstvedt, has persistently investigated the recreational activities of Norwegian children

(Enerstvedt, 1971a, 1971b, 1976, 1979, 1982, 1984). Indeed, this inquiry rests on her ethnographic expertise, for she developed the activity array used here and also conducted the field research in 1981 for this study with school children whose "recreational culture" she already understood.

Although this particular report deals with basic research, ultimately such inquiries may have larger implications. Today, games, both natural and artificial, are used for educational purposes in schools and elsewhere. It is important to know where such games fit in the world of the child and what understandings and motivations are associated with them if they are to be used insightfully and well.

In this exploratory research, pile sorts made by Norwegian girls and boys have been used to generate categories through the use of hierarchical clustering and multidimensional scaling. The child respondents were drawn from a single neighborhood in Oslo, Norway, but ethnographic research suggests that similar categories might well be found with samples from other Oslo neighborhoods. Although children aided in the naming of clusters and dimensions, these names are also based on conventional ethnographic knowledge. In fact this study is essentially a venture into the ethnography of Norwegian middle childhood.

The Research

In 1981 a true sampling design could not be implemented, but because the play activity culture appeared to be high in concordance for the children who knew it, it was held that available respondents could be used, at least at the level of an exploratory study. Certainly the results reported here appear to be in accord with the large ethnographic knowledge of this particular childhood culture.

Forty-seven girls and 31 boys engaged in the sorting tasks described below. In 1981 most of the children fell within an age span of 10 to 12 years with a modal birth year of 1970. The girls were born in 1969 ($n = 10$), 1970 ($n = 35$), and 1971 ($n = 2$). The boys were born in 1968 ($n = 1$), 1969 ($n = 10$), 1970 ($n = 19$), and 1971 ($n = 3$). The modal child lived in a block of flats, but some children lived in single and row houses. The girls resided in single houses ($n = 15$), row houses ($n = 11$), and blocks of flats ($n = 20$), with one residency undetermined. The boys resided in single houses ($n = 14$), row houses ($n = 9$), and blocks of flats ($n = 10$).

The occupations of some of the parents were determined ($n = 1$ except where otherwise specified). For the girls, the fathers' occupations were carpenter, charterer, civil engineer ($n = 2$), engineer, dentist ($n = 2$), designer (i.e., painter), doctor of medicine, marketing leader, marketing consultant, police inspector, printer, sales director, salesman, theater instructor, university teacher, and college teacher. The girls' mothers were primarily homemakers, with one bureau leader. For the boys, the fathers' occupations were consultant, director, assistant director, college professor, university teacher, designer, engineer, entrepreneur in heavy machinery, police inspector, sales consultant, secretary, and section leader. The boys' mothers were primarily homemakers, with one candidate in pharmacy.

The Oslo middle-childhood culture is rich in play activities. A full listing of these activities would have been much too long to permit the use of the pile sort technique, particularly with children who were only volunteering their time. Therefore a short list of 53 named activities was selected from the full array to illustrate the general range of activities. Only those activities were chosen that had familiar names within neighborhood childhood culture. These selected activities were varied enough to provide insight into the play activity categories characteristic of this particular childhood culture.

A full ethnographic description of each of the 53 activities could only be presented within the compass of a substantial monograph. Even acceptable summary descriptions of the activities would require too much space for this short paper. It is simply assumed that each reader will be sufficiently familiar with cognate play activities within his or her own culture to be able to recognize the activities from the brief descriptive entries offered in Table 1 (p. 12). There is a chance, however, that some of these brief entries may not be fully helpful, for the same activity may have different names elsewhere and sometimes a number of variants of any specific activity exist within the same culture.

A deck of 53 cards was created by writing the name of each activity in Norwegian on a card together with an identification number on the back. This deck was then thoroughly shuffled and given to a child respondent for sorting. Each sorter was treated individually, and other children were not allowed to watch or comment. The same oral instructions were given to each child. The children were told to deal the cards into piles based on the similarities they saw among the activities. Before the sorting began the children were allowed to look through the deck for as long as they liked. Later the children were also permitted to make as many changes in the sortings as they liked. Then the numbers of the cards in each pile were recorded for each respondent.

Each individual pile sort yielded a square 53 × 53 zero-one similarity matrix. The matrices were summed into single aggregate similarity matrices for the girls and for the boys. The similarities and differences between the two matrices were studied using the methodology of Nakao and Romney (1984). A quadratic assignment program (Hubert & Schultz, 1976) was used to compare and test the similarity of the two matrices. This program provides an index of association, the product moment distribution, along with the first two moments of a permutation distribution, allowing a normal distribution test. In studying the differences between the two matrices a method described by Hubert and Golledge (1981) was used. The data were standardized and then the girls' data were subtracted from the boys' data and compared with the boys' data. Any similarity can be interpreted as the unexplained part of the boys' data that is different from the girls' data.

The analysis of the two matrices followed the pioneering work of A. Kimball Romney (Romney, Shepard, & Nerlove, 1972; Shepard, Romney, & Nerlove, 1972) and Roy G. D'Andrade (1978). Categorizations were produced first through the use of the U-statistic hierarchical clustering method developed by D'Andrade (1978) and then through the use of a multidimensional scaling program, KYST (Kruskal, Young, & Seery, 1973).

The Results

An Initial Comparison of the Two Similarity Matrices

When the quadratic assignment program was used for the two similarity matrices, the correlation was .93 and the z-score was 32.45. These figures indicate that the girls and boys classified the 53 play activities in basically similar ways.

There were, however, some small differences between the two matrices. The Hubert and Golledge procedure provided a correlation of .186 and a z-score of 6.38. This small correlation indicates that the girls and boys were largely similar in their sortings, with only a small amount of data in each set that is not shared. The z-score of 6, however, indicates that this difference is significant (due mainly to a large N of more than 1,000 pairs of activities) even though the difference is very small. If one squares the correlations to estimate variance accounted for, it appears that the similarity is something on the order of 20 times the amount of difference. The difference could be accounted for with a movement of only a few games in the classification scheme. Once again it is clear that the girls and boys of this age classify the activities in a basically similar manner.

The Clustering Solutions

The U-Clust program (modified) provides some overall statistics of interest. For the 47 girls the solution had 5,245 "errors," 41,607 "correct," and 23,426 "unaccounted for." The solution for the 31 boys had 6,963 "errors," 39,889 "correct," and 23,426 "unaccounted for." These statistics, combined with ethnographic information, suggested that the girls may have had a slightly firmer cultural control of this domain of recreational activities than did the boys. Hence the material for the girls is presented first.

Figures 1 and 2 give the two hierarchical clustering solutions in outline. Simple inspection shows that the solutions are very similar for the girls and boys, although there are also differences of note. These solutions will be discussed later. In these figures each activity has been given a double identification number based on the order of its appearance in the girls' solutions and in the boys' solution. The girls' number is given first in Figure 1 and the boys' number is given first in Figure 2.

Tables 1 and 2 are based on the hierarchical clustering solutions portrayed in Figures 1 and 2. The girls' solution is presented in Table 1 and the boys' in Table 2. The clusters and subclusters have not been named in the figures, but they have been labeled in the tables. The two tables have the same format, but the ethnographic entries have only been presented in Table 1. In the tables each identification number is followed by an index number that purports to measure the degree of variation appearing in the sorting for that specific activity. The lower this number is, the less variation there was in sorting. The index numbers ranged from 51 to 560 for the girls and from 107 to 693 for the boys. The Norwegian name actually used in sorting is given for each activity. This name is followed by an English "tag" that is not necessarily a direct translation of the Norwegian name but is designed to aid the reader in identifying the activity.

In Tables 1 and 2 the specific activities are organized by clusters. The clusters have been assigned levels based on their positions in each solution tree. The first level is the lowest and represents the greatest level of similarity. Each cluster is also numbered in terms of the rank order of its "tightness." The clusters and later the dimensions have been labeled by the authors in consultation with both children and adults. These labels represent an attempt to identify a salient characteristic of groups of activities as they are combined in a cluster or arranged along a dimension.

Despite the great similarity found between the aggregate matrices of the boys and girls, a careful consideration of the clustering solutions shows that there are interpretable differences. The girls, for example, lump "Marbles" and the "Coin Game" with ball games. The boys, on the other hand, lump "Marbles" and the "Coin Game" with "Declare War," "Take Countries," and "Cutting Legs," which are quite distinct from the ball games. Thus the girls think of these two games as a sort of ball game, whereas the boys clearly regard them as a form of "war."

The girls also lump "King of the Street," "King of the Hill," and "King's Orders" together, whereas the boys place "King of the Street" and "King's Orders" with "Trickery Steps" and "Mother, May I?" The boys clearly attach a meaning to "King of the Hill" that is different from its meaning for the girls. A careful consideration of the clustering solutions will reveal other interesting examples. Space does not permit a discussion of each instance, but in the main these differences are interpretable.

The Multidimensional Scaling Solutions

The similarity matrices also supported multidimensional scaling. For the girls the three-dimensional solution had a stress value of .105. Dimension I, a "tough" dimension, appeared to range from activities involving strong active competition, such as "Hide and Seek," "Tag," and so forth, to those involving less dangerous competition, such as "Hopscotch" and "Long Rope Jumping." Dimension II, an "order" dimension, appeared to range from activities with a strong female social order,

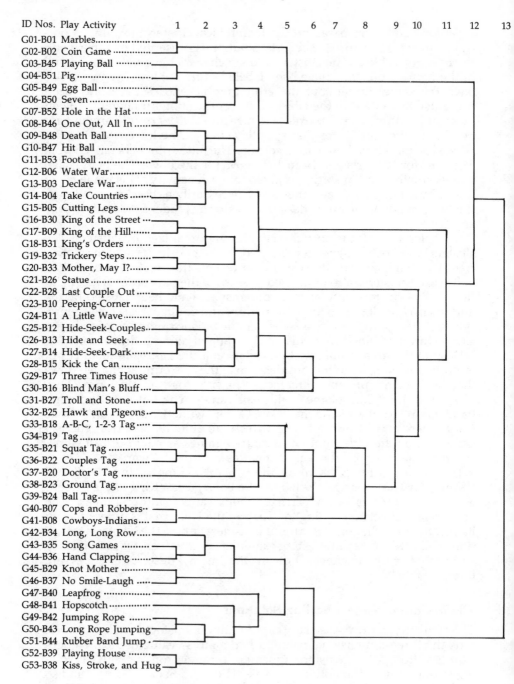

Figure 1.   Girls' hierarchical clustering solution

ID Nos.	Play Activity	1	2	3	4	5	6	7	8	9	10	11	12

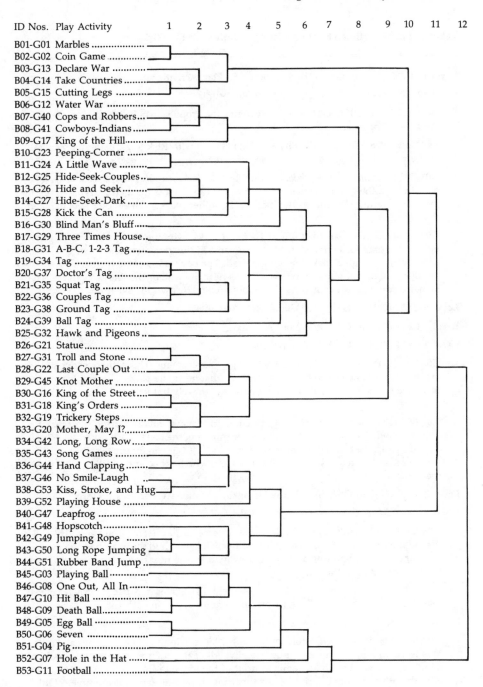

B01-G01 Marbles
B02-G02 Coin Game
B03-G13 Declare War
B04-G14 Take Countries
B05-G15 Cutting Legs
B06-G12 Water War
B07-G40 Cops and Robbers
B08-G41 Cowboys-Indians
B09-G17 King of the Hill
B10-G23 Peeping-Corner
B11-G24 A Little Wave
B12-G25 Hide-Seek-Couples
B13-G26 Hide and Seek
B14-G27 Hide-Seek-Dark
B15-G28 Kick the Can
B16-G30 Blind Man's Bluff
B17-G29 Three Times House
B18-G31 A-B-C, 1-2-3 Tag
B19-G34 Tag
B20-G37 Doctor's Tag
B21-G35 Squat Tag
B22-G36 Couples Tag
B23-G38 Ground Tag
B24-G39 Ball Tag
B25-G32 Hawk and Pigeons
B26-G21 Statue
B27-G31 Troll and Stone
B28-G22 Last Couple Out
B29-G45 Knot Mother
B30-G16 King of the Street
B31-G18 King's Orders
B32-G19 Trickery Steps
B33-G20 Mother, May I?
B34-G42 Long, Long Row
B35-G43 Song Games
B36-G44 Hand Clapping
B37-G46 No Smile-Laugh
B38-G53 Kiss, Stroke, and Hug
B39-G52 Playing House
B40-G47 Leapfrog
B41-G48 Hopscotch
B42-G49 Jumping Rope
B43-G50 Long Rope Jumping
B44-G51 Rubber Band Jump
B45-G03 Playing Ball
B46-G08 One Out, All In
B47-G10 Hit Ball
B48-G09 Death Ball
B49-G05 Egg Ball
B50-G06 Seven
B51-G04 Pig
B52-G07 Hole in the Hat
B53-G11 Football

Figure 2. Boys' hierarchical clustering solution

Table 1 Labeled Hierarchical Clustering Solution for the Girls

---

Level 13 C#52 (G01 to G53). The Full Set of 53 Play Activities.

Level 12 C#51 (G01 to G41). The Full Set less Stunts.

Levels 5 to 12 C#41 (G01 to G11). Games Requiring the Propulsion of Balls, Marbles, or Coins (i.e., round objects).

Levels 1 to 5 C#28 (G01 & G02). Physical Skill Games with Risk (e.g., being hit by a ball or the possible loss or gain of marbles or coins.

G01-B01 (348) *Spille med klinkekuler.* (Marbles). Object: winning. Players: boys. A hole or a circle on the ground is made. One boy at a time shoots his marble trying to reach the hole. If a marble touches the marble of another player, the shooter gets to claim that marble.

G02-B02 (233) *Kaste pa stikka.* (Coin Game). Object: winning. Players: boys. A game in the "Lagging for Pennies" family. The name of the game refers to tossing coins at a stick even though a stick is no longer used. The boys stand some meters away from a wall or a line and attempt to toss coins as near the wall or the line as possible. The owner of the nearest coin wins all the other coins thrown in that round.

Level 4 C#32 (G03 to G11). Ball Games and Activities.

Level 3 C#19 (G03 to G07). Catching Activities.

Level 1 C#14 (G03 to G04). Ball Activities.

G03-B45 (101) *Kaste ball.* (Playing Ball). Object: amusement. This activity is one of the first to be mentioned by a child who is asked what he or she plays. The term may refer to simple bouncing of a ball on the ground or off a wall, but it may also signify a team game.

G04-B51 (126) *Kaste gris* (Pig). Object: winning. Players: children up to the ages of 8 or 9 years old. The children stand in a circle throwing the ball to each other. Each time a child misses the ball, he or she gets a letter. A "P" is given for the first miss, an "I" for the second, and a "G" for the third. A child who has become a "PIG" must leave the game.

Level 2 C#12 (G05 to G07). Ball Throwing against Stationary Surfaces or Targets.

Level 1 C#7 (G05 & G06). Bouncing Off Walls.

G05-B49 (134) *Eggeball.* (Egg Ball). Object: amusement. Players: boys and girls. The children stand in a column, one behind the other. The first child throws a ball against the wall, and when it bounces back, jumps away to let the next one catch the ball. Then the thrower goes to the end of the row.

G06-B50 (101) *7'ern.* (Seven). Object: amusement. Players: girls. A ball is thrown against a wall in different ways. The girls go from one to seven in each turn.

Levels 1 to 2 (G07). Throwing at Stationary Players.

G07-B52 (238) *Hol i hatten.* (Hole in the Hat). Object: winning. Players: boys and girls. This is another game in the "Spud" family. All of the children except one stand on a line. The remaining child stands in front of the line and throws a ball to one child after the other. Before the child starts throwing, he or she says, for example, "Girl's name starting with an 'E' ". All of the others must say a name when throwing the ball back to the one who is "it." Then the thrower says, "Hole in the hat on _____," giving the name of the child who has said the correct name. The children run in all directions except for the child who got the "hole in the hat." He or she must catch the ball, then shout "Stop." Each child must stand wherever he or she is at that moment. The "hole in the hat" child then attempts to hit one of the others by throwing the ball. If the child is hit, he or she is eliminated from the game. The last child remaining is the winner of the game.

Level 3 C#22 (G08 to G11). Ball Games.

Level 2 C#3 (G08 to G10). Games Involving Hitting Girl and Boy Players with Balls.

Level 1 C#2 (G08 & G09). Tag Ball Games.

G08-B46 (108) *En ute, alle inne*. (One Out, Everyone In). Object: winning. Players: girls and boys. One child stands alone on the playground while the others stand in a line. Each child in the line hits the ball with a stick in turn. The lone child tries to catch the ball and to hit the batter with the ball while the batter is running to the other side of the play area.

G09-B48 (105) *Doball*. (Death Ball). Object: winning. Players: girls and boys. The game is similar to other games in which runners are tagged or hit with balls. In this game one team runs from one circle to another (four in all) marked on the playground.

Levels 1 to 2 (G10). Teams and Special Layout Emphasized.

G10-B47 (092) *Slaball*. (Hit Ball). Object: winning. Players: girls and boys. The game is similar to "One Out, Everyone In," but it is played by two teams. Children are eliminated if they are hit running from one side of the playing field to the other.

Levels 1 to 3 (G11). Boys' Football.

G11-B53 (083) *Fotball*. (Football). Object: winning. Players: boys. The game has special rules and it is not exactly like organized soccer.

Level 11 C#50 (G12 to G41). Mock Combat and Tag.

Levels 4 to 11 C#48 (G12 to G20). Dominance Activities.

Levels 2 to 4 C#30 (G12 to G15). Battle Games and Activities.

Level 1 C#32 (G12 & G13). Symbolic War Activity and Game.

G12-B06 (114) *Vannkrig*. (Water War). Object: amusement. Players: girls and boys. This activity is played in particular on hot summer days. The weapons are bottles, water-pistols, and paper bag "bombs" filled with water.

G13-B03 (131) *Melde krig*. (Declare War). Object: winning. Players: boys. A game in the "Spud" family. The children draw a figure on the ground that may be a circle or a square divided into as many sections as there are players in the game. Each section is given the name of a country. Each boy stands with one foot in his "country" and one foot outside the figure. Suddenly a boy may shout, for example, "I declare war on Sweden." Then "Sweden" has to run to the center of the figure while all the others run away. When Sweden has reached the center, he shouts "Stop." Each child has to stand where he is at that moment. Sweden tries to reach the nearest boy and takes three long steps toward him. If he is still too far from his target, he may spit as far as possible. From this point, he is allowed to lie down on the ground and to stretch out his arm. If he now touches the target boy, he goes back to the center of the figure

(Cont.)

Table 1 (Cont.)

and with a piece of chalk draws a line into the target child's country. The boy who in the end can claim the entire figure as his own country has won the game.

Level 1 C#15 (G14 & G15). Games Involving Knife Throwing.

G14-B04 (321) *Kappe land* (Take Countries). Object: winning. Players: boys and girls. A circle or square is drawn on the ground and divided into as many sections as there are players. These sections are "countries." One by one the children throw a knife into the ground. If the knife sticks in the ground, the thrower draws a line from "border" to "border" in the "country" where the knife is standing. Then the thrower chooses one of the sections. In the end the child who can claim the entire figure has won the game.

G15-B05 (250) *Kappe bein* (Cutting Legs). Object: winning. Players: boys. This game has similiarities to "Chicken." Two boys stand face to face. One throws a knife as near to the other's foot as possible. The target boy then takes the knife, moves his leg to the spot where the knife has hit, and throws the knife as near to the first player's foot as possible. With each throw, a boy has to move one leg. At last one boy will have his legs so far apart that he loses his balance and the other boy becomes the winner. The game is not as dangerous as it would appear from this description.

Level 3 C#42 (G16-G20). Boss Games.

Level 2 C#21 (G16 to G18). King Games.

Level 1 C#17 (G16 & G17). Maintaining Territory.

G16-B30 (261) *Kongen over gata.* (King of the Street). Object: winning. Players: boys and girls. One child is the "king." The others stand on the other side of the street discussing from what country they come and what their occupation is. Then they go up to the king telling him where they come from and beginning to mime their work. When the king understands, he runs to catch one of the children.

G17-B09 (264) *Kongen pa haugen.* (King of the Hill). Object: amusement. Players: usually boys. One boy stands on a hill or on something that is somewhat above ground level. He tries to defend his place against the other boys who attack him.

Levels 1 to 2 (G18). Stunts.

G18-B31 (307) *Kongen befaler.* (King's Orders). Object: amusement. Players: boys and girls. The child who is "king" orders the other children to do ridiculous things such as standing on one leg and singing a song.

Levels 1 to 3 C#26 (G19 & G20). Performance Activities.

G19-B32 (386) *Jukestritt.* (Trickery Steps). Object: amusement. Players: boys and girls. This game is similar to "Red Light, Green Light." The child who is "it" stands with his or her back to the other children. They, in turn, start at a line some meters away and try to steal up on the child who is "it." The "it" however suddenly turns to them and points out the children he or she saw moving. These children must return to the starting point.

G20-B33 (527) *Mor, far jeg lov.* (Mother, May I). Object: amusement. Players: boys and girls. The "mother" stands apart and the children stand on a line. Then the children ask, "Mother, please . . .?" and the mother replies with the type of steps the questioner may take, for example, two elephant steps," "five mouse steps," or even "one umbrella step."

Level 10 C#48 (G21 to G41). Central set of tag-like activities.

Levels 1 to 10 C#37 (G21 & G22). Holding and twisting activities.

G21-B26 (390), *Stiv heks.* (Statue). Object: amusement. Players: usually small girls. The amusement is played by children up to the ages of 9 or 10. One girl, the "witch," touches the other girls one after another. The children must "freeze" the movement they had when they were caught by the witch.

G22-B28 (328) *Siste par ut.* (Last Couple Out). Object: winning. Players: boys and girls. The children stand in pairs in a long column. A single child, the "widower," stands at the head of the line. When he or she shouts, "Last couple out," the last couple divides and one member runs on one side of the column and the other runs on the other. They attempt to meet at the head of the column without having been caught by the "widower," whose goal is to catch one of them.

Level 9 C#43 (G23 to G41). The Tag Family.

Levels 6 to 9 C#38 (G23 to G30). Broken Visual Contact Tags.

Level 5 C#33 (G23 to G29). Broken Visual Contact Tags without Blindfold.

Level 4 C#30 (G23 to G28). Simple Broken Visual Contact Games.

Levels 1 to 4 C#19 (G23 & G24). Two Forms of Hide and Seek.

G23-B10 (103) *Titten pa hjornet* . (Peeping Around the Corner). Object: winning. Players: boys and girls. A form of "Hide and Seek" where one child is "it" and the others hide around the corners of a house. The "it" tries to discover the others by peeping around the corners.

G24-B11 (123) *Et lite vink.* (A Little Wave). Object: winning. Players: boys and girls. This is a hide and seek game, similar to "release the peddler," where one child is "it." When a child is caught and put in jail, he or she may run away to hide again if any of the others wave to him or her from their hiding-places.

Level 3 C#27 (G25 to G28). Various Hide and Seek Games.

Level 2 C#19 (G25 to G27). Hide and Seek without a Can.

Levels 1 to 2 (G25). Hide and Seek with Couples.

G25-B12 (088) *Pargjemsel.* (Hide and Seek with Couples). Object: winning. Players: boys and girls. This is a hide and seek game in which the children hide in pairs.

Level 1 C#6 (G26 & G27). Simple Hide and Seek. Object: winning. Players: boys and girls.

G26-B13 (102) *Gjemsel.* (Hide and Seek).

G27-B14 (118) *Morkegjemsel.* (Hide and Seek in the Dark). Object: winning. Players: boys and girls.

Levels 1 to 3 (G28). Kick the Can.

G28-B15 (090) *Boksen gar.* (Kick the Can). Object: winning. Players: boys and girls. In this hide and seek game a tin can is placed on a certain spot. If one of the children is able to run and kick the tin can far away, the "prisoners" may hide again while the child who is "it" replaces the tin can on the original spot.

(Cont.)

Table 1   (Cont.)

Levels 1 to 5 (G29). Complex Hide and Seek.

G29-B17 (116) *Tre ganger rundt huset*. (Three Times Around the House). Object: winning. Players: boys and girls. This is a hide and seek game that resembles peeping around the corner, but is much more complicated.

Levels 1 to 6 (G30). Blind Man's Buff.

G30-B16 (149) *Blindebukk*. (Blind Man's Buff). Object: winning. Players: boys and girls. This game has many variations. Usually one of the children is blindfolded in one fashion or another and this child attempts to catch the others.

Level 8 C#41 (G31 to G41). Touch, Tag, and Capture.

Level 7 C#35 (G31 to G39). Touch, Tag, and Capture less "Good and Evil" Activities.

Levels 1 to 7 C#31 (G31 & G32). Transformation Activities.

G31-B27 (091) *Troll og stein*. (Troll and Stone). Object: amusement. Players: boys and girls. Trolls are believed to be stupid and sometimes evil supernatural creatures who live in the mountains. In this game some of the children are trolls. They cast a spell over the others, changing them into stone. Other children come to undo the spell.

G32-B25 (087) *Hauk og due*. (Hawk and Pigeons). Object: winning. Players: boys and girls. The game has similarities to "Fox and Geese." The child who is the hawk must catch the other children, the "pigeons," who run from one place to another. Anyone who is caught has to become a hawk.

Level 6 C#29 (G33 to G39). Forms of Tag.

Level 5 C#20 (G33 to G38). Tag less Ball Tag.

Levels 1 to 5 (G33). Touching under Unusual Circumstances.

G33-B18 (229) *A-B-C, 1-2-3 trakkesisten*. (A-B-C, 1-2-3 Tag). Object: winning. Players: boys and girls. The children stand in a circle holding each other's hands. They jump around saying the name of the game in a rhythmic fashion. On the last word they release their grips and jump as far away from each other as possible. They then try to touch each other with one foot without moving the other and losing their balance.

Level 4 C#11 (G34 to G38). Basic Tag Activities.

Level 3 C#8 (G34 to G37). Tags.

Level 2 C#5 (G34 to G36). Basic Tags.

Levels 1 and 2 (34). Fundamental Tag.

G34-B19 (064) *Sisten*. (Tag).

Level 1 C#4 (G35 & G36). Stunt Tags.

G35-B21 (051) *Hukesisten*. (Squat Tag). Object: winning. Players: boys and girls. Each time the child who is "it" tries to touch one of the other children, they may free themselves by sitting on their heels.

G36-B22 (054) *Parsisten*. (Couples Tag). Object: winning. Players: boys and girls. Pairs of children hold each other's hands. One couple is "it."

Levels 1 to 3 (G37). Tag with Unusual Requirements.

G37-B20 (060) *Doktorsisten* (Doctor's Tag). Object: amusement. Players: boys and girls. The players must keep their hands on the spots where they have been touched.

Levels 1 to 4 (G38). Avoidance Tag.

G38-B23 (056) *Hoydesisten*. (Ground Tag). Object: winning. Players: boys and girls. Here the tag is played without stepping on the ground.

Levels 1 to 6 (G39). Tag involving Hitting.

G39-B24 (291) *Ballsisten*. (Ball Tag). Object: winning. Players: boys and girls. The children hit each other with a ball.

Levels 1 to 7 C#25 (G40 & G41). Good and Evil Enactments.

G40-B07 (059) *Tju og purk*. (Cops and Robbers). Object: winning. Players: girls and boys. There are two teams, the robbers and the police. The robbers are in hiding, while the police attempt to find them and put them in jail.

G41-B08 (176) *Cowboy og Indianer*. (Cowboys and Indians). Object: amusement. Players: usually boys. Similar to the American game.

Levels 6 to 13 C#49 (G42 to G53). Interesting Activities.

Level 5 C#46 (G42 to G51). Physical Dexterity.

Levels 3 to 5 C#39 (G42 to G46). Exercise in Control.

Level 2 C#34 (G42 to G44). Unison Activities.

Levels 1 to 2 (G42). Unison Activity with Strong Physical Movement.

G42-B34 (341) *Lang, lang rekke*. (Long, Long Row). Object: amusement. Players: girls. The children form a row with their arms linked. An entire school class may go like a "wall" about the school yard. The child at one end changes places to the other end while the entire group shouts, "Long, long row, Eva out of the row." This process continues until everyone has changed places.

Level 1 C#18 (G43 & G44). Music and Rhythm.

G43-B35 (304) *Sangleker*. (Song Games). Object: amusement. Players: boys and girls. A collective term for several games in which the children use song and dance. These games are traditionally girls' games.

G44-B36 (334) *Klappeleker*. (Hand-Clapping Games). Object: amusement. Players: boys and girls. In the "Mary Mack" family. The rhythm is marked by pairs of children clapping their hands together.

Levels 1 to 3 C#36 (G45 & G46). Physical control.

G45-B29 (560) *Knutemor*. (Knot Mother). Object: amusement. Players: usually girls. One girls stands in a corner with her back to the others. The other children hold hands and then climb over and under their arms without loosening their grip. Finally they stand in a tight mass like a human "knot." Then the girl in the corner, the "mother," comes to undo the knot without loosening the grips of the children.

G46-B37 (411) *Ikke smile, ikke le*. (Do Not Smile or Laugh). Object: amusement. Players: boys and girls. The amusement is similar to the American "Quakers' Meeting." The children stand in a circle holding hands. They jump around saying "Do not smile; do

(Cont.)

Table 1 (Cont.)

not laugh; do not show the teeth.'' On the last word, they let go of their grips, jump as far away from each other as possible, and try to make each other smile or laugh.

Level 4 C#24 (G47 to G51). Patterned Jumping.

Levels 1 to 4 (G47). Vaulting Exercise.

G47-B40 (195) *Hoppe bukk*. (Leapfrog). Object: amusement. Players: boys and girls. One child stands in a bowed position with the head down and the hands on the knees while the other children leap over.

Level 3 C#13 (G48 to G51). Jumping Exercises.

Levels 1 to 3 (G48). Patterned Hopping.

G48-B41 (145) *Hoppe paradis*. (Hopscotch). Object: winning. Players: boys and girls. Boys play to win, but girls may not. Jumping or hopping within a pattern drawn on the ground.

Level 2 C#10 (G49 to G51). Jumping over Rope or Rope-Like Obstacles.

Level 1 C#01 (G49-G50). Rope Jumping.

G49-B42 (159) *Hoppe tau*. (Skipping Rope). Object: amusement. Players: usually girls. Conventional skipping with loop going overhead.

G50-B43 (142) *Slengtau*. (Long Rope Jumping). Object: amusement. Players: boys and girls. Conventional skipping over rope turned by two children each holding one end of the rope with the jumper in the middle.

Levels 1 to 2 (G51). Jumping with a Rubber Band.

G51-B44 (155) *Hoppe strikk*. (Jumping with a Rubber Band). Object: amusement. Players: usually girls. This game is sometimes called ''Chinese Jump Rope'' in America. Two girls stand face to face with a long rubber band around their ankles, making a tight double line between them. A third girl ''dances'' on and between the line.

Levels 1 to 5 C#44 (G52 & G53). Role Playing.

G52-B39 (215) *Mor, far og barn*. (Playing House). Object: amusement. Players: small boys and girls. A role playing game, literally ''Mother, Father, and Child,'' found most commonly among children up to the ages of 9 or 10.

G53-B38 (473) *Kyss, klapp og klem*. (Kiss, Stroke, and Hug). Object: amusement. Players: boys and girls. A game that belongs to the American ''Post Office'' family. The girls stay in a room while the boys wait outside. Each girl chooses one of the boys. Then one by one the boys are let into the room. Someone asks, ''Kiss, stroke, or hug?'' The boy chooses one of these and goes to a girl of his choice. If he goes to a ''right'' one, he must kiss, stroke, or hug depending upon the behavior he has chosen. If he goes to a ''wrong'' girl, he must leave the room.

Table 2   Labeled Hierarchical Clustering Solution for the Boys

---

Level 12 C#52 (B01 to B53). The Full Set of 53 Play Activities.

Level 11 C#51 (B01 to B44). The Full Set less the Ball Games.

Level 10 C#50 (B01 to B33). Domination Activities.

Levels 3 to 10 C#45 (B01 to B05). Games Involving Objects.

Levels 1 to 3 C#19 (B01 & B02). Games with Marbles and Coins.

   B01-G01 (486) *Spille med klinkekuler*. (Marbles).

   B02-G02 (328) *Kaste pa stikka*. (Coin Game).

Level 2 C#39 (B03 to B05). War Games.

Levels 1 to 2 Symbolic War.

   B03-G13 (397) *Melde krig*. (Declare War).

Level 1 C#11 (B04 & B05). Games with a Knife.

   B04-G14 (258) *Kappe land*. (Take Countries).

   B05-G15 (230) *Kappe bein*. (Cutting Legs).

Level 9 C#48 (B06 to B33). Chase and Obedience.

Level 8 C#46 (B06 to B25). Chase and Tag.

Levels 3 to 8 C#41 (B06 to B09). Friend and Enemy Activities.

Level 2 C#36 (B06 to B08). Mock Fights.

Levels 1 to 2 (B06). Attack with Water.

   B06-G12 (107) *Vannkrig*. (Water War).

Level 2 C#15 (B07 & B08). Good Guys and Bad Guys.

   B07-G40 (160) *Tju og purk*. (Cops and Robbers).

   B08-G41 (131) *Cowboy og Indianer*. (Cowboys and Indians).

Levels 1 to 3 (B09). One Against Many.

   B09-G17 (213) *Kongen pa haugen*. (King of the Hill).

Level 7 C#40 (B10 to B25). Catch Games.

Level 6 C#37 (B10 to B17). Vision Masked Games.

Level 5 C#32 (B10 to B16). Simpler Vision Masked Games.

Level 4 C#25 (B10 to B15). Hide and Seek.

Levels 1 to 4 C#14 (B10 & B11). Hide and Seek with Twists.

   B10-G23 (151) *Titten pa hjornet*. (Peeping Around the Corner).

   B11-G24 (163) *Et lite vink*. (A Little Wave).

Level 3 C#20 (B12 to B15). Variations of Hide and Seek.

Level 2 C#9 (B12 to B14). Hide and Seek less Kick the Can.

(Cont.)

Table 2   (Cont.)

Levels 1 to 2 (B12). A Variant with Couples.

   B12-G25 (122) *Pargjemsel*. (Hide and Seek with Couples).

Level 1 C#4 (B13 & B14). Day and Night Variants of "Hide and Seek."

   B13-G26 (145) *Gjemsel*. (Hide and Seek).

   B14-G27 (127) *Morkegjemsel*. (Hide and Seek in the Dark).

Levels 1 to 3 (B15). Hide and Seek with the Can.

   B15-G28 (142) *Boksen gar*. (Kick the Can).

Levels 1 to 5 (B16). Vision of "It" Masked by Blindfold.

   B16-G30 (164) *Blindebukk*. (Blind Man's Buff).

Levels 1 to 6 (B17). Complex Hide and Seek.

   B17-G29 (168) *Tre ganger rundt huset*. (Three Times Around the House).

Level 6 C#31 (B18 to B25). The Tag Family.

Level 5 C#29 (B18 to B24). The Simpler Tags.

Levels 1 to 4 (B18). A Special Tag.

   B18-G33 (180) *A-B-C, 1-2-3 trakesisten*. (A-B-C, 1-2-3 Tag).

Level 3 C#13 (B19 to B23). A Set of Tags.

Level 2 C#8 (B19 to B22). Variant Tags.

Level 1 C#2 (B19 & B20). Simple Touch Tags.

   B19-G34 (174) *Tag*. (Tag).

   B20-G37 (164) *Doktorsisten*. (Doctor's Tag).

Level 1 C#6 (B21 & B22). Special Feature Tags.

   B21-G35 (184) *Hukesisten*. (Squat Tag).

   B22-G36 (190) *Parsisten*. (Couples Tag).

Levels 1 to 3 (B23). Tag with a Taboo Feature.

   B23-G38 (196) *Hoydesisten*. (Ground Tag).

Levels 1 to 5 (B24). A Possible Harm Tag.

   B24-G39 (429) *Ballsisten*. (Ball Tag).

Levels 1 to 6 (B25). A Complex Tag.

   B25-G32 (203) *Hauk og due*. (Hawk and Pigeons).

Levels 4 to 9 C#43 (B26 to B33). Performances.

Level 3 C#42 (B26 to B29). Exercises in Control.

Level 2 C#38 (B26 to B28). Holding Position.

Level 1 C#24 (B26 & B27). Freezing Activities.

   B26-G21 (184) *Stiv heks*. (Statue).

   B27-G31 (347) *Troll og stein*. (Troll and Stone).

Levels 1 to 2 (B28). A Couple Variant.

B28-G22 (258) *Siste par ut*. (Last Couple Out).

Levels 1 to 3 (B29). Group Control.

B29-G45 (399) *Knutemor*. (Knot Mother).

Levels 2 to 4 C#34 (B30 to B33). Authority Figures.

Level 1 C#21 (B30 & B31). Activities with a Ruler.

B30-G16 (114) *Kongen over gata*. (King of the Street).

B31-G18 (274) *Kongen hefaler*. (King's Orders).

Level 1 C#28 (B32 & B33). Activities with an Authority Figure.

B32-G19 (261) *Jukestritt*. (Trickery Steps).

B33-G20 (337) *Mor, far jeg lov*. (Mother, May I?).

Levels 5 to 11 C#49 (B34 to B44). Stunts.

Level 3 C#47 (B34 to B39). Role Playing.

Level 3 C#44 (B34 to B38). Specific Roles.

Level 2 C#33 (B34 to B36). Rhythmic Activities.

Levels 1 to 2 (B34). Group Activity.

B34-G42 (282) *Lang, lang rekke*. (Long, Long Row).

Level 1 C#22 (B35 & B36). Rhythm and Sound.

B35-G43 (275) *Sangleker*. (Song Games).

B36-G44 (297) *Klappeleker*. (Hand-Clapping Games).

Levels 1 to 3 C#35 (B37 & B38). Emotional Control.

B37-G46 (456) *Ikke smile, ikke le*. (Do Not Smile or Laugh).

B38-G53 (318) *Kyss, klapp og klem*. (Kiss, Stroke, and Hug).

Levels 1 to 4 (B39). Role Assumption.

B39-G52 (159) *Mor, far og barn*. (Playing House).

Level IV C#27 (B40 to B44). Vaulting and Jumping.

Levels I to III (B40). Vaulting.

B40-G47 (310) *Hoppe bukk*. (Leapfrog).

Level 3 C#18 (B41 to B44). Hopping and Jumping.

Levels 1 to 3 (B41). Hopping on a Pattern.

B41-G48 (293) *Hoppe paradis*. (Hopscotch).

Level II C#7 (B42 to B44). Jumping with Obstacles.

Level I C#5 (B42 & B43). Jumping and Moving Rope.

B42-G49 (320) *Hoppe tau*. (Skipping Rope).

B43-G50 (314) *Slengtau*. (Long Rope Jumping).

(Cont.)

Table 2   (Cont.)

Levels 1 to 2 (B44). Jumping a Rubber Band.

B44-G51 (292) *Hoppe strikk.* (Jumping with a Rubber Band).

Levels 7 to 12 C#30 (B45 to B53). Ball Games.

Level 6 C#26 (B45 to B52). Ball Games less Football.

Level 5 C#25 (B45 to B51). Safe Ball Games.

Level 4 C#17 (B45 to B50). Less Onerous Ball Games.

Level 3 C#12 (B45 to B48). Throwing Games.

Levels 1 to 3 (B45). Simple Throwing.

B45-G03 (207) *Kaste Ball.* (Playing Ball).

Level 2I C#3 (B46 to B48). Throwing Games.

Levels 1 to 2 (B46). A Throwing Game.

B46-G08 (395) *En ute, alle inne.* (One Out, Everyone In).

Level 1 C#1 (B47 & B48). Hitting with Balls.

B47-G10 (240) *Slaball.* (Hit Ball).

B48-G09 (240) *Doball.* (Death Ball).

Levels 1 to 4 C#10 (B49 & B50). More Complicated Throwing Games.

B49-G05 (323) *Eggeball.* (Egg Ball).

B50-G06 (377) *Z'ern.* (Seven).

Levels 1 to 5 (B51). Game with Some Shame.

B51-G04 (693) *Kaste gris.* (Pig).

Levels 1 to 6 (B52). More Complicated Ball Game.

B52-G07 (582) *Hol i hatten.* (Hole in the Hat).

Levels 1 to 7 (B53). The Toughest Game.

B53-G11 (167) *Fotball.* (Football).

---

such as "Playing House" and "Kiss, Stroke, and Hug," to activities with a more male social order, such as "Seven," "Hit Ball," "Egg Ball," and "Football." Dimension III, a "war" dimension, seemed to range from activities with well-defined conflict, such as "Take Countries," "Water War," and "Declare War" to activities with less conflict, such as "Long, Long Row," "Song Games," and "Hand Clapping." The values for these dimensions are presented in Table 3.

The three-dimensional multidimensional scaling solution for the boys had a stress of .114. As in the solution for the girls, Dimension I appeared to be a "tough" dimension ranging from strong activities such as "Football," "Hit Ball," and "Death Ball" to such weaker activities as "Playing House," "Mother, May I?" and "Last Couple Out." The order of the

Table 3 Girls' and Boys' Multidimensional Scaling Solutions

		Dimensions					
		Girls			Boys		
		I	II	III	I	II	III
ID No.	Play Activity	Tough	Order	War	Tough	Chase	War
G26	Hide and Seek	0.870	0.724	−0.331	−0.050	0.827	−0.435
G27	Hide-Seek-Dark	0.824	0.720	−0.345	−0.018	0.921	−0.280
G25	Hide-Seek-Couples	0.813	0.620	−0.301	−0.253	0.679	−0.408
G37	Doctor's Tag	0.800	0.272	−0.079	0.134	0.422	−0.480
G38	Ground Tag	0.780	0.318	0.006	0.227	0.491	−0.322
G34	Tag	0.778	0.341	−0.036	0.217	0.471	−0.438
G40	Cops and Robbers	0.763	0.386	0.352	−0.043	0.758	0.229
G28	Kick the Can	0.747	0.002	0.026	0.138	0.872	−0.221
G36	Couples Tag	0.738	0.309	−0.066	0.157	0.420	−0.546
G35	Squat Tag	0.727	0.321	−0.048	0.010	0.354	−0.500
G24	A Little Wave	0.690	0.082	−0.473	−0.140	0.653	−0.107
G39	Ball Tag	0.666	−0.408	−0.128	0.757	0.106	−0.247
G23	Peeping-Corner	0.605	0.231	−0.512	−0.211	0.705	−0.156
G11	Football	0.494	−0.985	0.329	1.368	−0.324	0.122
G10	Hit Ball	0.466	−1.120	−0.270	1.246	−0.353	−0.098
G30	Blind Man's Buff	0.461	0.787	−0.095	0.167	0.794	−0.455
G09	Death Ball	0.460	−1.103	−0.314	1.246	−0.353	−0.089
G03	Playing Ball	0.459	−1.041	0.051	1.174	−0.501	−0.121
G29	Three Times House	0.456	0.250	−0.354	−0.506	0.493	−0.294
G31	Troll and Stone	0.430	0.339	0.226	−0.306	0.435	−0.141
G08	One Out, All In	0.422	−1.083	−0.322	1.050	−0.221	−0.054
G41	Cowboys-Indians	0.395	0.749	0.589	0.140	0.825	0.634
G32	Hawk and Pigeons	0.369	0.497	0.098	0.232	0.499	−0.086
G04	Pig	0.353	−0.946	0.060	0.759	−0.322	0.061
G06	Seven	0.277	−1.122	0.111	0.904	−0.612	0.024
G05	Egg Ball	0.272	−1.117	0.053	1.032	−0.501	0.034
G33	A-B-C, 1-2-3 Tag	0.165	0.539	−0.330	0.129	0.262	−0.510
G12	Water War	0.138	0.253	0.773	0.109	1.061	0.678
G3	Declare War	0.132	−0.013	0.709	−0.119	0.042	1.012

(Cont.)

Table 3 (Cont.)

G07	Hole in the Hat	0.023	−0.993	0.003	0.692	−0.651	−0.101
G22	Last Couple Out	0.011	0.141	−0.182	−0.876	0.184	−0.061
G02	Coin Game	−0.066	−0.571	0.719	0.649	0.047	0.895
G21	Statue	−0.081	0.303	−0.344	−0.638	0.154	−0.068
G15	Cutting Legs	−0.175	0.134	0.940	0.148	−0.242	0.957
G14	Take Countries	−0.214	0.002	1.182	0.014	−0.092	1.306
G16	King of Street	−0.226	0.008	0.269	−0.857	0.434	0.582
G19	Trickery Steps	−0.255	0.009	−0.505	−0.614	0.165	0.178
G17	King of Hill	−0.314	0.700	0.686	−0.235	0.544	0.875
G01	Marbles	−0.394	−0.737	0.239	0.471	−0.550	0.742
G18	King's Orders	−0.456	0.428	0.262	−0.887	0.105	0.617
G45	Knot Mother	−0.558	0.501	−0.590	−0.819	−0.391	0.004
G20	Mother, May I?	−0.584	0.187	−0.223	−0.964	−0.192	0.475
G53	Kiss, Stroke, Hug	−0.766	0.877	−0.104	−0.638	−1.051	0.650
G42	Long, Long Row	−0.822	0.112	−0.681	−0.620	−0.913	−0.135
G46	No Smile or Laugh	−0.869	0.325	−0.284	−0.422	−0.786	0.363
G44	Hand Clapping	−0.930	−0.072	−0.423	−0.222	−0.994	−0.097
G43	Song Games	−0.972	−0.35	−0.570	−0.342	−1,015	−0.014
G52	Playing House	−1.007	1.085	0.274	−1.316	−0.850	0.023
G47	Leapfrog	−1.216	0.302	−0.032	−0.302	−0.427	−0.971
G49	Skipping Rope	−1.364	−0.335	−0.020	−0.370	−0.512	−0.855
G51	Rubber Band Jump	−1.375	−0.335	0.025	−0.444	−0.596	−0.825
G50	Long Rope Jumping	−1.390	−0.349	−0.109	−0.437	−0.576	−0.719
G48	Hopscotch	−1.562	−0.206	0.085	−0.531	−0.702	−0.638

activities, however, was different for the boys than for the girls. Dimension II appears to be a "chase," or "pursuit," dimension ranging from strong chase as in "Water War," "Hide and Seek in the Dark," and "Kick the Can" to such less active pursuits as "Kiss, Stroke, and Hug," "Hand Clapping," and "Long, Long Row." Dimension III, like Dimension III for the girls, was also a "war" dimension that seemed to range from such high-conflict activities as "Take Countries," "Declare War," the "Coin Game," and "King of the Hill" to such low-conflict activities as "Leapfrog," "Jumping Rope," and "Long Rope Jumping." The values for the various dimensions are presented in Table 3.

Discussion

Specific play activities usually have multiple attributes, so it is not easy to specify in advance which of several attributes will be most salient in the minds of girls and boys as they sort. Once the categories have been generated through clustering and multidimensional scaling, however, it is relatively easy to determine the defining attribute, and the results appear to be quite interpretable. In other words, the categorizations offered here are not ethnographically surprising.

The categorizations, of course, rest solely on data elicited from Norwegian children. The labels of the various clusters and dimensions, however, represent the ethnographic work of the authors. In the future it would be desirable to systematically elicit category labels from the children. Even taxonomies such as those presented here, however, should be taken into consideration in planning recreational activities and in developing educational games. Such secondary developments must rest on the underlying cultural forms discovered by this and other studies.

Simple inspection shows that the conceptual domains defined by the 53 recreational activities were very much alike. This statement is also confirmed statistically. This high agreement simply shows that girls and boys are fine ethnographers of the playground culture. Perhaps there was a linguistic effect in that activities with similar names were sorted into the same piles even when there were behavioral differences among the activities, but we do not think that this effect was large. There probably are sex differences in the understanding of the rules of the activities, in the forms of actual play, in the frequency of play, in values attached to various activities, and so on, but at the fundamental level of activity names the two sexes do share in the same cognitive domain.

There are differences, all the same, to be seen when the clustering solutions and multidimensional scaling plots are compared. Some of these differences appear to be important and salient, and all of them seem to be interpretable. If the underlying similarity were not recognized, it would be easy to say that there are consequential differences between the domain of play activities perceived by girls and the domain of play activities perceived by boys. Surface differences may be misleading, and it would be interesting to know how often cultural anthropologists fall into this ethnographic trap. It is easy to see the differences but more difficult to prove underlying similarity.

This study must be viewed as laying a foundation for further research. We need a more sophisticated description of the play of these activities so that it would be possible to recreate not only the behaviors but also the associated emotional states, values, and attitudes. There is also a need for comparative research. This study has already been replicated among school children in Lima, Peru, and a report is forthcoming. The world of children's play activities is extremely complex from the viewpoint of the cultural anthropologist and is far from being understood.

Acknowledgments

The authors acknowledge the help of Richard G. Condon, Roy G. D'Andrade, Jose Flores Barbosa, Lawrence Knolle, A. Kimball Romney, and Lee D. Sailer in this enterprise. The contribution of Lee D. Sailer deserves special mention, for his help with the data analysis was invaluable. The authors also appreciate A. Kimball Romney's having processed the two similarity matrices through his computer programs and having interpreted the results.

References

Chick, G.E. (1984). The cross-cultural study of games. In R.L. Terjung (Ed.), *Exercise and sport sciences reviews* (Vol. 12, pp. 307-337). Lexington, KY: The Collamore Press.

D'Andrade, R.G. (1978). U-statistic hierarchical clustering. *Psychometrica*, **43**(1), 59-67.

Enerstvedt, Å. (1971a). Hoppe paradis, En barnelek. *Tradisjon*, **1**, 25-36.

Enerstvedt, Å. (1971b). *Kongen over gata*. Oslo: Universitetsforlaget.

Enerstvedt, Å. (1976). Om barnekulturen. *Forskningsnytt*, **5**, 20-26.

Enerstvedt, Å. (1979). Barnekultur: Et begrep med omstridt betydning. *Forskningsnytt* (Appendix).

Enerstvedt, Å. (1982). *Tampen brenn*. Oslo: Det Norske Samlaget.

Enerstvedt, Å. (1984). Barn och kultur. In L. Kohler and J. Merrick (Eds.), *Barns halsa och velfard* (pp. 63-72). Stockholm.

Hubert, L.J., & Golledge, R.G. (1981). A heuristic method for the comparison of related structures. *Journal of Mathematical Psychology*, **23**, 214-226.

Hubert, L.J., & Schultz, J. (1976). Quadratic assignment as a general data analysis strategy. *British Journal of Mathematical and Statistical Psychology*, **29**, 190-241.

Kruskal, J.B., Young, F.W., & Seery, J.B. (1973). How to use KYST, a very flexible program to do multidimensional scaling and unfolding. Unpublished manuscript, Bell Telephone Laboratories.

Nakao, K., & Romney, A.K. (1984). A method for testing alternative theories: An example from English kinship. *American Anthropologist*, **86**(3), 668-673.

Roberts, J.M., Arth, M.J., & Bush, R.R. (1959). Games in culture. *American Anthropologist*, **61**, 597-605.

Roberts, J.M., & Chick, G.E. (1979). Butler County eight ball: A behavioral space analysis. In J.H. Goldstein (Ed.), *Sports, games, and play* (pp. 262-291). Hillsdale, NJ: Erlbaum.

Roberts, J.M., & Chick, G.E. (1984). Quitting the game: Covert disengagement from Butler County eight ball. *American Anthropologist*, **86**(3), 549-567.

Roberts, J.M., Chick, G.E., Stephenson, M., and Hyde, L.H. (1981). Inferred categories for tennis play: A limited semantic analysis. In A.T. Cheska (Ed.), *Play as context* (pp. 181-195). West Point, NY: Leisure Press.

Roberts, J.M., & Luxbacher, J.A. (1982). Offensive and defensive perspectives in soccer. In J.W. Loy (Ed.), *The paradoxes of play* (pp. 225-238). West Point, NY: Leisure Press.

Roberts, J.M., & Nattrass, S.M. (1980). Women and trapshooting: Competence and expression in a game of physical skill with chance. In H.B. Schwartzman (Ed.), *Play and culture* (pp. 262-291). West Point, NY: Leisure Press.

Romney, A.K., Shepard, R.N., & Nerlove, S.B. (1972). *Multidimensional scaling: Theory and applications in the behavioral sciences: Applications* (Vol. 2). New York: Seminar Press.

Schwartzman, H.B. (1978). *Transformations: The anthropology of children's play*. New York: Plenum Press.

Shepard, R.N., Romney, A.K., & Nerlove, S.B. (1972). *Multidimensional scaling: Theory and applications in the behavioral sciences: Theory* (Vol. 1). New York: Seminar Press.

von Glascoe, C.A. (1976). The patterning of game preference in the Yucatan. In D.F. Lancy & B.A. Tindall (Eds.), *The anthropological study of play: Problems and prospects* (pp. 119-134). Cornwall, NY: Leisure Press.

CHAPTER 2
Play in the Elementary School Cafeteria

Stuart Reifel
The University of Texas at Austin

The study of children's play in natural settings has typically looked at play either in classrooms or on the playground. Many have argued that we need to leave schools entirely if we want to take a look at children as they "really" play, because adults in schools have tended to institutionalize play (Opie & Opie, 1969; Schwartzman, 1983). What children would do "on their own" is supposedly not demonstrated in schools. Observation of many classrooms and playgrounds would confirm this view. Alternatively, it could be argued that children's play, in its childlike form, does still occur in schools. To find it, we need to look in places where play might not be expected. We will look in the grade school cafeteria to see what children are doing there and why they might be doing it.

Some notice has been taken of play in lunch rooms. Opie and Opie (1959) documented British children's commentary on the food they were served in their dining halls. They found a rich variety of descriptive language used by the children to describe their food, as well as irreverent sayings such as "For what we have put back on the dish, may the school chickens be truly grateful" (p. 164). They did not report much in the way of games or other forms of play.

What does occur in the cafeteria? If the Opies' observations are still relevant, we would expect to find in that school setting a good deal of description of food. If other observers are correct (Schwartzman, 1983), we will find little in the way of child-initiated play at all in the schools.

The Settings

Observations were conducted in the cafeterias of three public schools located in middle-class and upper-middle-class neighborhoods. One school housed kindergarten through grade 3, one kindergarten through grade 4, and one kindergarten through grade 6. The neighborhoods were minimally integrated, and there was some busing to increase the minority population in one of the schools. All of the schools could be typified as basic skills oriented, with a high expectation of academic achievement.

Children were expected to work their way through publisher-prepared materials, which were supplemented with teacher-designed lessons. The school day was tightly scheduled, with children moving from one subject matter topic to the next in rapid succession. There was usually one 20-minute recess period in the morning only; kindergarten may have had an additional afternoon outdoor period. Physical education was provided on alternate days, conducted by a specially trained teacher. It would appear that there was not much time for children's play in any of the schools.

Children were rotated into the cafeterias for their 30- to 40-minute lunch periods. Kindergarten children entered the cafeterias at about 10:40 in the morning for their lunch, and children in successive grade levels were funneled into the room in 20- to 30-minute intervals. Roughly one quarter to one third of the children brought lunches from home, and the rest bought prepared lunches. Teachers seldom ate with their classes; they took their lunches to a faculty room. Children were supervised by monitors, who were typically older men and women with little or no prior experience working with children. Their primary task was to maintain order, defined as peace and quiet. The children's task was to eat lunch, as quietly as possible, and to remain seated. A number of control systems operated to help maintain order. In one school, a child who needed something (e.g., a fork) had to raise his or her hand to attract the monitor, who then allowed the child to act. Another school had the monitor warn children if they were getting too loud or if they were acting up (e.g., pushing); if the child's misbehavior continued, he (for it was usually a boy) was sent onto the stage in the front of the cafeteria, where he finished his lunch. (Of course, some children loved this.) Another school had a stoplight system that indicated the noise level in the cafeteria; green allowed talk, yellow meant be quiet, and red meant be silent.

Monitors in the cafeterias were supplemented by university students who were assigned to classrooms as part of their teacher training courses. These students sat with their classes at lunch, talking and eating with the children. Supervision of these students allowed me relatively unobtrusive entry into the cafeteria.

Varieties of Play

Opie and Opie (1959, 1969) present examples of the varieties of games and play that British children enjoy. They include a number of types of play, including "Wit and Repartee," "Just for Fun" (i.e., pure nonsense), "Riddles," "Guile," "Jeers and Torments," "Pranks," and "Pretend." The frequencies of each type of play found in this study are presented in Table 1.

Since the categories are relatively self-explanatory, they will not be elaborated upon other than by examples of the play events found in each category.

Table 1   Types of Play Events Observed (percentages)

Play event	% of total
Wit and Repartee	12.9
Just for Fun (nonsense)	3.2
Riddles	19.3
Guile	22.6
Jeers and Torments	9.7
Pranks	9.7
Pretend	22.6

Wit and Repartee/Nonsense

There were a number of examples of ''wit and repartee'' in the cafeteria. One kindergarten girl responded to a slight from another child with the following:

> I'm gonna tell on you,
> That you put ants in my pants
> and made me do a boogie dance.

More of the witticisms were not provoked, as with this kindergarten child:

> Look left;
> Look right;
> Look everywhere.
> Na Na Na Na Na Na!
> Your pants are falling down.

By second grade, there was more of a rhyme in a variation of the same saying:

> Look up, look down. Look all around.
> Your pants are falling down.

Some kindergartners' sayings related to disliked food:

> Skunk in the barnyard; P.U.!
> Somebody ate it; that's you!

Other rhymes were shared "just for fun." Groups of kindergarten girls would recite the following:

> Bubble gum, bubble gum, in a dish.
> How many pieces do you wish?
> One, two, three, four . . .

The counting in the rhyme was accompanied by bouncing fists on top of one another. This is similar in form to jump rope rhymes found by Knapp and Knapp (1976).

Riddles

Language play also took the form of ever-popular riddles. Many of them were food related:

> What's green and flies through the air?
> Super pickle.   (second grade)

> Why do you salute the refrigerator?
> Because it's General Electric.   (third grade)

> What goes up white and comes down yellow?
> An egg.   (kindergarten)

> What's green and red and goes 30 miles an hour?
> A frog in a blender.   (second grade)

These riddles also lead to an occasional knock-knock joke:

> Knock! Knock!
> Who's there?
> Banana.
> Banana who?
> Knock! Knock!
> Who's there?
> Banana.
> Banana who?
> Knock! Knock!
> Who's there?
> Orange.
> Orange who?
> Orange you glad I didn't say banana?   (second grade)

A good number of the play activities verged on the cruel (Sutton-Smith, 1983), some in a general way and others becoming specifically mean:

> Child 1: Say I.
> Child 2: I.
> Child 1: Your mommie had a baby at the FBI.   (second grade)

Guile

Some of these games involved guile, specifically self-incrimination or either-way tricks.

> Are you a P.T.?
>
> If yes: Then you're a pregnant teacher.
> If no: Then you're not a pretty teacher.
>
> Are you an S.K.?
>
> If yes: Then you're a stupid kid.
> If not: Then you're not a smart kid.   (second grade)

This game continued with any number of variations. Some of the letter combinations were made to mean more cruel things, if the target child was less well liked.

This form of teasing play took a subtle form with one kindergarten girl.

> Child 1: What's your name?
> Child 2: Sarah.
> Child 1: [Pretends to be deaf, thereby irritating Sarah.]

In a first grade, a game of "telephone" was begun at one end of a table. The message was "Happy Birthday," but it was no one's birthday. The message was passed around the entire table anyway.

In the school where monitors required children to raise their hands when they needed something, the kindergartners learned how to use this rule in their play. The trickster-leader of the play directed, "Anyone with a blue shirt, raise your hand" or "Anyone who likes pizza, raise your hand." When the children raised their hands, the monitor came over, and they got in trouble.

Kindergartners and first graders were also seen to use the cafeteria environment as a tool for teasing. Tables had fixed seats, alternating in color (blue and orange). One child made a rule, after everyone was seated: "The orange seats are the girls. The blue seats are the boys." Any girl on a blue seat was teased that she must be a boy, and boys on orange seats were teased that they must be girls. Some children panicked; others denied it violently. The organizers of the game had a big laugh.

Jeers and Torments

Unpopular children were sometimes the butt of the following jokes. In certain instances they were picked out by name.

> Whoever looks at _____ is a nerd.   (second grade)
> Whoever looks at _____ has cooties.   (second grade)

These reminded me of my own youth in the cafeteria, when the game was to avoid eating whatever Charlotte was eating. If we drank milk while she did, we would have cooties, like she did. We had to watch her throughout lunch, so as not to eat what she did when she did.

Unpopular children were also mimicked in kindergarten. One unfortunate girl who chewed her fruit roll with her mouth open was laughed at and imitated by the boys around her.

Pranks

Pranks were more difficult to get away with, but did show up in the cafeteria. They usually took a simple form, such as kindergartners throwing napkins at one another or putting food in milk cartons. One second grader was observed perpetrating a more complex prank. When a classmate left his or her seat to get something, the prankster ran quickly to the vacant seat, took the tray or lunch box, and moved it to a new location. The returning child would miss the lunch and have to search all around for it.

Pretend

There were a good many more benign play activities. Many of them involved pretense. A few kindergarten boys would sneak Matchbox cars into the cafeteria, and pretend to race them during lunch. Most of the other play centered on food. Blowing air into chocolate milk with straws made a pretend "milk shake" (second grade). Children of all ages rolled white bread into little balls to make pretend "pills," to be popped into the mouth. Second graders chewed around the edges of graham crackers to form toy "guns," then shot the guns at one another.

Pairs of kindergarten boys who had bananas in their lunches used the bananas as telephones. They carried on long conversations, discussing lunch, friends, and television shows. Two first grade boys pretended to be a baby and a monkey. They fed each other pizza, using the voices of a baby and a monkey, asking each other if they liked the food. Apparently, monkeys did like pizza.

The most sustained example of pretend play involved role playing at a table of third graders. One day the monitor limited to three the number of boys at a table. None of the eight children at the table was willing to let this adult prohibition stand. One of the boys asked, "How do girls eat?" All of the children, boys and girls, began to eat their lunch "the way girls eat": Boys and girls lifted their little fingers as they brought food to their mouths; they all tilted their heads and took delicate little bites of food; they all raised the pitches of their voices as they talked to one another; they all giggled like girls. Then they decided to eat "like boys eat." Everyone's elbows went out to the sides as they held their food, and they hunched over their trays or lunch boxes. They all took big bites of food and chewed with their mouths open. Voice pitch dropped for everyone, and they all laughed in a false robust tone.

This same group of third graders continued the role playing as they carried their lunch trays to the kitchen. They all left the table as boys, taking heavy, stomping steps, still with their elbows out to the side. They then shifted into the "girl" mode. All the children took little steps, wiggling and pretending to be walking on high heels. They held their trays daintily. Again, all their voices were pitched high to sound like girls', and everyone giggled.

Discussion

It appears that there is a relatively unrecognized locus of child-initiated play in schools in the school cafeteria. Children did engage in many forms of play while they ate lunch, although they did not seem to engage in the same kinds of verbal food play that the Opies (1959) had observed. The various commentaries on food found by the Opies were not present in the cafeterias that were investigated. What was found were general food-related jokes, riddles, and wit, some pranks and jeering, and a good deal of pretense. A wide range of play is found in the cafeteria. Many of the jokes, rhymes, and riddles are similar to the data provided by Knapp and Knapp (1976) on American child lore, although they make no reference to cafeterias as a location where such play can be found.

It is interesting that a good deal of the play found in cafeterias does relate to food (e.g., jokes about eggs, using bananas as telephones) or to food equipment (e.g., blenders, refrigerators). The cafeteria environment seems to trigger food associations that surface in play. It may be worthwhile to consider how the content of play is evoked by environments. Play themes have received scant research attention, except in the analytic literature (e.g., Hartley, Frank, & Goldenson, 1952). It is possible that some environments may stimulate certain thematic content in play, whereas other environments may not.

Just as child-initiated play can serve many functions in other natural settings, it appears that it can meet a number of social needs in the cafeteria. Leadership is exercised by those who initiate play, as demonstrated by the telephone game and "boys-on-blue-seats-girls-on-orange" game. Maintenance of status and scapegoating also occur, in nerd and cootie games and other teasing events. Social roles are explored in the many pretense games, such as "everyone-be-boys-everyone-be-girls." Perhaps most important is the fact that children are finding ways to entertain themselves in what is basically a constrained and seemingly uninteresting situation. The adult-supervised, subdued atmosphere found in cafeterias is the epitome of institutional drabness. The physical and social environment is sanitized and streamlined for efficiency; everyone is channeled in to do what they must do, with no frills or interest provided. Children's ways of responding to this situation are to generate fun and to minimize the tedium. Just eating is boring; play fills the void.

How is it that children get away with all this frivolity in an adult-regimented setting? The answer is simple. The adults focused their attention on two, and only two, matters in the cafeteria: relative quiet and food intake. Everything else was overlooked. The adults were oblivious to the fact that play was going on. After some initial observations, the project was mentioned to a number of university students and teachers who spent time in the cafeterias. They guaranteed that no play was taking place. They claimed that all that took place was talk and eating. After our discussions, these adults began to notice jokes and pretend activities that they had failed to overhear before. It seems that the adults viewed lunchtime only as a time to eat. All else was irrelevant, unless it interfered with the adult-set goal of eating. Our discussions on cafeteria play brought background play into the foreground for those adults. It is hoped that those discussions did not lead to adult intrusion in that play.

The examples provided in this study point to the fact that schools are a site where we can learn about naturally occurring, child-initiated play. There is something so essential about child play that it survives even in settings where many efforts are made to regiment every minute of the child's day. The few glimpses into the cafeteria presented here reveal that there is a lively variety of play activities interwoven into school life. We should not underestimate children's ability to maintain play in spite of adult efforts to regiment their lives.

References

Hartley, R.E., Frank, L.K., & Goldenson, R.M. (1952). *Understanding children's play*. New York: Columbia University Press.

Knapp, M., & Knapp, H. (1976). *One potato, two potato*. New York: W.W. Norton.

Opie, I., & Opie, P. (1959). *The lore and language of school children*. London: Oxford University Press.

Opie, I., & Opie, P. (1969). *Children's games in street and playground*. London: Oxford University Press.

Schwartzman, H.B. (1983). Child-structured play. In F.E. Manning (Ed.), *The world of play* (pp. 200-214). Champaign, IL: Leisure Press.

Sutton-Smith, B. (1983). Play theory and cruel play of the nineteenth century. In F.E. Manning (Ed.), *The world of play* (pp. 103-110). Champaign, IL: Leisure Press.

CHAPTER 3

Masked Desire: Adolescent Play Fighting at Boys' Home

Robert Horan
University of Pennsylvania

Boys' Home is my name for a residential treatment center for emotionally disturbed male adolescents. The Home is situated in an exurban county of a northeastern state and occupies about 10 acres. There are nine buildings housing 36 boys and 51 full-time staff members. The boys come from throughout the state, but primarily from its major urban areas, the nearest of which is an hour's drive away. Founded in the latter half of the 19th century to care for homeless boys and girls, the Home has evolved, particularly in its last 30 years, into an institution claiming to treat emotionally disturbed and learning-disabled young men.

I entered this community as an employee, armed with a plan to report on the folklore of the institution. My job was and is coordinator of activities therapy, and my study was conducted while I worked at the Home. The information in this report is based on 2 years of observation, notes, interviews, audiotapes of group counseling sessions, agency documents, and my general experience as a member of this community. My description of the play fight sequences is based on field notes of 28 extended play fight bouts and observations of more than 100 briefer play fights.

Description of Play Fighting

At Boys' Home, play fighting occurs among networks of friends; it is primarily, though not exclusively, dyadic; and it occurs in a sequence of framed actions that are marked throughout by signals that "this is play." The play signals consist of role reversals, smiling, laughing, holding punches, kicks, or bites, and an alternation between muscular tension and relaxation. To the observer, a play fight looks like wrestling or like boys trying to start a fight by hitting one another and running off. It may also look like boys actually preparing to fight, facing off and trading punches or kicks. The physical resemblance to real fights is considerable, and it is understandable that this would generate anxiety in adult onlookers; nonetheless, the affective tone is altogether different from a real fight. Whereas the play signals seem to serve primarily to mark the boundaries of the activity for the participants, the muting or masking of those signals forms yet another kind of play that seems specifically designed *for* spectators. The following example is from my notes. George was 15 years old, 6 feet, 1 inch tall, and about 230 pounds. Joe was 14, 5 feet tall on a good day, and perhaps 100 pounds; he was George's primary play fight partner. Larry was also 15, 5 feet, 9 inches tall, and a well-developed 140 pounds.

> We had just finished a barbeque dinner outside. Some boys were lingering by the picnic tables talking; a few had drifted over to the basketball court. George, Larry and Joe were by the dumpster, throwing away their paper plates. George grabbed Larry from behind. Larry bent forward and walked around with George on his back, yelling to George that he was being hurt and every few steps trying to throw him off. Joe had been involved since the beginning of this interaction; he had gotten things rolling by saying that Larry had said he could beat up George. Now, Joe rushed in and punched George in the chest. George screamed that it hurt, but he held on to Larry. Larry continued to yell that George was hurting him and that he should let him go. Joe rushed in two more times and punched George in the stomach and the ribs. George stopped complaining and looked hurt. He then let go of Larry and ran after Joe. Joe turned and half-ran, laughing away. Although he was not as quick as Joe, George caught him almost immediately. George pulled him to the ground from behind and then crawled up to a sitting position on the small of Joe's back. He knelt forward and seemed to be biting Joe's neck, whispering in his ear. Joe alternately laughed and yelped for George to get up. Mrs. Mooney, who was dispersed with 3 other staff members at the picnic tables throughout these goings-on, hollered over for George to stop. I then walked over toward them. George started to raise up—he put one knee on the small of Joe's back and his big hand on the back of Joe's head, covering it entirely. Then he said, "All right, Joe," and got up. Joe then leaped up; he looked enraged. I was surprised because he had been laughing only seconds earlier. He screamed at George, "You bitch!" George started to lope away from us, toward the cottage. Joe picked up a small stick and threw it at George; it hit him in the back. "So take that," Joe said, and started to walk toward the dumpster, where I was now talking with Larry. George turned back toward us and started to walk our way too. When George approached, Larry stepped forward—extending his fist—and said, "OK, George, you want some of this?" "No," George said. The three boys then walked over toward the school. I left to do something else. About ten minutes later, when I next saw them, George and Larry were wrestling. George was on the bottom; Joe was circling about them, his head bent toward them, talking all the while.

These play fights illustrate the formal, sequential order alluded to earlier. Both "horizontal" play fights, in which the players wrestle or tumble on the ground, and "vertical" play fights, in which the players keep on their feet, begin with a push, a shove, or a grab. There is then usually a quick role reversal, with the active player turning and running as Joe did in the example above after punching George. Once the originally active player backs up or runs, his eyes are trained on his partner. Thus focused, he both is alert to the quick retaliatory blow and has created the physical and affective space for the play to continue. As the originally passive player assumes the active role, the fleeing partner moves quickly enough to invite a chase but slowly enough to be caught. When the catch occurs, the now active player delivers his blows, punches, kicks, or slaps to the now passive player; he may grab him in a headlock or wrestle him to the ground.

When this sequence is followed by a move to the ground, the active player generally takes his turn on the ground and the passive player moves to top position. In the example given above, George and Joe did not reverse positions, possibly because the staff was after them to stop. In the wrestling that followed, however, George and Larry did reverse roles, and when Joe later joined in the wrestling, he had his turn on top as well.

Throughout these exchanges, role reversal, smiling, laughing, and pulling punches signal that "this is play." Frame breakdown can occur during any of the sequences—generally by a boy hitting, punching, or pulling too hard, or else "body-slamming" his partner to the ground. One boy, Paco, explained that a fight under discussion one day was a "real fight" and "not play" as had been claimed (by the staff) because "you could hear it" when one boy slapped another. This definition is similar to that employed by the boys in basketball to determine an indisputable foul— the only kind called on the playground. When a player is hit hard enough that others hear it, play will generally stop and the offender is expected to provide some conciliatory gesture. In the case of frame breakdown in play fighting, when the conciliatory gesture is slow in coming, a boy may pick up a stick or a brick and pursue with intent to harm.

In the case of horizontal play fights, the top player may simply sit atop his partner, occasionally slapping his partner's face, or he may lower his torso so that their heads are close and bite his partner, nuzzle him, spit at him, kiss him, or pull at his ears or cheeks. Throughout, the smiling and laughing are displayed, except in the case of a player like Joe, who was masterful at masking his signals; it was extremely difficult to determine when Joe was playing and when he was being hurt. Like other staff members, I found it economical to assume that he was usually playing and tended to ignore his pleas for help.

Play fights last from a few minutes to a half hour at Boys' Home. The longer ones take place on the carpet in the cottages at night, when there is a lenient staff member on duty, or else on the wide lawn in front of the cottages in the afternoons or evenings of warm days. Residents have 15-minute outdoor breaks during their school day and play fights occur then as well; these tend to be shorter and to be vertical. Most play fights are of the vertical kind. They can consist of boys making a series of raids on one another, or they can occur in the most casual ways—one boy slapping another, running, stopping, and looking back with a smile on his face. Events of this type are so common at Boys' Home that they are virtually uncountable.

Studying Play Fighting

One of the most obvious difficulties of researching a situation in which you are employed is separating the roles of observer and participant. As an observer, I was inclined to be passive and lenient because I was interested in what people would do on their own. As a participant and an adult, however, I was consistently drawn into interaction on the basis of my job role or age status. And after all, I was working for Boys' Home. I attempted to deal with this by looking for previously documented genres such as stories, songs, insult and exchange rituals, beliefs, and so forth for the study and handling the ongoing flow of social activity as my employment required. As might be expected, this approach, convenient though it would have been, was short-lived. Those regularly occurring forms that lent themselves to study were not central to the experiences of either the residents or the staff. By contrast, the ongoing flow of social life, the daily dramas with which we were all involved, was fascinating, frustrating, and implicating. It was some months before I began to look for the expressive patterns of daily life, thus blurring my roles further, giving up a certain amount of control, and opening the door to confusions I would rather have kept at bay.

Play fighting was not even a thought as I reformulated my study, and it might never have emerged at all were it not for the appearance of the boy I have called George. George entered Boys' Home in December, 1982, after being expelled from another residential treatment center for "fighting." He was and is an effervescent young man with a seemingly insatiable appetite for play fighting. Within days of his admission, he was embroiled in difficulty stemming from too much play fighting. It was in George's first weeks at the Home, and specifically in the interminable meetings that concerned his play fighting, that it began to dawn on me that what George was doing might be something besides, or in addition to, acting out. I had seen and discussed numerous play fights and play fighters up until this point, but I had always viewed play fighting as either acting out or a nuisance behavior. That the behavior might have other, more significant meanings to the participants was an idea that had never occurred to me nor, apparently, to anyone else at Boys' Home. In this respect, my attitude was similar to that of Mrs. Jones, the First School Dinner Lady quoted by Andy Sluckin (1981), who made the following statement:

> Sometimes they have their little games and it would appear that they're fighting and I go up and say "What's happening here?", and they say, "Oh, it's all right, it's only play, we're not fighting." And you just keep your eyes open to make sure it's playing, and invariably it is. (p. 41)

Play fighting was only visible for the length of time it took to determine whether or not it was "real" fighting; in itself, it was nothing, play. As adults charged with keeping control of supposedly unruly boys, we were vigilant in our fight watch. And yet fights at Boys' Home are rare.

Play fights, "not fights," are common. While my socialized concern as a staff member had been to sense and prevent "real" fights, I slowly began to develop a curiosity about what George and the other residents were doing. Once I looked, it seemed that play fights were everywhere; I couldn't believe I had missed them. I observed and questioned. The players, however, had little to say. Beyond asserting that they weren't fighting, they seemed not to have a language for what they *were* doing. As I proceeded, I began to see that staff members, usually young men in their 20s, also play fought, both among themselves and with the residents. Some kind of thing was going on, yet the only language for it was a language of what it was not: this isn't fighting, and this isn't sexual.

I searched for the literature on adolescent play fighting. Like the boys and staff at Boys' Home, however, scholars seemed more concerned with real fights and aggression. There are several studies of play fighting, notably Blurton-Jones (1967) and Aldis (1975), but Blurton-Jones studied nursery school children and Aldis looked at 7- to 10-year-old boys. However, Blurton-Jones's report on "rough and tumble play" and his connection with the human ethologists seem to have alerted other scholars to play fighting, even though they may have had other research goals.

In Smith and Connolly's *Ecology of Preschool Behaviour* (1980) they find rough and tumble play to be discouraged by staff members and, consequently, to occur less frequently than in a setting that allows freer peer interaction. They also point to the dearth of research and the contradictory claims made about play fighting when they state that they can make no recommendation as to whether to allow or forbid play fighting in a preschool.

In McGrew's *An Ethological Study of Children's Behavior* (1972), the author uses a category, "quasiagonistic behavior," that he correlates with Blurton-Jones's "rough and tumble play." I should, however, interject a word about Blurton-Jones's study; in it, he offers "rough and tumble play" as a way of separating play fighting from real fighting. Previous investigators had not separated these and had considered them to be part of the same phenomenon. Still, developing this discovery seems to have been more troublesome. McGrew's effort leaves him with 43% of his "interaction endings" representing "intermediates between agonistic and quasiagonistic interactions in which the participants seemed uncertain about the interaction's nature" (pp. 128-130).

In the studies cited, children are observed "as if they were monkeys," as Schwartzman (1978) put it. From a naturalist's perspective, however, excepting Aldis, these studies move too quickly toward generating quantifiable data and do not provide enough observation and description. From an ethnographic perspective, these studies seem to suffer from not knowing the children they consider. Nonetheless, they do serve to suggest the pervasiveness of play fighting and several of its patterns. Notably, boys play fight more than girls and there is little verbalization in the interaction; children seem to know, or tolerate not knowing, what's going on without talking much about it. Sluckin (1981) reports that the 5- to 6-year-old boys he studied spent four times as much time at chasing games as the 5- to 6-year-old girls did and twice as much time in pretend role games, such as cops and robbers or Starsky and Hutch. His 7- to 8-year-old boys spent twice as much time as the girls in teasing, arguing, or fighting. And among the 9- to 13-year-olds, the boys specialized in "soft punches" and "gentle strangulation," while the girls' repertoire included practically no such behavior.

Functions of Play Fighting

These points in an admittedly sparse literature suggest that play fighting is primarily a male phenomenon, particularly when it occurs in adolescence. Regardless of its wider distribution, it is certainly a male phenomenon at Boys' Home. Fagen's (1976) paper "Exercise, Play and Physical Training in Animals" rightly, I think, outlines the physiological benefit of vigorous play. He concedes, however, that "there may be more to social play than physical training" (p. 210) and suggests that this could be the opportunities provided for "testing and comparing physical strength, endurance and skill without the risks" (p. 210) of actual combat. Yet, as in the earlier example, it is common at Boys' Home for regular play fight partners to be of widely disproportionate size; there is no question of who is physically stronger. The argument that play fighting prepares predation and hunting skills (Symons, *Play and Aggression: A Study of Rhesus Monkeys*, cited in Smith and Connolly, 1980, p. 290) only exaggerates the difficulty of comparing analyses of nonhuman and human play. The argument that play fighting fosters social bonds (Poirier and Smith, "Socialising Functions of Animal Play," cited in Smith and Connolly, 1980, p. 290) seems incomplete; certainly it has been argued that girls do a better job of forming social bonds than boys do and they apparently use play fighting very little.

I would prefer to argue that play fighting seems to foster a very particular kind of male bond. It is one that I have come to think of as "a way to get close and keep your distance," a peculiar style of approaching and interacting with another, but not fully "being there" with him. Using McGrew's data, this affective texture of play fighters should be differentiated from approach-withdrawal behaviors, simply because the play fighters at Boys' Home do interact physically. It is the affective texture, the personal desire, that is absent in a strictly ethological report.

The sequences of play fighting serve as an internal frame to the activity, whereas the fact that play fights tend to occur in public means that the presence of spectators provides additional frame external to the activity. A play fight is firmly bounded, and we can suppose that this supplies a certain safety to players familiar with it. The lines drawn by these frames would seem to rule out both aggressive and sexual display. I can only allude to this here, but both fights and homosexual behavior have rules and frames of their own at Boys' Home; neither are public in the seemingly calculated fashion of play fights.

The role reversals of play fighting suggest a rather more fluid notion of dominance and submission and control than we often hear in discussion of male socialization. In effect, the boys play at being on top and on the bottom, at being the pursuer and the pursued. Above all, this is a physical and nonverbal genre—"hands-on," as they say. The success of the frame seems to depend on how well the players know each other's needs; they need to know when it really hurts and, presumably, when it feels good. An error could incite someone to throw a brick at you and, more important, it could endanger your relationship.

It is important to ask why boys who are so concerned about their sexuality, their aggression, and their bodies engage in this physical display of mimed sexuality and aggression. It seems to me that it is *because* they are concerned about these issues—though that concern has not been frightened into severe neurotic or psychotic symptoms—that they play fight. It is just this concern with the newly emerging eroticism and power of their bodies that causes boys to adopt active and passive roles, lie expectantly on their stomachs or backs while their partners mount them, and bite and even kiss each other. Again, this behavior is rarely mistaken for homosexual behavior at Boys' Home. While it would be foolish to argue that boys receive no sexual pleasure from such play, public displays of sexual arousal are subject to much comment, contempt, and ridicule. The presence of spectators would serve to assure frame maintenance in such instances.

What starts and stops a play fight is an instance of the other player's desire. Although stereotypically said to be trained out of such sensitivity, residents of Boys' Home are finely attuned to what their partners want and don't want. The very rudiments of relationship, what one wants and what the other wants—intimate knowledge, if you will—is here displayed as it is played, physically and nonverbally. Whereas many adults lack the verbal sophistication required to talk about such issues, play fighting boys explore the themes hardest to talk about, the emergent self in all of its physicality, the other in all of his.

References

Aldis, O. (1975). *Play fighting*. New York: Academic Press.

Blurton-Jones, N.G. (1969). An ethological study of some aspects of social behaviour of children in nursery school. In D. Morris (Ed.), *Primate ethology* (pp. 437-463). Garden City, NY: Doubleday.

Fagen, R. (1976). Exercise, play and physical training in animals. In P.P.G. Bateson & P. Klopfer (Eds.), *Perspectives in ethology* (pp. 189-219). New York & London: Plenum Press.

McGrew, W.C. (1972). *An ethological study of children's behavior*. New York & London: Academic Press.

Schwartzman, H. (1978). *Transformations: The anthropology of children's play.* New York: Plenum Press.

Sluckin, A. (1981). *Growing up in the playground.* London: Routledge & Kegan Paul.

Smith, P.K., & Connolly, K.S. (1980). *The ecology of preschool behaviour.* Cambridge: Cambridge University Press.

CHAPTER 4

Talking Nonsense and Other Types of Spontaneous Speech Play

John R. Bowman
Pembroke State University, North Carolina

A good pun ought to be drawn and quoted. —Roland L. Holter

The following chapter presents additional data on the organization of spontaneous forms of adult play. Elsewhere (Bowman, 1978) I have described situations in which the structures and procedures of play emerge over the course of the social interaction. I concluded that such play forms should be regarded as dynamic in nature, with participants actively engaged in creating and negotiating these playful occasions. Above all, I argued that the study of the organization of spontaneous forms of social play should put primary emphasis on how such play states are achieved through a communicative process.

This paper is concerned with the elements of communication in spontaneous forms of adult play. Although not all communicative exchanges are verbal, the focus of the present analysis is limited to speech or conversational communication. Nonverbal elements of interaction will not be explicitly covered in this discussion.

After a distinction is made between playfulness expressed through language (i.e., talk) and playfulness created by actively manipulating language, cases of naturally occurring instances of adult speech play will be considered. As will be demonstrated, any of the organizational levels of language may be manipulated for playful purposes.

Furthermore, given that speech is an interactional event, major emphasis will also be placed on sociolinguistic rules and the role of such rules in the production of speech play. Many essential features of conversational cohesion, such as topic selection and the distribution of talk between participants, as well as the objectives of speech, are potential resources for playful interactions. Finally, it will be demonstrated that one of the ways of recognizing as well as accomplishing speech play is the disruption (or suspension) of the conventional orderliness of ordinary talk.

Play Materials

The topic of spontanous forms of adult speech play was approached and described through a variety of methods. In addition to personal observations and a limited number of audiotapes, information about speech play was collected from some 500 accounts written by individuals who were involved in such play experiences. These accounts provide us with first-hand descriptions of what went on in these social situations by supplying such details as the context (setting) of the interaction, who was involved, and how these types of play were routinely recognized and accomplished. Moreover, these accounts provide us with a unique subjective orientation to the experiences they describe. Because the accounts are written from the point of view of the social participants themselves, necessary background information on the intentions of the players as well as the purpose of the conversation can be ascertained.

The Importance of Talk

Much of the understanding of what is happening in a social setting is achieved through talk, and perhaps even structured by it (Speier, 1973). Cicourel (1974) has noted that talk is important for participants in that it provides information about the appropriateness of occasions. Thus talk is seen as being reflexive in that particular forms of speech will give a setting the appearance of something recognizable and intelligible.

Bateson (1972), in his elaboration of the concept "metacommunication," describes a situation involving monkeys engaged in play fighting. Bateson observed that their actions and signals were similar, but not identical, to those of combat. Hence the accomplishment of play fighting presupposes a recognition that "this is play." Speech acts are subject to similar transformations. Although verbal forms of play fighting may appear to be serious to unsuspecting observers, for participants such exchanges are intended to be playful.

In certain respects, talk may be seen as being more susceptible than other activities to playful transformations. Garfinkel (1967), as well as others, has suggested that speech is essentially indexical, in that part of its meaning and intelligibility requires contextual information. For hearers to interpret the meaning of whatever is said, they must consider the possible meanings of the words as well as their grammatical relationships. Nilsen and Nilsen (1978) describe this process in the following way: "In order to sift out the inappropriate meanings, they must use the compatibilities and incompatibilities of the various words as well as whatever is known about the real world" (p. 6).

Furthermore, to hear talk as either an instance of playfulness or a statement of fact requires making a reference to other features of the conversational context. In order for participants to decide the meaning of the contents of speech, consideration must be also given to *how* something is said. In the words of Farb (1973), ''A speech act is made up of both form and content; in other words, how something is said is part of what is said'' (p. 38).

Playfulness Expressed Through Language

As previously noted, states of playful interaction are achieved through a communicative process, and typically this involves conversations of various kinds. Conversations may be defined as communicative acts of speech among individuals involved in face-to-face interaction (Speier, 1972). An examination of various accounts of adult play reveals that playfulness is often expressed through speech. Even if play-intention signals are not explicitly verbal in form, the types of activities that adults engage in while playing frequently involve talk. For example, this can be readily observed in the following account where two friends engage in a mock verbal fight:

Martha: Well, let's ask Susan who she'd rather play with.
Susan: Of course, I'd rather play with Martha.
Dorothy: Ok, I'd rather not play than play with you, Susie.
Susan: Good, why don't you play with some of your friends, Brinley?
Dorothy: What do you mean?
Susan: Oh, Lipster and ''the Dude'' and all those winners.
Dorothy: At least I have friends.
Susan: I wonder what you do to get them!
Dorothy: I happen to like my friends and I don't *do* anything.
Susan: That's not what A.T.O. says.
Dorothy: Listen, I'm sure that Crawford has a few good ones about you.
Susan: Maybe it's your skin-tight pants.
Dorothy: You bitch!
Susan: Brinley, I'm only kidding.
Dorothy: I know—but you're still a bitch.

Dorothy concluded her description as follows:

The play ended when we both started laughing. Throughout the play it was important that neither of us cracked a smile. I don't think that Martha realized we were merely playing until we started to laugh.

Another illustration of play expressed through speech can be observed in instances where adults pretend to be something they obviously are not. For example, two individuals can talk as if they were at a racetrack when in fact they are eating dinner in their apartment:

In the apartment above mine there is a person who has a very large dog. Very often the dog runs back and forth across the apartment, and when he does that the walls of our apartment shake. We now call the dog a horse.

One day when I was having dinner with one of my roommates, the dog began running around. I said to her, "It sounds like a racetrack up there." She immediately picked up the subject and began to "play" the part of the announcer at the horse races. She began a monologue that went something like this: "In the third race of the evening the competition is great! They're off and running and Sugar has taken the lead. And now they're coming into the final stretch and Friday is gaining the lead . . . "

And individuals can pretend they are "popular," as in the following conversations between two college students who discover their names are again not present on the message board:

A: Oh, look at all the messages for us. How are we going to answer them all?
B: I think we better get a secretary. I don't know where to start.
A: It's so hard being this popular. I mean when the girls call you wanting to go out, how can you turn so many of them down?
B: I know, last weekend when I had 20 girls at my door, I had to be fair, so I didn't go out with any of them.

Similar examples were also described where participants engaged in playful conversations about such pretend topics as being wealthy, being Chinese spies, living in a coal-mining town, and being members of a family on television. Actually adults, like children, can make believe they are a number of things, and express this sense of play through their speech.

A more obvious form of speech play involves talking nonsensically (or what some participants described as "silly talk"). The following two examples represent conversations where the intention of the speakers is to produce talk that is unintelligible:

A: I just bought a pair of new jeans.
B: I don't know how you can say that. My parents don't spoil me!
A: My eyes aren't brown, they're blue.
B: He called me the other night to ask me out.

Kathy: I walked into a store today and walked out.
Friend: My shoes are red.
Kathy: The clock is running away.
Friend: Well, the earphones are brown.
Kathy: But the car turned the 90 degree turn in 0.5 seconds.
Friend: But the noodles I bought in China turned sour.

Usually the talk involved in these types of play becomes more and more exaggerated (or ridiculous) to the point where laughter breaks out.

The contents of these types of conversations are obviously playful for participants, for as one player noted, "It was apparent that we were playing because if it were serious it wouldn't have made any sense." Furthermore, players report that they experienced a sense of fun, excitement, and enjoyment as a result of engaging in these types of conversations. Indeed, the purpose of such conversations is beyond the mere communication of basic information (cf. Nilsen & Nilsen, 1978).

Playfulness expressed through language is one of the ways players produce recognizable playful scenes. As was shown, the content of these playful conversations often makes use of make-believe topics and nonsense. Other ways that participants identify such play forms will be taken up later in a discussion of the ways in which playful conversations differ from ordinary conversations. Now let us consider ways that language itself can be manipulated.

Playing With Language

Regardless of its purpose, language can be defined as "a hierarchical system of arbitrary symbols related to each other by rules and used by humans for communication and socialization" (Nilsen & Nilsen, 1978, p. 3). A delineation of this system reveals the following four organizational levels of language: phonology (sounds), morphology (words), syntax (grammar), and semantics (meanings). Any of these organizational levels of language can be manipulated for playful purposes.

An examination of the data reveals a number of ways individuals can establish a sense of play through the sounds of their speech. Sometimes playful sounds can be inserted into a conversation, even though these sounds have no apparent meaning. This can be seen in the following account:

> At dinner with all my roommates one night, we were talking regularly like we always do. Susan, the roommate who always gabs, was telling us about a phone call she had gotten from her mom. She said, "Mom said she had played golf yesterday and blah, blah, blah." She kept repeating blah, blah, blah. . . .Then one of my other roommates jokingly said to Susan, "Did she really say blah, blah, blah?" Then two of my other roommates started in on the blah, blahs and then all of a sudden they were all having this mock, silly conversation using blah, blah, blah instead of real words. After laughing crazily they all quieted down and resumed normal conversation.

A number of other accounts described similar episodes of making strange noises and speaking "crazily." Another college woman reported the following play episode that followed several hours of studying:

> Rick has this habit of making strange noises and speaking as if he is synthesized. Lisa and I were laughing so hard at him we could hardly catch our breath. Then Lisa began to speak back to him in a similar voice. Then we all began to make funny noises together. It evolved into an intricate pattern that sounded as though we had practiced beforehand.

Sometimes playful manipulations of sounds can become game-like in character, as in the following:

> About a month ago on our dormitory floor we started saying people's names with a W at the beginning instead of the correct letter. So my name would be Wenny Wembold instead of Jenny Rembold! It began because so many people

on our floor have last names which begin with the letter *R*. So someone was saying all the names which began with *R* and her speech slipped and they all came out with *W*s instead of *R*s. So now we all just do it for fun. We call Lisa Wisa and Cary Wary. This play has not ended.

Furthermore, another person reported, "I have two friends who, whenever they get together, give each syllable of every word the same amount of stress. Their conversations are therefore amusing even when they are about a serious topic."

Other cases of playing with sounds involved numerous example of spontaneous rhyming and repetition. Although the rhyme in the following conversation began quite unintentionally, it was, however, playfully continued:

I was in the vegetarian cafeteria line the other night and I asked the worker for some "cheese and peas, please." The girl behind me started laughing and said, "You mean please cheese and peas." Then the worker said, "Cheese please and please peas." We all started laughing, then continued on through the line acting crazy!

Similarly, another student wrote the following account:

Six of my suitemates and I were just sitting in our living room when one of them began to tell a story about what had just happened to her. She explained how she had put down some books, a small painting, and a large can of candy corn in the parking lot so she could unlock her car door. While unlocking the door two children came by and kicked over the can. She then said, "I could kill that kid who kicked my can of candy corn." Immediately everyone started laughing at the rather lengthy alliteration she had just recited.

Then the play began. We all began creating our own alliterations, trying to make them as long, if not longer, than hers. The rules sprang up as quickly as the play itself did. They were that you had to have at least five words in one sentence that started with the same sound or letter, and tongue twisters that everyone had heard before were not allowed.

Another frequently reported type of language play involved talking in accents. For example, individuals described instances of talking as if they were German, English, French, Chinese, Jewish, babies, sexy, rich, hillbillies, or from New Jersey, Boston, or the South. And sometimes a series of incomprehensible sounds is stated and assumed to be a foreign language, as in the following:

Jon: Ching chang we wong tong?
Kim: Ai ding ying yang kin!

The following account describes a conversation over the telephone between two adults who talk in a baby-like voice:

Mr. Frye: Who's this? (in a real baby-like voice)
Lori: Oh . . . ahh . . . this is Lori. (Right away I knew who it was.)
Mr. Frye: Oh, it's my Lori. How's my sweetheart doing?
Lori: I'm pretty good. How are you? (I also started to talk baby-like.)
Mr. Frye: Well, I'm fine since I'm talking to you! I was wondering if you wanted to go down to the ice cream shop and get a malt with me?
Lori: Is this a real date?
Mr. Frye: It sure is and I hope you'll go with me.
Lori: Well, wait a minute and I'll go ask my mommy!

I then laughed on the phone. The man on the phone was a neighbor, and while most people would think he was crazy or something, once you get to know him you tend to play along with him until you realize what you're doing.

Another level of language play involves word and sentence play. By far the most numerous examples of this type of language play involve the use of puns. A pun exists when a word or phrase unexpectedly and simultaneously combines two unrelated meanings (Sherzer, 1978). Almost always the pun involves words that sound like other words. Puns may occur either intentionally or accidentally in conversations, and as Sacks (1973) has noted, "Puns are recognizable, though not always recognized" (p. 135). Each of the following puns represents words or sentences that were recognized as examples of playful conversation:

1. Two students who are friends are walking across campus.
   Lisa: You sure walk funny, kind of like a duck.
   Dave: That's a fowl thing to say. Here, take a gander at this.
2. One woman who is complaining to two others about the noise they are making states the following:
   Carey: All I can hear are your loud voices. Your voices penetrate the walls.
   Lisa: Oh, but your voice carries.
3. A couple is passing a football around and one of them dives for the ball and lands in the middle of a bush.
   Sheila: Are you all right?
   Tom: Yea, I'm OK. Just a little bushed.
4. A man is watering his house plants when a friend walks into the room.
   John: Your fern is really looking good.
   Todd: You better "be-leaf" it.
5. A man is introducing his friend to the pilot of the airplane.
   A: Huh, I can spot you pilots a mile away. There goes one now (pointing up).
   B: Oh yea, what's so special about pilots?
   A: Nothing, pilots are just plain people, with a special air about them.

The last illustration involves a case of more than one pun in the conversation. Occasionally puns may act as initiators for further speech play, and sometimes a playful competition develops where one person tries to out-pun the other, as in the following cases:

6. A man and a woman are in the middle of a conversation about how they would landscape a golf course.
   Tom: I couldn't use bushes because whenever you ask them how they're feeling, they always say they're bushed.
   Amy: And evergreens are always pining away for something, so you can't use them either.
   Tom: If I didn't like elm trees I could always ask them to leave.
   Amy: You could always spruce up the course.
   Tom: Yea, people would really go *for* that.
   Amy: But who knows, some might get *teed* off.
7. Two men are teasing a woman at a party when she jokingly threatens to throw an egg at them.
   Jim: I think we should make an exit.
   Friend: You're "eggsactly" right.
   Jim: But, that would be a poor "eggsample" of courage.
   Friend: "Eggsplain."
   Jim: We would "renegg" on our masculinity.
   Friend: "Eggscuse" me.

All of the above examples (no pun intended) illustrate how all of the various components of language can be manipulated by puns. Furthermore, all of these conversations involving pun, as well as the previously mentioned cases, are considered obviously playful by the participants.

Playful Versus Ordinary Speech

Speier (1973) has noted that speech involves far more than sentence production. "It is social exchange and social coordinations. Talk is interactional" (p. 59). We will now examine some of the ways speech play is recognized and accomplished through social interaction.

Speech must be considered more than a system of grammar, since its production also requires sociolinguistic rules. For example, various studies in conversational analysis and the ethnography of speaking have attempted to describe some of the basic features of ordinary conversational exchanges. Some of the more important properties of conversations recognized by members of our society are the following:

1. Conversations have beginnings and endings.
2. The number of parties involved in conversation can vary.
3. The distribution of talk between participants is regulated.
4. Generally one party speaks at a time.
5. Conversational systems are highly sensitive to cohesion.

Although members of our society may not be able to clearly state the above properties, they will nonetheless recognize something unusual about conversations that do not have these features. Indeed, one of the ways that playful conversations are achieved is the disruption (or suspension) of one or ore of these conversational features.

As noted, one property of ordinary conversation is that one party speaks at a time and that extensive interruptions are to be avoided. Therefore, the sequence of talk in a two-party conversation is alternating and would be described by the formula ABABAB, where "A" and "B" are the parties to the conversation (Schegloff, 1968). An examination of the following transcript produced from an audiotape of a playful conversation reveals that this feature is routinely violated (the symbol // refers to interruptions):

Steve: Give me the Okies, just give them to me!
David: Hey, Steve, I haven't harmonized with you on "Home on the Range" in a long //
Steve: Well //
David: How about //
Steve: If you, if you, if you //
David: Wait, wait, wait, wait. Let me bring over the old kazoo.

As can be seen, a great deal of overlapping and interruption occurs in the above talk.

Perhaps one of the more obvious ways that playful conversations are socially recognized and achieved occurs when the meaningfulness of what is said during conversational talk is disrupted. In the previously mentioned examples of nonsense, the various speech utterances did not seem to fit together; that is, what was said in one turn of talk did not make sense with the previous turn of talk. The following account illustrates a case of speech play involving noncohesive (although repetitive) turns at talk:

A: When you go downtown, could you buy me some gum?
B: Well, how about when I go downtown, I'll just buy you some gum.
A: What you could do is *buy* me some gum when you go downtown.
B: Or better yet, I could buy you some *gum* when I go downtown.
A: No, no. I got it. When you go downtown, you could just *buy me* some gum.
B: Great idea.

The point to be made about this conversation, as well as the examples of overlapping and interrupting talk, is that no particular attempt is made to correct or remedy the observably disruptive effects that such talk has in these conversations.

Finally, another socially recognized feature of playful conversations relates to the objectives of speech. Whereas ordinary conversations tend to be concerned with the practical communication of basic information, playful conversations do not necessarily have this concern. Like other play forms, speech play can be characterized by its emphasis on process rather than goal. In short, speech play is used primarily for fun (cf. Sherzer, 1976).

Summary

The primary concern of this paper has been with the various communicational ingredients of spontaneous forms of adult speech play. An analytical distinction was made between types of playfulness expressed through language or speech and types of playfulness created by language or speech manipulation. It was demonstrated that *how* something is communicated through speech must be considered an important part of what is said. Specifically, it was pointed out that one of the ways of recognizing as well as accomplishing speech play involves the disruption or suspension of the conventional orderliness of ordinary talk. Topic selection, the distribution of talk between participants, and other essential features of conversational cohesion, as well as the objectives of speech, were all found to be potential resources for playful interaction.

References

Bateson, G. (1972). *Steps to an ecology of mind*. New York: Chandler.

Bowman, J. (1978). The organization of spontaneous adult social play. In M.A. Salter (Ed.), *Play: Anthropological perspectives*. Champaign, IL: Leisure Press.

Circourel, A. (1974). *Cognitive sociology*. New York: Free Press.

Farb, P. (1973). *Word play*. New York: Bantam Books.

Garfinkel, H. (1967). *Studies in ethnomethodology*. Englewood Cliffs, NJ: Prentice-Hall.

Nilsen, D., & Nilsen, A.P. (1978). *Language play*. Rowley, MA: Newbury House.

Sacks, H. (1973). On some puns: With some intimations. In R. Shuy (Ed.), *Sociolinguistics: Current trends and prospects*. Washington, DC: Georgetown University Press.

Schegloff, E. (1968). Sequencing in conversational openings. *American Anthropologist*, **20**, 1075-1095.

Sherzer, J. (1976). Play languages: Implications for (socio)linguistics. In B. Kirshenblatt-Gimblett (Ed.), *Speech play*. Philadelphia: University of Pennsylvania Press.

Sherzer, J. (1978). Oh! That's a pun and I didn't mean it. *Semiotica*, **22**, 335-350.

Speier, M. (1972). Some conversational problems for interactional analysis. In D. Sudnow (Ed.), *Studies in social interaction*. New York: Free Press.

Speier, M. (1973). *How to observe face-to-face communication*. Pacific Palisades, CA: Goodyear.

PART II

Theories of Play

A theory can be a tightly constructed nomological network of propositions that yield testable hypotheses; it can be a guiding organizational principle; it can also be an interesting and intellectually efficient statement of relations between ideas and observations. The first type of theory is quite rare, though one may read an experimental study that approaches this type in Johnson's contribution here. The other papers in this theory section are more loosely constructed, which allows the reader greater room to speculate in company with the various authors. Given the fascinating breadth of possibilities for theories of play, this makes sense.

Biesty's paper, "If It's Fun, Is It Play?" is a decided example of the use theory as an organizing principle. He creatively applies modes of analysis taken from G.H. Mead's social role theory to the game of amateur baseball. Though not for the neophyte, this paper will entice the reader who appreciates closely reasoned argument and creative interpretation of questionnaire data.

Using data gathered from fifty-five male and female respondents, Biesty has examined their reflections on playing and observing baseball games. His central concepts rest on seeking baseball as a social envelope that allows for role engrossment. A player's embracement of his or her own role, as well as the ability to perspective-take and to participate in another player's role and to be part of a group that defines a "game," will define the role playing necessary for play that is also "fun."

Although Biesty dismisses their relevance, it would be interesting to have more detail of his subjects' responses according to their ages (17 years to 45 years) and sex. We are also not given much detail on the process of gathering the data on participation or game experience. These may seem superfluous facts from his perspective, but they are the data that allow his interpretations and hence would be a worthwhile inclusion.

Biesty tells us that "play requires an achievement of a unique, social self," but little attention is paid to the discrete social organism in his paper. This is consistent with the theoretical position of this first paper but leaves the developing "self" out in the cold. Therefore, the second paper in this section, "The Lighter Side of Play," by E.P. Johnsen and Kathlee Snyder, strikes a good balance with the first offering. The authors are concerned with presenting a view of children's play that is adaptive and that reflects the positive capacity of the organism.

Johnsen and Snyder content that fantasy play and other imaginal activities with young children promote their increased self-control and improved ability to withstand environmental stresses. They support their proposition with a review of studies that have employed fantasy groups, structured imagery skills, and prosocial TV experiences with young children. These autors point out that more psychodynamic interpretations of children's play have usually stressed the expression of instinctual conflicts, namely the "darker side of play." Their argument is that play may obviously also serve as adaptive problem solving for children. Although this is the briefest paper in this section, it certainly does not lose by its brevity. The authors' critique of conclusions or methods from several studies makes this an even-handed, worthwhile presentation.

The third paper in this series, "Play as Adaptation: The Work-Play Dichotomy Revisited," is a closely worked argument to see play as a form of adaptation to a sometimes harsh reality. Rather than Karl Groos's notion of play (primarily mock-aggressive) as an approximation of adult forms, author Blanchard's idea of adaptation rests on play producing a fundamental difference in the experience of reality; the idea of playfulness as "a mechanism which human beings employ to remove themselves from the angst of reflecting on the realities of existence." He follows Bruner's lead in seeing play as adaptive in an evolutionary perspective. The illustrative material is taken from his obvious sensitive knowledge of Native American habits of thinking and activity—more specifically from the structure of games, the indirect nature of manipulation in games, religious systems that are *not* hierarchical, and a notion of time in which events in themselves are the measure, not time-over-event. Blanchard has introduced very articulately a notion of play strange to our Puritan, rational culture: play and playfulness not as a subtype of thinking, a "turn of mind," but rather as a cognition itself.

The fourth paper in this section, "Attitudes Toward Play and Belief About Development," has been mentioned as an exemplar of an experimental investigation drawn from a hypothesis-producing network. In this instance, it is Vygotsky's notion of the "zone of proximal development." Johnson's research attempts to examine the context of adults' beliefs about preschool play. The author expected that specific background characteristics (e.g., education level) of parents and teachers would produce different beliefs regarding play versus school activities and preferences for some kind of play (e.g., convergent) over others. Although the statistical analyses are somewhat unclear, Johnson's results do present evidence for his hypotheses.

Dealing with the complexity of the relationships between cultural belief systems, individual adult roles, and the consequent valuing of *sorts* of play of one's own child requires many levels of analysis and abstraction. Johnson has presented this material clearly and deserves praise for his ambition to explicate these difficult relationships. He provides another facet to our view of children's play, distinct from Johnsen and Snyder's previous paper.

Mergen's contribution, "Travel as Play," is the fifth and last paper in this section. This is the most playful paper of the five presented here. Mergen reviews four books by famous and not-so-famous travel authors (e.g., Twain, Nickerson) as illustrative that there are qualities of play similar to most travel (e.g., escape from routine, risk taking of a safe sort, a spirit of fun). Mergen's engaging narrative style and the obvious deft selection of vignettes from the books discussed produce much enjoyment; it almost makes reading the books cited superfluous!

The topic of play has been well served, judging from the five papers in this section. Theory should have flexible boundaries, at least at this point in the infancy of knowledge of human development and social systems. Play is one of the most inventive and extensive human behaviors and therefore should have great latitude for theory. After all, we range from the frolic of chimps or monkeys to the subtle pretense of a "drink" for baby to the verbal pyrotechnics of Tom Stoppard's "play" with language. These five papers give credence to the creative potential possible of play as a subject area. They inform, speculate, and spark imagination; they are indeed a "good read."

Linda J. Brandt

CHAPTER 5

If It's Fun, Is It Play?
A Meadian Analysis

Patrick Biesty
County College of Morris, New Jersey

One of the widely acknowledged means of defining play has been to contrast it to what appear to be its opposites, for example work and duty. Huizinga (1955) writes, "Play is superfluous. The need for it is only urgent to the extent that the enjoyment of it makes it a need. Play can be deferred or suspended at any time. It is never a task" (p. 8). Similarly, Caillois (1961) writes, "In effect, play is essentially a separate occupation, carefully isolated from the rest of life, and generally is engaged in with precise limits of time and place. . . . Nothing that takes place outside this ideal frontier is relevant" (p. 6).

More recently, however, the categorical distinction between play and work has been questioned. Csikszentmihalyi (1975) has outlined the similarities between enjoyable work and play by focusing on flow patterns and intrinsic motivation:

> A society could not survive long if people were exclusively involved in playful pursuits. We assumed, however, that there is no unbridgeable gap between "work" and "leisure." Hence, by studying play one might learn how work can be made enjoyable, as in certain cases it clearly is. (p. 5)

Csikszentmihalyi's emphasis on "flow" questions play's separateness, especially when it requires accomplishment and expertise. If flow is a shared criteria of play and enjoyable work then the accomplished pianist is playing not only musically but ludically, despite the fact that he or she is being paid for the performance. To agree with this perspective we would also have to consider whether the stalking lioness is playing when she attacks and kills her prey, if that action is experienced as flow. Both the pianist and the lioness enjoy what they are doing; their actions flow back and reinforce further actions; and both "make their living" through these actions. The variety of behaviors that flow is limitless.

A different critique of play's distinctiveness comes from Sutton-Smith (1984), who catalogues how unideal actual play can be. "In general, *academic play theories* have been created by professionals who work with children in nursery schools, in therapy clinics or in laboratories. One might tentatively call them play theories for the rich" (p. 8). Rather than a means of socialization to approved behaviors, Sutton-Smith argues that play is a parody of human folly that is often very unpleasant and even brutal. To take but one of Sutton-Smith's examples, however, those who are the subjects of such unpleasant activities as being urinated on would find it difficult to convince themselves and others that their involvement is play. Second, although the perpetrators might claim to be playing, the dominance goals they betray mark their behavior as an odious form of fun making. Their behavior is not play by at least two criteria: The actors are not making believe, they are after real status and power in their group; and their actions are not rule-governed, but rather are characterized by rule breaking. Sutton-Smith acknowledges that participation in such brutal events is rarely voluntary in the usual sense.

The Problem

If both work and play can flow and be enjoyed for themselves, then the distinction between them either disappears or must be found elsewhere than in flow. Second, if so much of what is called play is in reality brutal and dominance-oriented, the use of the label "play" for these actions needs to be questioned. Such social labeling might be better understood as a legitimation strategy. Both these recent works confuse play with fun. The issue, then, is to focus on the relationship between fun, an outcome, and play, an activity, so that play can be distinguished from other fun activities such as autotelic work and brutalizing dominance games.

In this paper I argue that the concept of play is an ideal in two ways. First, play is an ideal in Weber's sense of an ideal type. We use the concept to clarify our understanding of behavior and to distinguish play from work, recreation, and fun activities that are not play. Thus theorists use the term *play* differently than do the subjects they study.

Second, the term *play* is an ideal that arises in social interaction and serves as a referential and regulatory guide to the conduct of action. When a child says, "He hurt me, I'm not playing anymore," he is using a referential concept that represents an ideal that he feels should govern play. When a coach yells at a player, "Stop goofing off and play the game," he is using a reference that he trusts both he and the player share. A sociologist observing these interactions will note that the ideal is not so much fixed as being negotiated. From observations of negotiated referential ideals the theorist proposes an abstract ideal type.

The Argument

Despite the claim that "the fun of playing resists all analysis, all logical interpretation" (Huizinga, 1955, p. 3), some clarity can be shed on the concept of fun. In a useful essay entitled "Fun in Games," Goffman (1961) locates fun in the reflection on actions made from a game's surrounding framing interaction. The fun of a card game, for example, comes not from the moves of the game but from the reflection of these moves from the role of participant: "While it is as players that one can win a game, it is only as participants that we can get fun out of this winning" (p. 37).

Winning is fun because it is characterized through the framing interaction as a unique event in the game. Losers can also have fun by reflecting on and framing their own unique plays, for example, bluffing or raising the stakes. In Goffman's study fun is defined as the positively affected reflection upon a novel, unique, or original action. This definition accords with De Charms's (1968) argument that intrinsic motivation and the fun of doing something comes from the feeling of having originated an act.

Because something is fun to do does not mean it is play. As stated, the definition of play is negotiated by reference to players' expectations. This social element makes play dependent upon mutual enjoyment, specifically upon making the other person's enjoyment part of one's own. It will be argued that Mead's (1934) description of role playing is an accurate account of the way fun and play are related. The argument here is that each of the three acts that constitute role play—taking the role of the other, taking the role of the generalized other, and role enactment—result in types of fun that, when the three are taken together, constitute play. When one or more types of fun are missing the action is not truly play, although it may be labeled as such in the negotiation of definitions.

True play is not, however, simply the addition of three types of fun. Such a conception would be narrow and particularistic. True play achieves a measure of the player's referential ideal by expanding the players' experience of themselves as part of a group reality. Play requires achievement of a unique social self, at least temporarily. In summary, this paper addresses the question "If it's fun, is it play?" by arguing that actions are play when the players have three types of fun that achieve a realization of the social embeddedness of their fun.

Focus and Definitions

In line with the theoretical tradition of George Herbert Mead, whose conceptual framework is used to analyze the data, I have chosen to investigate amateur baseball to illustrate the fun of play. If there are three acts in any role play, it follows that each act can be analyzed from the perspective of the social achievement of fun. An ideal play in a game, for example, a particular pitch, hit, catch, throw, or tag, should have three fun-achievement moments, and the experience of the game should vary according to the accumulated experiencing of these three moments.

The variable that strings the three fun moments into really good play is role engrossment. Engrossment is defined as the full physiological experiencing of the role one is playing (Goffman, 1961). The continuity of engrossment requires the stringing together of three taken roles in one enacted role. The first taken role is a director, telling oneself to do something; the second taken role is the position in the game that structures the expected action; and the third taken role is the audience that observes or references the action. Engrossment is the embracement of these three roles in an ordered yet simultaneous way. If the player is distanced from any one of the three roles he or she is limiting his or her experience of play.

The argument relies on concepts of role playing, role taking, role embracement, and role distance. Although these concepts are widely used in social-psychological studies, they are used here with some refinements.

Role playing is used to mean the person is playing when enacting the role. When the person is not playing, role behavior will be referred to as *role acting*. This usage follows Mead (1934) in a literal sense; role playing in a game requires a simultaneous role taking of the other and the generalized other.[1]

Role taking is divided into two types. The first type I designate *pretend* role taking. The pretend role taker considers the other's role moves as indications or possibilities. Pretend role taking accompanies role acting in everyday encounters. The second type is *make-believe* role taking. The make-believe role taker feels the other's role moves as if they were his or her own. Role takers literally make themselves believe they are the other when role taking. The child playing at adult roles is make-believe role taking. However, the coordinated role play of a game also depends on an ability to make believe. The continuity between play at roles and role play will be developed in the discussion of the make-believe reality of taking the play away from the other.

Role embracement refers to the physiological involvement of a person in a particular role. When a person embraces a role he or she lets go of the self that stands outside the role (Goffman, 1961). The concept of embracement will be used here to describe both role taking and role playing, and will help explain the difference between pretend and make-believe role taking. The pretend role taker does not embrace the role of the other, whereas the make-believe role taker does.

Role distance refers to the psychological space between the self that stands outside a role and the self in role and is therefore a way of expressing a contrast to embracement. In introducing the concept Goffman (1961) used the example of a young child having fun embracing the role of a merry-go-round rider, who as he gets older exhibits increasing degrees of role distance by clowning or being "cool" while riding. With each degree of distance, the enactment of the role of merry-go-round rider is further from play. The fun now comes from embracing and observing the role that provides the distance, for example the "cool" role.

Methodology

Data on baseball were collected from narrative questionnaires that asked the respondents to report their internal dialogues before, during, and after both exceptional and typical plays. Fifty-five male and female respondents, aged 17 through 45, participated. The responses were not analyzed for age or sex differences as the focus was on the common experience of play. Selected respondents were interviewed to exploit the most promising surveys.

The self-reports on the fun of playing baseball were analyzed to determine how role-taking actions before, during, and after a "good play" facilitated and/or detracted from the play experience. The objectifications of play in the game rules, in the dialogues that referenced the ongoing action, and in the reflections on what was done indicated possible types of fun. The responses were analyzed to see if "a really good play" encompassed a composite of the three types of fun and the realization of a unique social self.

Playing Baseball

Amateur baseball is a game set aside from everyday activity and engaged in for fun and winning. As with any game, what is intended as fun can become work if too much emphasis is placed on achievement, and conversely the game can disintegrate into masquerade if too much emphasis is placed on fun. It is not argued that when baseball becomes a masquerade it is no longer play, but rather that baseball play and not masquerade is the subject of this study.

Baseball is sequential. Each side takes turns at bat, each inning follows the previous one, and batters come up in order. It is also sequential in the series of actions that constitute an "at bat" in an inning. A typical sequence might include these moves: a pitch to the batter, a hit to the outfield and run to a base, a catch and a throw to the infield, another catch and a tag. This sequential character provides a focus for looking at each "play" as one possible instance of the experience of the play of baseball. The focus will be on these individual plays because they constitute the empirical reality the players use to conclude that they played the social reality we call baseball.

In contrast to its referential ideal, the actual play of baseball players may embrace none, one, two, or all of the roles that intrude upon them. Actual game play is characterized by periods of embracement and distancing from roles. Instead of keeping an eye on the ball the player may slip into keeping an eye on one or more of these roles or be distracted by other players. In contrast, embracing the appropriate role at the appropriate time requires focusing on the ball. The following analysis of play sequences will illustrate the continuity of embracement in the ideal and the sequential hesitancy of the real.

Embracing the Role of the Other

Mead called the make-believe play of the three-year-old who acts at being mommy, daddy, or policeman "playing at roles" because the child is not integrating his or her play with the role structure of the surrounding world. This integration occurs at a later age in games. In the play of a game, however, play at roles is not simply supplanted by role playing, that is, the integration of role actions with others. Instead, play at roles continues as role-taking adjustments to one's role play. One continues to pretend or make believe one is the other, but in an attenuated, subvocal manner.[2] The make-believe action of role taking in a competitive game is trusting oneself to take a role that is in another's ongoing control. Making believe is therefore restricted to momentary and attenuated role-taking actions that are experienced as taking the other's indications into account.

Embracement of the role of the other in a game is complex because the other is initiating challenging behaviors as the game proceeds. Nevertheless, one's play depends upon gaining a sense of control or direction of the other's role by making believe through embracement and at the same time responding in one's appropriate role to that make-believe action. Players do not talk of making believe they are the other but rather of "having the other's number." When one has the other player's number sufficiently, the fun of one's own role is supplemented by the novelty of embracing the other's role.

Players define their sense of the other as a kind of "knowing" what's going to happen. One respondent expressed the fun of embracing the other's role as follows:

> Pitching can at times *seem* to brink on supernatural or better, ESP, experiences. I'm not saying it in a scientific way, I just can relate experiences when I know a batter is going to get a hit, or maybe strike out. . . . When I'm in the groove, a game flies by and is one enjoyment after the other.

Another way of embracing the other in role is to take the other by surprise:

> Unless the first pitch looks absolutely perfect, I let it pass to gauge the pitcher's aim and speed. (If it's "perfect" in appearance, I swing for the fences, and since I rarely miss it takes the players on the opposite team by surprise and gets me to first or second.) Ah, success!!

A successful play confirms the make-believe reality of directing the other. When fellow players concur with cheers of "Good play!" it validates the action as play.

Taking the other by surprise is taking the other's role so well that the other cannot respond immediately. The play is literally taken away from the other. The batter is in this case experiencing the play as a direction of the situation brought about by taking the role away from the pitcher and embracing it as part of himself or herself. The fun of role playing the other in baseball is expressed as follows: "the feeling of being in control of the game"; "catching a very hard ball to catch"; "the most fun is when I succeed and have gotten on base and act as if it was the simplest thing to do."

Playing the Position

Strictly speaking, role playing consists of three simultaneous acts: taking the role of the other, enacting one's role, and taking the role of the generalized other. Consequently I will refer to actions specific to the role as playing the position. As with the role of the other, the encumbent takes (or embraces) the position as a direction to his or her own upcoming action.

Embracing one's role makes it one's immediate make-believe reality. To refer to one's game role as make-believe is to emphasize that it is a believed socially constructed reality, not that it is socially false. While acting in a role, one's validation remains subjective, measured by the feeling of having done it right and by reference to one's ideal of the play.

The central fun of playing baseball is feeling oneself in a role-taking action that is at the same time the response one is directing at the other. One focuses his or her "I" and "me" by acting "spontaneously," that is, by suspending the indications to oneself from the two roles. One directs one's play from the fusion of the two taken roles, as in the following examples:

> I would concentrate less on the play, forget everyone else, the ball was all I could see.
>
> I don't vocalize during a play because it can break concentration.
>
> If the ball is hit at me, I usually am caught up in the play and say nothing to myself until it is finished.

Spontaneity is a way of defining engrossment, the suspension of self-talk that accompanies a good play. In contrast, an unreflected response that results in a flub is considered impulsive and untrained. "Keep your eye on the ball," the player is warned once again. "Spontaneity" therefore only refers to the successful plays that result from coordinating the two role-taking acts. In other words, "spontaneity" or naturalness is the well-trained and executed play. It is an achievement.[3]

The embracement of the role of batter is batting, of pitcher is pitching, of fielder is fielding, and so on. Embracement leads to a fusion of the "I," or actor, and the "me," or reflected-upon self, in the position. For example, the batter unquestioningly accepts his or her self-instructions, "Keep your eye on the ball, level swing, watch for the curve." The batter then acts on these directions because he or she has embraced the role they constitute.

In the reality of the game the batter may or may not hit the ball right. Nonetheless, embracing the position is how he or she plays, as opposed to acting the role. When embracement results in that successful swing, successful hit, or successful catch, the player senses himself or herself as suspended in time. In terms of the ideal, he or she is suspended in the (self-) embrace of the generalized other. In fact, the batter may embrace himself or herself from any number of roles. For example, he or she might coolly define it as a normal, superior performance that astonishes others.

This feeling of suspension is expressed by many players. The following dialogue illustrates two sides of the experience:

> Sometimes the pitch looks like it takes 15 seconds to get to the plate. I know I'm going to slam it then.
>
> Do you ever miss those pitches?
>
> Never.
>
> Do you ever feel you wait too long?
>
> That's when my timing is off. I start thinking about what to do.

It is unclear whether the two experiences of batting are objectively different or simply subjectively experienced as different depending on whether the swing was successful or not. In the case of failure, the batter acknowledges his or her ongoing reflection during the play and blames the reflection for the failure. In the case of success, the batter goes on embracing the memory of the act as he or she replays it. Whether successful or a failure, fun is experienced when the embracement of the other has been consummated by taking the play away from the other. The emphasis for both winner, the taker, and loser, the taken, is how they played. In other words, winning and losing happen in the game and are only make-believe.

That many players report suspending the "I/me" dialogue during a good play does not mean that their play is not observed, defined, and acknowledged. Other players are taking in the action in order to respond to it. Thus although the player fuses his or her "I" and "me," a real or imagined observer is available, from whose perspective the player can continue to embrace himself or herself after the action. The reflected-upon "me" of the just-completed action is embraced with the support of this audience. Embracement of self from the audience's role extends the player's subjective validation into the broader social world.

Embracing the Generalized Other

The third embraced role is the generalized other that is concretized by those who define baseball as play. Each ball player participates in the definition of the situation from beginning to end. Goffman (1961) distinguishes between two activities, participating and playing, by referring to those who define the situation in the surrounding gaming encounter as participants and those who enact the roles as players. Of course, the players are both, but some, for example those who sit on the bench or in the stands, are only participants. Their participation requires role taking the actions and defining them as degrees of play using generally understood criteria.

The play of a game is defined by two sets of criteria. One, codified in the rule books, covers the allowable plays of the game. The other, the rules of moral and entertaining sportsmanship, covers the demeanor of participation. I refer to these as the effective, or play, rules, and the affective, or participatory, rules. The gaming encounter of the fans, of course, does not exist solely for support of the play of the game. Much of the fun for fans comes from being a fan. For the moment, however, the fun of gaming is examined as a part of a player's participation in it.

That actions of participants are essential to play is clear from player reports of things that hinder or ruin play:

> If anything negative was said aloud I would feel more guilty and hate the game even more, but I would play even harder the next play to make myself feel better.
>
> An umpire who was either stupid or biased against one team (always mine).
>
> An opponent who was always moaning or playing dirty.
>
> Intentionally breaking rules and then denying it.
>
> A coach who *always* yells at his players.
>
> Laziness.
>
> High spiking.
>
> Calling nasty names.

Not all players find these gaming jousts disruptive. Some in fact find them helpful. As one put it, "Things that are said (good or bad) are always inspirational reinforcement." Nevertheless, there is a point where play is ruined by participant behavior.

As some social validation of play is required to fulfill the definition of having played the game, the players must take the role of some defining agent. Of course, a player can define his or her own actions as play, but this narrow behavior cuts the player off from the fun of a broader and therefore additional novel experience of self. The fun of validation is available from embracing the role of the generalized other as it is displayed in the vocalizations and actions of one's teammates. "The team is the generalized other insofar as it enters—as an organizing process or social activity—into the experience of any one of the individual members of it" (Mead, 1934, p. 154).

Umpires, opposing players, and fans also contend for a share of the validating role. Umpires display the effective criteria of the generalized other; fans usually display the affective criteria; coaches may display both effective and affective aspects of the generalized other.

The third part of a player's fun comes from embracing and then playing at various displays of the generalized other. The simplest way of playing a validation is to smile. The smile not only displays the player's own confirmation of the act as play but also, when given in response to the comments of others, displays an embracement of their validation. Thank you's, agreement with statements, and elaborate recountings of what one did ("Did you see that, I almost dropped it!") are other ways of validating actions. Technology, such as photographs, films, and tapes, is also used to display and therefore validate specific actions as play. Here, however, I am concerned with a player's validating action at the time of play.

Taking the role of the generalized other is an ongoing cognitive-affective action. However, it is embraced most openly after a play when players accept and recount their actions as play. By embracing the role of others in the definition of play, the player completes the round of role taking.

Discussion

In summary, the fun of playing a game comes from each of three role embracements and their subsequent actions that together constitute engrossment. These are (a) embracing the role of the other(s) so that one "directs" the other's play, (b) embracing one's own role and acting, and (c) embracing the role of a generalized other and displaying a social validation of the play act on reflection.

The three fun moments are three instances of the fusion of the "I" and the "me." Two of these are types that Mead identified as the fusion of the "I" and the "me" in teamwork and fusion of the "I" and the "me" in religious and patriotic feeling. In teamwork "the full concreteness of the 'me' depends upon a man's capacity to take the attitude of everybody else in the process which he directs" (Mead, 1934, p. 277). Here, Mead is discussing actions in which two or more people do the same thing, as when people pile up sandbags during a flood. In patriotic or religious feeling, the fusion of the "I" and the "me" comes about by identification of the self with the generalized other.

In a baseball play the fusion is more discrete because it is an individual rather than a team action and more momentary because it is only one of a series of actions. When successfully acting in a role the player fuses the "I" and "me" in the momentary reality of the move. The player is calling out in himself or herself what teammates and fans are calling out in him or her. Once that player's action passes, however, the calling out is directed at the next player. The fusion of the "I" and the "me" that comes from enacting the role of generalized other likewise lasts only as long as the cheers. At the end of the game fans and players, especially of the winning team, may share another measure of group fusion.

The most characteristic fusion of the "I" and the "me" in baseball play, however, is the make-believe fusion that occurs by taking the play away from the other. In the opposing player's reality there is no fusion. He or she remains in a competitive posture. Nevertheless, the fun of the play is essentially the make-believe reality of directing the other to do as one wants. The batter or pitcher must subjectively feel he or she has a directed control of the other.

Fun in baseball is the reflection on one's actions, but this fun only becomes the play of baseball when the three types of fun are included. To play a game as an ongoing interaction the player must play reciprocal roles in turn. The batter must become a participant who roots his or her teammates on and must likewise accept being taken by surprise or out-played. Only when players reflect on their involvement can they experience the fun of what they are doing.

Conclusion

I have argued that play in games consists of three actions, each of which is fun. Play involves (a) embracing a novel object, (b) acting in the world as if that novel object were part of oneself so that the "I" in the ensuing action is novel, and (c) validating that novel action so that the "me" or reflected-upon self is also novel in the social world. Each of these novel experiences of self is a form of fun. Only in play are all three forms of fun enacted as an ongoing and interrelated entity.

Play varies between narrow and broad performances that approach a negotiated ideal. The narrow player has fun. The broad player acknowledges the debt his or her play owes to others.

In agreement with Goffman, I have argued that the fun of an action can only be had by participating in a surrounding transformational interaction that supports engrossment. I have argued, however, that fun in play must be understood separately from the fun of other focused events. For example, the flow experienced by a skilled surgeon who embraces his or her role fails to measure up to the ideal of play because (a) the action is a matter of life and death—there is no make-believe role he or she can embrace, and (b) the action does not allow for the intrusion of participants who define the action and urge the player on to greater exploits.

Notes

1. The term *game* is also often used as a sociological metaphor for serious social encounters. Such a use runs the risk of reifying the concept and misrepresenting the reality of those encounters. Here, the term *game* is used literally to mean an organized event intended for play outcomes.
2. The concept of hypothetical instantiation applies here. Sarbin and Coe (1972) argue persuasively that role taking is not so much imagining oneself as the other as it is attenuated acting as the other.
3. On the issue of being spontaneous or, in a broader sense, a natural ball player, the following response of Joe DiMaggio is instructive. "As for being a natural, well nobody ever worked harder than I did. In spring training I'd have Earle Combs hit me grounders in the outfield, and hit balls over my head, and to my right and to my left. And effortless? Let me tell you, every time I take a step today I'm reminded of my baseball career." (Quoted by Ira Brokaw, "The Presence of DiMaggio," *New York Times*, January 1, 1984.)

References

Caillois, R. (1961). *Man, play and games.* New York: The Free Press.

Csikszentmihalyi, M. (1975). *Beyond boredom and anxiety.* San Francisco: Jossey-Bass.

De Charms, R. (1968). *Personal Causation*. New York: Academic Press.

Goffman, E. (1961). *Encounters*. Indianapolis: Bobbs-Merrill.

Huizinga, J. (1955). *Homo ludens: A study of the play element in culture*. New York: Beacon.

Mead, G.H. (1934). *Mind, self and society*. Chicago: University of Chicago Press.

Sarbin, T.R., & Coe, W.C. (1972). *Hypnosis: A social psychological analysis of influence communication*. New York: Holt, Rinehart & Winston.

Sutton-Smith, B. (1984). Recreation as folly's parody. *A TAASP Newsletter*, **10**(4), pp. 4-13, 22.

CHAPTER 6
The Lighter Side of Play

E.P. Johnsen
Kathleen Snyder
University of Kansas

An activity as universal to children as play must have numerous developmental functions and correlates. Indeed, some outcomes of play have been productively researched. For example, some cognitive manifestations of imaginative play, such as the increase of creative verbal production, seem to have been relatively well established (Christie & Johnsen, 1983). Likewise, the role of play in the functioning of unconscious processes has been emphasized by psychoanalytic psychologists. This "dark side of play," as some authors refer to it, has been discussed by Lidz (1968) as follows:

> One reason why unacceptable ideas can remain isolated, and can emerge in play and still not be clearly conscious, is that many of the little child's sensuous feelings, desires, and thoughts, as well as his primitive hostile feelings, originated before language was well developed and they were never properly linked up with words; and some were . . . in a form that could not be communicated. . . . There are no simple words for many of the diffuse ideas and fantasies that the child has felt or symbolized visually, and they are not a topic for discussion by elders or with elders. They remain very much of a private world, and are thought about in an amorphous combination of feeling states and mental pictures. (p. 247)

Thus play becomes a medium by which psychiatrists can help children explore and dissipate the id impulses and their associated feelings of anxiety and depression. In spite of questions that can be raised about the empirical adequacy of these psychoanalytic assumptions, play therapy seems to hold a powerful capacity for exploring the darker issues troubling children who cannot cope with powerful feelings.

Recent research also suggests, however, a lighter side to the role of play in child development. Specifically, if play is intimately connected with the images mentioned above, it can also be hypothesized that playful activities deal not only with taboos but also with one positive side of social development, the emergence of self-control.

Self-control, according to Harter (1983), should be viewed as a broad array of intellectual and emotional mechanisms that transform a child's social learning into internalized contol over his or her behavior. This ability to intentionally manage mental events for the purpose of self-regulation has been linked to the emergence of images (Berkowitz, 1982). Let us examine briefly how this occurs.

Self-control in young children is usually operationalized as the ability to delay pursuit of a desirable object, to wait, or to cope with frustration. Each of these abilities is considered an important landmark in the process of maturation within our society. In order to delay attainment of a reward, children are said to either distract themselves from the desirable object or think about the object in a transformed way, for example, to think of foods as if they were pictures of edibles rather than the real thing. Both of these approaches involve transforming mental images of objects. Mischel (1981) reported that children under 5 years of age have difficulty separating themselves from the motivational aspects of real-world desirables because they do not have the image manipulation strategies that would enhance their self-control.

What does all of this have to do with the issue of play? If the capacity of children to formulate images as well as to retrieve and reformulate them is linked to the initial displays of behavioral self-control, then play activities that enhance fantasy and imagery manipulation may be connected to this developmental process. Tower (1983), in her review of the role of imagery in child development, strongly suggests that imaginative skills promote emotional regulation, behavioral control, and resources for coping with stress. A few studies in the literature have examined these relationships.

Saltz, Dixon, and Johnson (1977), in a complex training study investigating the effects of play and fantasy on disadvantaged preschoolers' thinking and social behavior, used a resistance-to-temptation format to assess children's self-control. Children were left unsupervised in a playroom with desirable toys but were instructed not to touch them because they belonged to someone else. As a measure of self-control, unobtrusive observers recorded the amount of time that elapsed between the instructions and actual manipulation of the toys. Children in the play groups were able to withhold interest for a longer period of time than children who had received no training, but there was an even stronger effect for children in the group that was also given distraction strategies such as "Think about your favorite story while you're waiting for me to come back." This suggests that children in both play conditions used manipulation of images and attention control, but the effects for this particular sample of youngsters were greatest with the more direct manipulation.

In addition, Saltz, Dixon, and Johnson tested all subjects on the Matching Familiar Figures Test, a problem-solving device that requires children to search for perceptual commonalities among ordinary everyday objects. The test is scored on a latency basis to measure the "reflectivity" of children, that is, the amount of time they use to detect solutions. This test has been described as an indirect measure of impulse control in children. Play groups once again scored somewhat better than nonplay training groups in not jumping to conclusions.

Singer (1961, 1973) reported that children who engaged in substantial make-believe play were also capable of engaging in delay. Delay was specifically defined in these studies as the amount of time children would wait in a simulated space capsule in a play area. The degree of make-believe engaged in is usually measured in such studies through interviews or by projective tests, but the reliability of such data with children this age is usually relatively low. The ecological validity of the self-control tasks is often criticized for violating the natural complexity of the self-control phenomenon by defining relevant dimensions in ways that would never occur in real-world settings.

Friedrich-Cofer, Huston-Stein, Kipnis, Susman, and Clewett (1979) designed a field study to assess the impact of prosocial television on the social behavior of children. In one training condition, subjects were exposed to the television program alone ("Mr. Roger's Neighborhood"), and in another, to the program accompanied by sociodramatic play materials that were used by the classroom teachers of these students in whatever way they wished. Observations revealed that children in the combined treatment conditions, television plus play materials, engaged in significantly more imaginative play and self-regulation. Self-regulation was defined as fulfilling social responsibilities such as working during the clean-up period without help from peers or supervision from teachers. Although this definition differs from that used in the delay studies, both types of measurement are commonly used to operationalize the self-control construct. Interestingly, students in the combined condition increased not only in self-regulation but also in aggressive responses to peers. In a third training condition in which teachers were also trained in the use of the play materials, for example role-taking episodes, increases in play and self-regulation were reported without concomitant increases in aggression. Incidentally, positive social interactions such as comforting and giving affection or praise also increased in the two play conditions.

Finally, Udwin (1983) conducted a well-controlled study in which children who had been placed in institutional foster care because of neglect at home were given imaginative skills training. These children, aged 4 years, 8 months on the average, either received imaginative skills training for 4 weeks or were placed in a control condition with no training but with equal exposure to the adult experimenters. Variables controlled in the study included time in foster care, IQ, and predisposition to fantasy as measured by the Children's Thematic Apperception Test and by Guilford's Unusual Uses Test, a creative measure. After the treatment period, observations of play behavior showed significant increases in imaginative play and cooperation with peers and significant decreases in aggressive behavior for the play group but not for the control group. Before treatment, children in both groups had engaged in imaginative play with less frequency than home-reared children, but after treatment the play group's frequency increased to a comparable level. Although children in the study were clinically described as displaying aggressive behavior more frequently than non-foster care children, none of the sample had problems sufficient to refer them for therapy or special treatment. The degree of training effectiveness may be accounted for by the initially low levels of play and self-control; it is unknown whether a similar but noninstitutional sample would respond in the same way. Udwin does indicate that age emerged as an important factor in that younger children seemed more responsive to imaginative play training. Because the sample included children as old as 6 years, 2 months (an age at which, among noninstitutionalized children, games with rules become prominent), there may be some effect due to normative change in the characteristics of pretend play itself.

What are we to conclude from consideration of the development of mental imagery and the concomitant emergence of self-control? On the one hand, there are those who insist that children's play is a mask for sexual impulses, irrational fears, and hostile aggression. Play, from this point of view, serves as a mechanism allowing internal, unconscious factors some degree of expression. Whatever the accuracy of this view, it seems equally probable that children are also stimulus bound, that is, dependent on the concrete and sensory stimulation of their environment to direct their behavior. The capacity for imaging may be a crucial process for freeing the child from this dominance of the environment. Specifically, the initial display of self-control may indeed be mediated by some type of internalization process. This process may involve the acquisition of imaginative content as well as the skills of retrieval and transformation that allow the child additional control of his or her own behavior.

Imaginative play training, with its emphasis on the use of fantasy and the development of roles, has been shown to enhance spontaneous occurrences of pretense among preschoolers. The literature reviewed above suggests that when the capacity for pretense is enhanced, there is an accompanying increase in certain forms of self-control. As the child grows older, such factors as increased self-awareness and self-monitoring, along with the emergence of language, self-evaluation, and social comparison capabilities, contribute to self-control. While the cognitive and emotional processes inherent in managing one's own behavior become increasingly sophisticated as these capabilities develop, perhaps children gain their initial sense of self-control within the context of early imaginative play experiences. Some authors suggest that play experiences are a wellspring of the darker side of human personality, revealing antisocial and negative motives. However, we believe that play, by providing the imagery and transformation skills necessary to free oneself from the control of the environment, becomes not merely an infantile way of thinking of experiences (Erikson, 1940) but rather a way of exercising independence and self-direction.

References

Berkowitz, L. (1982). Self-control development and relations to prosocial behavior: A response to Peterson. *Merrill-Palmer Quarterly, 28*, 223-236.

Christie, J., & Johnsen, E.P. (1983). The role of play in social-intellectual development. *Review of Educational Research*, **53**, 93-115.

Erickson, E. (1940). Studies in the interpretation of play: I. Clinical observations of play disruption in young children. *Genetic Psychology Monographs*, **22**, 557-671.

Friedrich-Cofer, L., Huston-Stein, A., Kipnis, D.M., Susman, E., & Clewett, S. (1979). Environmental enhancement of prosocial television content: Effects of interpersonal behavior, imaginative play and self-regulation in a natural setting. *Developmental Psychology*, **15**, 637-646.

Harter, S. (1983). Developmental perspectives on the self-system. In P. Mussen (Ed.), *Handbook of child psychology: Vol. IV. Socialization, personality, and social development* (pp. 19, 275-386). New York: Wiley.

Lidz, T. (1968). *The person*. New York: Basic Books.

Mischel, W. (1981). Metocognition and the rules of delay. In J. Flavell & L. Ross (Eds.) *Social cognitive development: Frontiers and possible futures*. New York: Cambridge University Press.

Saltz, E., Dixon, D., & Johnson, J. (1977). Training disadvantaged preschoolers on various fantasy activities: Effects on cognitive functioning and impulse control. *Child Development*, **48**, 367-380.

Singer, J. (1961). Imagination and waiting ability in young children. *Journal of Personality*, **29**, 396-413.

Singer, J. (1973). *The child's world of make believe*. New York: Academic Press.

Tower, R. (1983). Imagery: Its role in development. In A. Sheikh (Ed.), *Imagery: Current theory, research and application*. New York: Wiley.

Udwin, I. (1983). Imaginative play training as an intervention method with insitutionalized preschool children. *British Journal of Education Psychology*, **53**, 32-39.

CHAPTER 7

Play as Adaptation:
The Work-Play Dichotomy Revisited

Kendall Blanchard
Middle Tennessee State University

Historically, Western society, Euro-America in particular, has had problems with the idea of play. Despite the occasional emergence of a leisure ethic (e.g., Mergen, 1977) and a continuing preoccupation with sport in this country, play has been viewed by most as only marginally legitimate. It has been reserved for the young and understood as antithetical to work. Work has been seen as meaningful, purposeful activity, the driving force behind progress. Play, on the other hand, has been the antonym of work. It is treated as having limited importance, as being nonproductive and in some cases impeding progress. This dichotomy has found its clearest expression in the ideological milieu fostered by labor intensive industrial capitalism, early Protestantism, and frontierism. It continues to be a significant force in Western political economy.

The problem is not work nor the enthusiasm some manifest for work as a value. Work, defined here as activity undertaken for the purpose of achieving an objective, is essential to human existence. Work does make the world go around. A problem arises, however, when work is glorified at the expense of play. Play is also an important human activity and, as does work, it may have meaningful objectives and consequences. Most important, it is not the polar opposite of work. Play does not preclude work. Nevertheless, this false dichotomy persists. The dangers of such a dichotomy have been discussed in earlier contexts (e.g., Stevens, 1980), but here I am suggesting that the dichotomy is particularly problematic as an impediment to cross-cultural understanding and concomitantly a boon to ethnocentric bias.

Work and Play as Adaptive Activities

If work and play are not mirror images of each other, what *are* their appropriate respective counterparts? Work appears to be better understood in contradistinction to leisure instead of to play. In fact, the idea of work may have evolved as a means of describing the not-leisure state (DeGrazia, 1962). Work is an activity directed toward external objectives, leisure is activity undertaken for its own sake. The distinction is clear. Unfortunately, there is no generally accepted English word to describe the counterpart of play. Perhaps the best alternative is the concept of "not-play" (Blanchard & Cheska, 1984). I use play and not-play to describe the opposite ends of the playfulness continuum (see Figure 1).

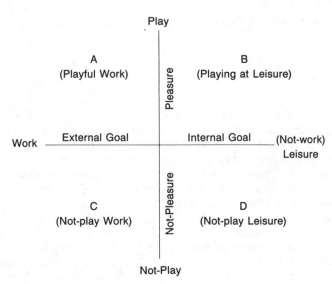

Figure 1.   The dimensions of human activity.

Using Bateson's (1972) definition, I suggest that play is best understood as metacommunication (i.e., communication about communication) and paradox. In the act of playing one communicates, albeit subtly, that one is not in fact doing what one appears to be doing. In this sense, play becomes a form of symbolic distancing. It is a message about reality, but one expressed indirectly. Thus play is distant, not-play proximate; play is metacommunication, not-play communication; play is paradox, not-play logically intact; play is open-ended, not-play closed.

As Bateson (1972) has explained, play as metacommunication has evolutionary implications. In other words, play is a major factor in evolution. The precise role play has filled in that process has been debated. Bateson himself sees its primary significance in the evolution of language. Bruner (1975), however, suggests that play is important to human existence because it provides models of behavior that are self-motivating and thus instrumental to learning and task completion:

> There is a well known rule in the psychology of learning, the Yerkes-Dodson Law, that states that the more complex a skill is, the lower the optimum level

of motivation required to learn it. That is, too much motivation arousal can interfere with learning. By deemphasizing the importance of the goal, play may serve to reduce excessive drive and thus enable young animals and children to learn more easily the skills they will need when they are older. (p. 82)

Consistent with Bruner's theme, I suggest that play is an important mechanism of adaptation, that in fact, play *is* adaptation. In the process of primate evolution, adaptation and survival become increasingly cognitive, as opposed to mechanical or instinctive. Human beings, in comparison to other anthropoids, are forced to think more about and reflect on the mechanics of adaptation. This reflexive thought is both a gift and a dread responsibility of self-consciousness. Whether it be the anxiety that comes with contemplating the inevitability of death or the pleasures of anticipating a tasty meal or an exciting sexual encounter, this unavoidable reflecting on existence represents an important dimension of human adaptation. In other words, the struggle for human survival is not a mindless struggle. It is a symbolic act. And it is a source of tension, a tension generated by conflict between the perceived demands of survival and the will to act. At an instinctive level, such tension is present but limited. At symbolic levels, however, the tension is both unavoidable and intense.

This is the evolutionary importance of play. Play is a mechanism that human beings employ to remove themselves from the angst of reflecting on the realities of existence. Play is a symbolic distancing that relieves or at least limits that tension. Yet it is not a form of escapism, not pure fantasy. Play, like work, addresses those vital issues of survival. Unlike work, however, it does so indirectly. Play may reverse or abstract, but it deals with the fundamental problems of adaptation nonetheless.

The extent to which play characterizes adaptive styles varies from one culture to another. As Dobkin de Rios and Schroeder (1979) have suggested, the variable role of play between cultures may be rooted in different styles of left and right brain use. They also raise the possibility that "play in human society is neurologically adaptive behavior" (p. 13).

Regardless of its physiological basis, cultural variability, and function, play is universal. All cultural systems are more or less playful. The quantitative distinctions that exist between play orientations can, however, be instructive in understanding cultural differences and variable adaptation styles.

Understanding Native America via Its Play

As a means of illustrating the adaptive significance of play and its potential as a perspective for understanding cultural differences, consider Native America. While one must be careful not to overgeneralize about Native American societies, it is safe to suggest that as a rule they have a playful air about them. This playfulness is perhaps most evident in their games and sports, from the ubiquitous ball game of prehistory to the many sports, hand games, gambling games, and other playful activities of the post-Columbian period.

The proliferation and importance of Native American games and sports—treated here as subsets of play—have been noted numerous times since the first contacts between Indians and Europeans. Travelers, explorers, and military men were intrigued by the intensity and level of commitment characterizing Native American games. Early writers frequently described the commitment as "addiction," suggesting that it obstructed the pursuit of "more serious" activities (e.g., Adair, 1775/1966; Bartram, 1793; de Paina, 1676). There is an obvious playfulness to Native American lifestyles.

The Problem of the "Playful" Stereotype

Unfortunately, much of the reference to Indian playfulness is implicitly or explicitly racist. Wittingly or not, writers have often portrayed this playfulness in ways that make negative stereotypes credible. This has been particularly true outside the social sciences and most evident in the early historical accounts. In many of these cases, the writer's suggestion that Indians love to play is tantamount to his saying they are lazy, not industrious, and difficult to motivate. Underscoring the reality of Indian play can also suggest childishness and naiveté. For example, Bartram (1793) commented, with reference to the Creeks, "they are fond of games and gambling, and amuse themselves like children in relating extravagant stories, to cause surprise and mirth" (p. 211-212). To emphasize the skills of hand and string games is to imply that Indians are "crafty." To cite their use of magic in the attempt to manipulate game outcomes is to reiterate their "trickery" and lack of trustworthiness. Other games suggest "paganism," "idolatry," "immorality," and various forms of offensive impiety. The gambling that so often accompanies Indian games can be used to portray the Native American as wasteful and economically irrational. And finally, descriptions of their play can also be used to reinforce notions about the "senseless brutality" and "bestiality" of aboriginal Americans (e.g., de Paina, 1676).

The easy translation of observations about Native American play into degrading stereotypes creates a dilemma for social scientists interested in the objective analysis of Indian games and sports. Does this mean they must abandon the pursuit or downplay this important dimension of Native American life? I think not. Rather they must rethink the concept of play, remove it from the realm of fantasy, and take it beyond the false juxtaposition to work. Play is a meaningful form of adaptation and its elaboration a major achievement of Native America. This perspective makes possible a more humanistic appreciation of Indian games and sports as well as a better understanding of other areas of Native American life. It also allows the anthropologist to admit to the playfulness of aboriginal American life without apology or fear of misinterpretation.

The Adaptive Significance of Games and Sports in Native America

Adaptation is defined herein as the process by which a system effectively interacts with the natural, social, and historical forces comprising its total environment. It is assumed that culture is an adaptive mechanism and that all facets of a particular culture are elements of that adaptive process. Defined in the broadest sense, adaptive mechanisms are those activities or institutions that lead to a more effective integration of the social system and its eco-niche.

As Roberts, Arth, and Bush (1959) have noted, games and sports can be viewed as adaptive mechanisms. This is particularly evident among Native American groups, being most obvious at technological and economic levels. Skill games develop coordination and dexterity, affect redistribution, and may have other less obvious functions (e.g., as population control devices). Native American games affect social organization by assisting in the social maintenance process (Cheska, 1979) and reinforcing social definitions (Blanchard, 1976). They have important political (Haas, 1940) and ritual dimensions (Culin, 1907). The games and sports of American Indian groups also are significant factors in the process of their adaptation to change (Fox, 1961).

Games and sports are important to the adaptive strategies of traditional Native American societies. Furthermore, they tend to manifest a particular flavor, a playfulness that may be endemic not only to games but to the total Native American adaptive process. This play element is witnessed too in myths about games, in attitudes toward competition, in the response to rules and the enforcement of these rules, and in the frequently incongruent relationship between means and outcomes (see Blanchard, 1981). To the Euro-American observer, this playfulness is obvious, since it contrasts sharply with typically middle-class American notions about competition. It is also often misinterpreted as a lack of seriousness or commitment. It is not that at all. Instead, it is the actualizing of that paradox of play Bateson has defined, the communication of the metamessage that is play via a game medium.

Recognizing this inordinate amount of playfulness and its importance makes certain features of Indian games more understandable. For example, Culin's (1903) conclusion that among Native American groups "games of pure calculation, such as chess, are entirely absent" (p. 58) makes obvious sense. Games of strategy imply a direct attempt to control outcomes that in a playful world view can only be affected by circuitous manipulations. If one is successful in altering his or her fate, it is because he or she worked around rather than directly attacked the problem. Nevertheless, as Cheska (1979) has observed, to say that Indians do not engage in games of strategy is not to say that Indians do not employ strategy in other types of games. They do. But it is a playful strategy, indirect rather than direct, cooperative rather than coercive, and more deceptive than forceful.

If this is the case, the "addiction" to gambling often credited to Indians (e.g., Adair, 1775; Williams, 1927) can also be understood. Gambling is an activity that allows the forces of fate to make decisions for the participant. One may manipulate, coax, deceive, bargain with, or trick the gods. These are the skills and strategies of gaming, and they may in some cases prove effective. In most instances, however, such efforts are futile. The expected happens. But when the unexpected does occur, the strategy is validated, and chance becomes hope. This element of possibility keeps such playfulness from being fatalism. A playful social system invariably finds gambling games more compatible than those of pure calculation. Thus it should come as no surprise that Native Americans have appeared preoccupied with betting. It is also no wonder that this preoccupation frequently manifests itself as moral commitment (e.g., in connection with betting on ball games in Mesoamerica and in the Southeast).

Play as Adaptive World View

This playful quality of Native American life can be observed in areas other than games and sports and provides some insight into the ideological conflicts between Indian and Euro-American traditions. Consider, for example, the conflicting attitudes toward nature. What is often viewed as the Indians' greater respect for the environment is in fact a manifestation of their playful world view. This reverence for the land and its flora and fauna is but an illustration of playful distancing. Hunting and fishing are viewed not as the exploitation of animal life, but as a cooperative relationship between hunter and hunted, between fisher and fish. The ritual surrounding the hunt reflects the paradox that is play. The hunter entreats the prey, and the message is ultimately metamessage: "I am killing you, but I am really not killing you." At the same time, land is to be used, not sold, owned, or destroyed. Playfulness is reflected in the implicit assumption that "land is not controlled, even though it appears that way." The less playful world view of Euro-America is more direct: nature is to be exploited, land to be mastered and owned. There is little or no paradox or uncertainty in the message. Therefore, there is nothing unexpected in the conflict of the two general ecological perspectives. One is simply more playful than the other.

Native American cosmologies also tend to reflect the playful element. They limit categorical distinctions between "this world" and "other worlds," are more circular than hierarchical in nature, and emphasize harmonious relationships between parts rather than unilateral dominance and submission (see Figure 2). The mythological figures in these systems frequently reflect this playfulness. Tricksters are often prominent personalities and by their behavior provide models for skirting the obvious and in so doing outmaneuvering the inevitable (e.g., Radin's [1956] Winnebago trickster).

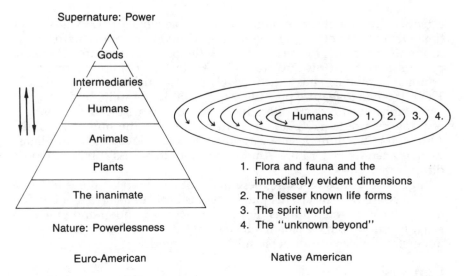

Figure 2. Euro- and Native American cosmologies.

Native American religious systems, consistent with the suggested playful theme, exhort to practical morality by reasoned advice and sound example. They have little room for the belief imperative and lose much of their significance if taken too seriously. Furthermore, proselytizing, a form of intellectual manipulation and control, is viewed as both strange and distasteful. This play factor in Indian religions is manifested in the personalities, roles, and styles of its practitioners. There is the curing shaman who reorders the patient's universe rather than the patient's body, the clown whose performance employs a subtle humor to chide and reaffirm moral principles (Heib, 1979), and the witch whose very existence is paradox.

Indian political styles and relationships can also be understood from the perspective provided by this notion of play as adaptive. Political process in Native America is often marked by deliberations that address issues through circumvention and perpetual discussion. Leadership is generally accomplished by example as opposed to coercion, and authority defined in terms of one's willingness to relinquish that authority. The wisdom that so frequently accompanies effective leadership in Native America is a playful intellect, a distancing from rather than a direct confrontation with the issues. The wars that often color political patterns in Native America are in many cases more aptly viewed as sporting events, playful encounters in which skirting, tricking, or outmaneuvering the enemy is the preferred alternative to killing.

The playful social systems of Native America structure time in ways that Euro-Americans find disconcerting. Time for the Indian is not a progression of specialized, inflexible, sacrosanct categories that organize activities. Instead, it is a setting within which events occur. Events order time, not time events. Time is generalized and more important for structuring the past than for reckoning with the present or future. There are progressions of events and chronologies, but they simply happen.

Indian humor also has a distinctively playful quality about it (Deloria, 1969). It tends to feature playful teasing, self-deprecation, and the obviously ludicrous. Jokes are often characterized by plays on words, twinges of irony, or riddle-like paradoxes. In most cases, the humor is subtle. Although Indian humor can be appreciated and enjoyed by non-Indians, there is a tendency for Euro-American humor to be less subtle and more direct.

In general, I am suggesting here that Native American life is tied to a playful sense of reality. This playfulness is basic to its styles of adaptation and self-understandings. From hand games to hoop-and-pole contests, from economic exchange to healing, the play theme is there. To understand play is to understand Native America.

Conclusion

Playful adaptation is an effective survival mechanism. Play, like work, has important functions and consequences. The critical distinction in the comparison of adaptive styles is not between work and play, but rather between levels of playfulness. More playful systems (e.g., Native America) reflect a distancing style that is indirect, flexible, curvilinear, and often circuitous. Less playful systems (e.g., Euro-America) tend to operate with a direct, inflexible, linear, and confrontational mode. Both styles ultimately lead to the achievement of adaptive goals, at least ideally, but in different ways.

Those social and behavioral scientists who study play must be cautious in their attempt to defend the work/play dichotomy. To do so is to overlook the adaptive significance of play, its functional similarity to work, and its potential for understanding cultural differences. Most important, the dichotomization of work and play lends itself to ethnocentric bias in the description and interpretation of those cultural systems that are traditionally more playful in orientation than that of Euro-America.

References

Adair, J. (1966). *History of the American Indian.* New York: Argonaut Press. (Original work published 1775)

Bartram, W. (1793). *Travels.* Charlottesville: University of Virginia Press.

Bateson, G. (1972). *Steps to an ecology of mind.* New York: Ballantine Books.

Blanchard, K. (1976). Team sports and social organization among the Mississippi Choctaws. *Tennessee Anthropologist,* 1(1), 63-70.

Blanchard, K. (1981). *The Mississippi Choctaws at play: The serious side of leisure.* Urbana, IL: University of Illinois Press.

Blanchard, K., & Cheska, A.T. (1984). *The anthropology of sport: An introduction*. South Hadley, MA: Bengin and Garvey.

Bruner, J. (1975). Play is serious business. *Psychology Today, 8*, 81-83.

Cheska, A.T. (1979). Native American games as strategies of social maintenance. In E. Norbeck & C. Farrer (Eds.), *Forms of play and Native North Americans* (pp. 227-247). St. Paul, MN: West.

Culin, S. (1907). Games. In F.W. Hodge (Ed.), *Handbook of American Indians* (pp. 483-486) (Bulletin 30). Washington, DC: Bureau of American Ethnology.

De Grazia, S. (1962). *Of time, work and leisure*. New York: Twentieth Century Fund.

Deloria, V., Jr. (1969). *Custer died for your sins*. New York: Avon.

de Paina, Father J. (1676). Origin and beginning of the ball game which the Apalachee and Yustage Indians have been playing from pagan times up to the year 1676. In J. Granberry (Trans.), *Archivo general de Indias, Seville, Escribania de camara, legajo 156. XXX*. Part of unpublished manuscript by J.M. Goggin. (Photostats in Stetson Collection, University of Florida Library, Gainesville.)

Dobkin de Rios, M., & Schroeder, R. (1979). American occupations, leisure time use and left brain/right brain dialectics: Some explorations. In E. Norbeck & C. Farrer (Eds.), *Forms of play of Native North Americans* (pp 1-16). St. Paul, MN: West.

Fox, J.R. (1961). Pueblo baseball: A new use for old witchcraft. *Journal of American Folklore, 74*, 9-16.

Haas, M.R. (1940). Creek inter-town relations. *American Anthropologist, 42*, 479-489.

Heib, L. (1979). The ritual clown: Humor and ethics. In E. Norbeck & C. Farrer (Eds.), *Forms of play of Native North Americans* (pp. 171-188). St. Paul, MN: West.

Mergen, B. (1977). From play to recreation: The acceptance of leisure in the United States, 1880-1930. In P. Stevens, Jr. (Ed.), *Studies in the anthropology of play* (pp. 187-200). Champaign, IL: Leisure Press.

Radin, P. (1956). *The trickster: A study in American Indian mythology*. New York: Schocken Books.

Roberts, J.M., Arth, M.J., & Bush, R.R. (1959). Games in culture. *American Anthropologist, 61*, 597-605.

Stevens, P., Jr. (1980). Play and work: A false dichotomy? In H. Schwartzman (Ed.), *Play and culture* (pp. 316-323). Champaign, IL: Leisure Press.

Williams, S.C. (Ed.). (1927). *Memoirs of Lt. Henry Timberlake*. Johnson City, TN: Watauga Press.

CHAPTER 8

Attitudes Toward Play and Beliefs About Development

James E. Johnson
Pennsylvania State University

Probably no single researcher would even want to attempt to explicate the relationships among play, development, and the environment in a single research study or even in a lifetime program of research. On the other hand, most would agree that it is necessary to conceptualize research problems in multivariate terms and to be able to locate where a given study fits into a general scheme of things. To accomplish this, one usually first identifies distinct areas within the research domain and then proceeds to study intensively the relations within and among areas. In understanding the relationships within and among research areas, one is able to construct a systematic view or model of the topic area under study that represents both a comprehensive overview of the area and an agenda for continuing and future research.

A general perspective for the current work is depicted in Figure 1. Although neither all-inclusive nor prioritized, the diagram illustrates major research areas dealing with the environment and the play behavior and development of children, a general topic that has concerned numerous investigators in early childhood education and developmental psychology in the United States for over 20 years. The autors cited in Figure 1 representing the various areas have been selected for illustrative purposes from among other equally prominent investigators. Furthermore, the authors (with the exception of Schwartzman and Sutton-Smith), it should be noted, do not directly represent the anthropologic-folkloric, animal, social psychological, gestalt, historical, theoretical, or games, sport, or leisure literatures. The researchers listed were selected because their theoretical or empirical (experimental or correlational) work in developmental psychology or early childhood education is related to some degree to the research areas identified in the figure and the current study is done within the traditions of these disciplines. Researchers' names are given to suggest evidence for the model.

The general research area depicted in Figure 1 is vast and spans the entire spectrum from demographic and family structure variables (on the left side of the figure) to the individual child and development variables (on the right side of the figure). The model suggests that play activity

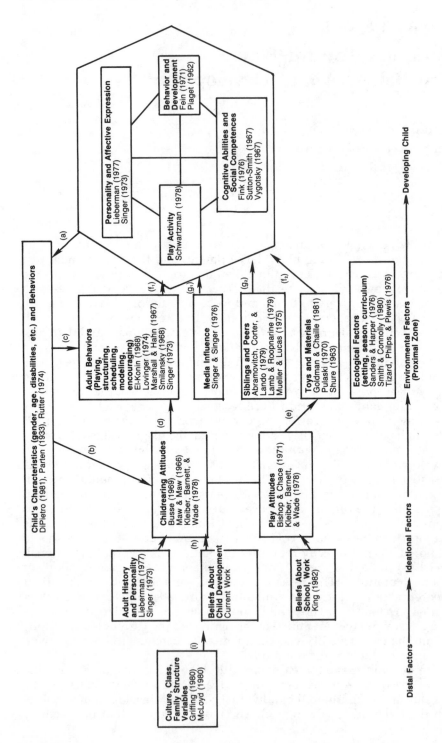

Figure 1.   Diagram of relations among cultural and environmental factors and play and development in young children.

and behavior and development in early childhood are reciprocally related and that each has important significant correlates in the areas of personality and affect on the one hand and cognition and social competence on the other. Line *a* in Figure 1 suggests that the developing system just described relates to the behaviors and characteristics of the child that serve, in turn, as stimulus factors influencing childrearing and play attitudes (line *b*) and adult behaviors (line *c*) in a given culture. Childrearing and play attitudes and adult behaviors themselves are associated with each other (line *d*), as shown in the work of Bishop and Chace (1971) and Kleiber, Barnett, and Wade (1978) among others. These adult ideations are implicated in the selection of toys and materials and certain curricular events and scheduling (ecological factor) for children (line *e*), which together with more direct adult play-related behaviors, such as encouraging play, modeling play, or serving as an audience or producer or as a passive play prop for children's play, shape the proximal environmental zone affecting the play of young children (lines f_1 & f_2). This proximal zone, as shown in Figure 1, also consists of media influences and the presence and behaviors of siblings and peers that have a direct or indirect influence on play in young children (lines g_1 & g_2).

Current work reported here can be located on the left side of Figure 1. Beliefs about child development are hypothesized to be related to distal status factors on the one hand (line *i*) and to childrearing and play attitudes on the other hand (line *h*). Second, Figure 1 suggests that adult history and personality and other belief systems, such as beliefs about school and work, also influence childrearing and play attitudes (line *h*), as well as being related to distal status factors (line *i*). The latter pair of relationships—how beliefs about work and school or achievement and success in a society are associated with distal variables or with childrearing and play attitudes—will not be pursued further in this paper, although their relevance to the present focus on play attitudes and child development beliefs would appear to be considerable.

A number of investigators have sought to delineate the extent and direction of the relationships among play, the play environment, adult ideations, and distal or structural factors. Since this literature is most germane to the current study, the main points made by these researchers will be summarized briefly.

Bishop and Chace (1971), in a classic study, reasoned that young children do not decide for themselves what, where, how, when, and with whom to play. Parents, teachers, and other providers of play experience make these decisions for young children. Adults, moreover, do not make these decisions randomly or haphazardly or based on temporary feelings or moods but based on basic and stable values and beliefs. Because adults' fundamental assumptions about childrearing in general and about sex roles, morality, and achievement specifically no doubt are important in making these decisions affecting the play of young children, it is imperative for researchers to consider the psychological and sociological characteristics of parents. Many such characteristics appear to be related to decisions about play activities, settings, procedures, and content.

Bishop and Chace (1971) considered socioeconomic status, educational level, and various cognitive style and personality traits of parents as pertinent to playfulness-engendering decisions and behaviors. Personality traits such as ability to cope with spontaneity, open-mindedness, adaptability, and role-taking ability were mentioned as important but were deemed not likely to occur as a determinant in isolation. Hence, Bishop and Chace opted to study the conceptual level of parents in relation to measures of the home as a play environment, with the former estimated by Harvey, Hunt, an Schroders (1961) "This I Believe" test, and the latter indexed by a questionnaire containing items such as "Boys should be discouraged from playing with girls' toys and games," "How should a parent react to a child's using a toy in an incorrect but enjoyable manner?" and "Where in the home is your child allowed to play?" Although no significant relationships were found for fathers, significant relationships for mothers were found among conceptual levels, measures of the home as a play environment, and potential creativity in children. Mothers with more abstract conceptual levels provided more play opportunities in the home and this was related to higher creativity in children. These measures were not related to age, income, educational level, or occupation of the parents.

In a more recent study, Kleiber, Barnett, and Wade (1978) began by citing evidence that children from more permissive homes are more creative and playful (e.g., Dreyer & Wells, 1966; Watson, 1957). Kleiber et al. (1978) used Lieberman's (1977) 12-item scale for measuring playfulness in 106 5-year-olds and used Bishop and Chace's (1971) home inventory as the parent measure. They found no evidence that permissiveness in the home was related to playfulness in children but did find for boys a significant negative correlation between playfulness and parental emphasis on skill training in sports and athletics. In addition, higher levels of playfulness in males were related to *not* owning sports equipment, having both parents watch sporting events, having both parents likely to play ball with their child, and longer play sessions.

Maw and Maw (1966), in an earlier study, also reported a gender difference in socialization factors related to playfulness in young children, specifically curiosity. Again, no significant home antecedents were found for girls, but for boys high levels of curiosity were predicted by their fathers' high scores for equalitarianism on the PARI (Parent Attitude Research Instrument) and mothers' low scores on the PARI subscales for fostering dependency, excluding outside influences, and intrusiveness. Finally, in another earlier study, Busse (1969) examined parental characteristics related to flexible thinking in fifth-grade black children. Busse reported that maternal commandingness and paternal rigidity were negatively related to flexibility in children but that moderate parental control predicts flexible thinking. Together, these research studies suggest that different socialization attitudes may be responsible for playfulness in boys and girls, and that permissive childrearing attitudes per se are probably not associated with play in young children.

In the present study, beliefs about development held by mothers and teachers are compared and related to attitudes toward play in young children. Beliefs about development are viewed as an integral feature of a culture's childrearing pattern worthy of study in its own right. Moreover, play attitudes of adults in a society are known to be associated with the play opportunities provided for young children. How teachers and mothers are alike and differ in beliefs and attitudes is the important focus of this study. A group of highly educated mothers were contrasted with a group of mothers with less education to explore the hypothesis that a dissemination or modernity gap exists within the United States concerning mainstream childrearing ideology: Highly educated mothers would have more in common with preschool teachers' stated beliefs and attitudes than would mothers with less education. Second, it was hypothesized that interactionist and environmentalist developmental beliefs would be positively and significantly correlated with mother and teacher attitudes favoring divergent or imaginative play over other play forms in preschool children and favoring divergent thinking or cognitive process learning over convergent thinking or content learning in young children. The basis for this hypothesis rests on previous research suggesting the value of the latter over the former kinds of play experiences in childrens' development. These research generalizations would be reflected in mothers' and teachers' beliefs and attitudes. Modernity in developmental beliefs would go hand-in-hand with modernity in attitudes about play.

Design Features

Participants

A total of 30 preschool teachers participated in this study from nine centers in two university towns and surrounding rural areas—one located in the Eastern United States and one in the Midwest. All teachers were either college graduates or were completing their senior year student practicum. A total of 60 mothers of preschool children participated in the study. Thirty mothers were college graduates and 30 were high school graduates, some of whom possessed vocational school or junior college backgrounds. The income level of the participants and their ethnic and racial backgrounds varied.

Procedure

Permission was obtained from each teacher and mother participating in this study to administer three questionnaires. Each participant was administered a Beliefs About Development questionnaire (Martin, 1983), an Attitudes About School and Play questionnaire (Johnson, 1982), and a Play Attitudes questionnaire (Johnson, 1983). Participants were instructed to complete these questionnaires at home without advice from others and to return them within one week. A subset of 4 teachers and 20 mothers from the total sample were administered the questionnaire in person. Their responses to the three instruments did not differ significantly from the responses of the remaining sample.

Instrumentation

Beliefs About Development questionnaire (BAD). This instrument was designed to measure general beliefs about the nature of young children and how they change over time. A forced choice format requires the respondent to rank three possible answers to 30 hypothetical situations. One item from the scale is "Why are children able to make up imaginative stories? (a) Make-believe is a natural part of childhood; (b) Teachers and parents encourage and foster the child's imagination; (c) As children play with others and think about objects, their imagination develops." The three answers represent different theoretical positions worded in everyday language. During instrument development, people versed in child development theory assisted in evaluating face and content validity by indicating which responses represented environmental (learning theory), maturational, and interactional (cognitive-developmental theory) perspectives. Because this was an untested instrument, only items that generated 100% agreement were retained from the original item pool. Reliability information was obtained using test-retest (1 month apart) and internal consistency procedures. Overall test-retest reliability of the instrument was .80. Alphas were .79, .75, and .69 for the three subscales (environmental, maturational, interactional).

The Attitudes About School and Play questionnaire (TAASP). This instrument was developed to assess general attitudes about school activities and play activities for preschool children. A paired comparison format requires the respondent to select one of two activities as the preferred one for preschool children to spend their time doing. This technique was used to produce rankings of items. Ranking of school and play activities is in a basic way more informative than ratings because in deciding what is important for a child to spend time doing neither the mother nor the teacher has the liberty of responding as if everything were equally important. This is realistic in that time constraints require that we set priorities, and a decision to spend time on one objective necessarily implies that we will spend less time on some other objective.

The actual instrument consists of 18 paired comparisons among 12 items, three items each for four categories: content skills, process learning, convergent play, and divergent play. Mothers and teachers were asked to indicate which item of each pair they believed "was the more important for the child to spend time doing." Test-retest reliability on the scale is .84. Experts in child development and education were asked to review the instrument to provide an indication of its face and content validity.

Play Attitudes questionnaire (PA). This instrument was developed to assess attitudes about specific types of play activities for preschool children. A paired comparison format requires the respondent to select one of two play activities as the preferred one for preschool children to spend their time doing. This instrument consists of 20 paired comparisons among 10 items, two items each for five play categories: convergent play, divergent play, game play, physical play, and expressive play. The respondents indicated which of each pair they believed "was the more important for the child to spend time doing." Test-retest reliability is .71. Experts in child development and education were asked to review the instrument to provide evidence of its face and content validity.

Analysis of the Data

The mean rankings for the three BAD subscales, the 12 items and four subscales of the TAASP questionnaire, and the 10 items and five subscales of the PA questionnaire were computed for each group of respondents. The design of the BAD questionnaire was such that total endorsement scores for each theoretical position could range from 0 to 60; the design of the TAASP questionnaire was such that each subscale could receive from 0 to 9 total points and each item of each subscale from 0 to 3 points; the design of the PA questionnaire was such that each subscale could receive a total ranking from 0 to 8 with each item under the general category chosen from zero to four times. Analyses of variance on the data were performed to indicate whether the patterns of responses of teachers and high- and low-educated mothers were significantly different. The fact that the data were ranked implies that a high score in one category necessarily leads to a lower score in the other categories. This property of the data, referred to as "ipsativity" in statistics, makes it inappropriate to apply further statistical tests to determine individual items on which mothers and teachers differ significantly. The differences are inextricably differences in the pattern of rankings. Still, one can examine the patterns to point out areas of greatest difference. Finally, correlations were computed between respondents' total subscale scores on the BAD questionnaire and their total scores on the general categories of the TAASP and PA questionnaires. Ipsativity makes redundant some of the correlational patterns found.

Findings

Tables 1, 2, and 3 summarize the data from the BAD, TAASP, and PA questionnaires. The major findings were as follows:

1. Teachers and mothers with a high educational level demonstrated the same general response pattern on the BAD questionnaire: Interactionist views and environmental views were ranked very closely together as

Table 1　Mean Scores on the BAD Questionnaire

Beliefs	Teachers	College-educated mothers	Non-college-educated mothers
Interactionist (Cognitive-Developmental)	24.9	23.9	21.9
Environmental (Learning Theory)	23.3	22.3	20.8
Maturational (Biological-Based)	12.2	13.3	18.5

Table 2　Mean Rankings of Preferred School and Play Activities for Preschoolers on the TAASP Questionnaire

Categories and Items	Teacher	College-educated mothers	Non-college-educated mothers
Content Skills	3.6	4.4	4.5
Counting out different numbers of objects	1.9	1.8	.9
Learning the sounds of the letters of the alphabet	1.0	1.7	1.4
Learning color and shape names	.7	.9	2.2
Process Learning	5.0	4.6	3.7
Figuring out how something is wrong	1.3	1.4	.5
Thinking about how two objects are alike	1.5	1.4	1.5
Planning what to do next	1.9	1.9	1.7
Convergent Play	3.7	3.9	4.8
Painting a picture of something	1.5	1.6	1.6
Forming clay into different objects	1.1	1.2	1.7
Making something with blocks	1.1	1.1	1.5
Divergent Play	5.6	5.2	4.7
Make-believe using puppets	1.8	1.7	1.9
Pretending with dress-up clothes	1.9	1.8	1.9
Imagining with miniature toys	1.7	1.5	.9

Table 3 Mean Rankings of Preferred Play Activities for Preschoolers on the PA Questionnaire

Categories and Items	Teacher	College-educated mothers	Non-college-educated mothers
Convergent Play	3.7	3.8	4.9
Making something from different materials	1.9	1.9	2.5
Building something with table blocks	1.8	1.9	2.4
Divergent Play	4.8	4.9	4.6
Make-believe with small figures	1.9	2.0	2.1
Pretending to be a favorite character	2.9	2.9	2.5
Game Play	1.8	1.9	1.8
Playing a board game	1.3	1.3	1.1
Playing connect-the-dots-game	.5	.6	.7
Physical Play	4.2	4.4	4.5
Climbing and exercising	2.0	2.1	2.2
Balance and coordination activities	2.2	2.3	2.2
Expressive Play	4.7	4.8	3.9
Singing children's songs	2.2	2.4	2.0
Dancing and movement expression	2.5	2.4	1.9

first and second choices with maturational views a distant third. Mothers with lower educational levels, although not significantly different from the other two groups, ranked environmental and interactionist views of child development as first and second choices with maturational views a not-so-distant third.

2. Comparing the preschool teachers' and college-educated mothers' rankings of the items on the TAASP questionnaire revealed a generally similar pattern, with divergent play and process learning ranked high and content skills and convergent play ranked low. Mothers who were not college-educated ranked convergent and divergent play high and content and process learning low. The teachers and college-educated mothers were clearly able to differentiate among the school and play activities in the priorities that they assigned to them, as evidenced by the large spread in the combined mean ranks among the categories: 5.4, 4.8, 4.0, and 3.8 for divergent play, process learning, convergent play, and content learning, respectively. Mothers with less education, on the other hand, failed to make sharp distinctions: Combined mean ranks were 4.8, 4.7, 4.5, and 3.7 for convergent play, divergent play, content learning, and process learning, respectively. For all three groups of respondents, the fact that the individual items chosen usually were given quite similar ranking suggests that the respondents shared our view that these items were similar in content.

3. Comparing the preschool teachers' and the college-educated mothers' rankings of the items on the PA questionnaire also revealed a generally similar pattern, with divergent play ranked the highest, followed by expressive play, physical play, convergent play, and then game play. Mothers with less education ranked the play categories as follows: convergent play, divergent play, physical play, expressive play, and game play. With the exception of game play, which was ranked lowest by a wide margin by all three groups of respondents, the spread across the play categories was not great, indicating less ability or inclination to discriminate among the five play categories. Rankings given to individual items under the play categories generally were quite similar.

4. For preschool teachers and college-educated mothers, generally similar correlations were found relating beliefs about development and attitudes about school and play activities for preschool children. Because of the ipsative nature of the ranked data, only the most outstanding correlation will be reported. Maturational beliefs were significantly and negatively related to divergent play scores ($r = -.57$). For non-college-educated mothers, the largest correlation found was between convergent play and maturational beliefs ($r = -.39$).

5. Across all respondents, there was a tendency to rank divergent and convergent play similarly on the two questionnaires. Divergent play was generally ranked less favorably on the PA questionnaire than on the TAASP questionnaire.

Conclusion

The results are consistent with the hypotheses. First, there are differences in beliefs about development and attitudes about play and learning held by teachers and college-educated mothers compared to those held by less educated mothers. This finding suggests a dissemination problem or modernity gap in awareness of mainstream childrearing ideology as defined by current knowledge about development and socialization of children. Support was found for the hypothesis that modernity in developmental beliefs goes hand-in-hand with modernity in attitudes about play. Similar results have been reported by Marianne Bloch and Wiwan Wichaidt (1984) with a comparable Thailandese sample of teachers and parents of different social and economic status using the same questionnaires as used in this study. In Thailand, more positive attitudes toward play were expressed by teachers, especially those in the public schools, than were expressed by parents of either lower- or middle-class backgrounds.

In sum, a nomological network (Figure 1) was proposed that served as the point of departure of this investigation. Relations among distal culture and family structural characteristics on the one hand, and a proximal zone of play behavior and child development on the other hand, were conceptualized to be mediated by an ideational zone that includes adult attitudes toward play and beliefs about development. The latter relationship was the focus of this study. Limitations of this study include the use of questionnaires with no known concurrent or predictive validity; observational research is necessary to evaluate this. Coupling interview methods with the questionnaire data, furthermore, would provide information about respondents' reasons for their judgments and choices, thus revealing subtleties and complexities in adults' thinking about play and development that unquestionably exist. Finally, the model itself is limited in that it is a two-dimensional representation of relations and constructs frozen in time. By incorporating generational or cohort change in a society, and a notion that "the child is father to the man," a more dynamic, recursive, and potentially useful model could result. These methodological and conceptual limitations notwithstanding, the present study suggests a significant and positive relationship between beliefs about development and attitudes toward play in the sample investigated. Differences in responses by the groups of participants, moreover, suggest that adult groups within a society have different access to mainstream ideological beliefs, values, and attitudes concerning play and development in children.

References

Abramovitch, R., Corter, C., & Lando, B. (1979). *Sibling interaction in the home*. Paper presented at the Biennial Meeting of the Society for Research in Child Development, San Francisco.

Bishop, D.W., & Chace, C. (1971). Parental conceptual systems, home play environments, and potential creativity in children. *Journal of Experimental Child Psychology, 12*, 318-338.

Bloch, M.N., & Wichaidt, W. (1984). *Parents' and teachers' attitudes toward play and work in early childhood schools in Thailand*. Paper presented at the Annual Meetings of the American Educational Research Association, New Orleans.

Busse, T.V. (1969). Child-rearing antecedents of flexible thinking. *Developmental Psychology, 1*, 585-591.

Dreyer, A.S., & Wells, M. (1966). Parental values, parental control and creativity in young children. *Journal of Marriage and the Family, 29*, 83-88.

El'Konin, D.B. (1968). Some results of the psychological development of preschool-age children. In M. Cole & I. Matteman (Eds.) *A handbook of contemporary Soviet psychology*. New York: Basic Books.

Fein, G. (1971). A transformational analysis of pretending. *Developmental Psychology 4*, 203-210.

Fink, R.S. (1976). Role of imaginative play in cognitive development. *Psychological Reports, 39*, 895-906.

Goldman, J., & Chaille, C. (1981). *Object use in the preschool: An under-developed resource.* Paper presented at the Biennial Meetings of The Society for Research in Child Development, Boston.

Griffing, S.P. (1980). The relationship between socioeconomic status and sociodramatic play among black kindergarten children. *Genetic Psychological Monographs, 101,* 3-34.

Harvey, O.J., Hunt, D.E., & Schroder, H. (1961). *Conceptual systems and personality organization.* New York: Wiley.

Johnson, J.E. (1982). *The Attitudes About School and Play questionnaire.* Unpublished manuscript.

Johnson, J.E. (1983). *Play Attitudes questionnaire.* Unpublished manuscript.

King, N.R. (1982). *Children's play as a form of resistance in the classroom.* Paper presented at The American Educational Research Association Annual Meeting, New York.

Kleiber, D.A., Barnett, L.A., & Wade, M.C. (1978). *Playfulness and the family context.* Paper presented at the SPRE Research Symposium of the National Recreation and Parks Association, Miami.

Lamb, M.E., & Roopnarine, J.L. (1979). Peer influences on sex-role development in preschoolers. *Child Development, 50,* 1219-1222.

Lieberman, J. (1977). *Playfulness.* New York: Academic Press.

Lovinger, S.L. (1974). Sociodramatic play and language development in preschool disadvantaged children. *Psychology in the School, 9,* 313-320.

Marshall, H., & Hahn, S.C. (1967). Experimental modification of dramatic play. *Journal of Personality and Social Psychology, 5,* 119-122.

Martin, C.A. (1983). *Children's self-perceptions in relation to mothers' developmental beliefs and mothers' perception of the child.* Unpublished doctoral dissertation, University of Wisconsin, Madison.

Maw, W.H., & Maw, E.W. (1966). Children's curiosity and parental attitudes. *Journal of Marriage and the Family, 28,* 343-345.

McLoyd, V.C. (1980). Verbally expressed modes of transformation in the fantasy play of black preschool children. *Child Development, 51,* 1133-1139.

Mueller, E., & Lucas, T.A. (1975). A developmental analysis of peer interaction among toddlers. In M. Lewis & L.A. Rosenblum (Eds.) *Friendship and peer relations* (pp. 223-257). New York: Wiley.

Piaget, J. (1962). *Play, dreams and imitation in childhood.* New York: W.W. Norton.

Pulaski, M.A. (1970). Play as a function of toy structure and fantasy predisposition. *Child Development, 41,* 531-537.

Sanders, K.M., & Harper, L.V. (1976). Free play fantasy behavior in preschool children: Relations among gender, age, season, and location. *Child Development, 47,* 1182-1185.

Shure, M.E. (1963). Psychological ecology of a nursery school. *Child Development*, **34**, 979-994.

Singer, D.G., & Singer, J.L. (1976). Family television viewing habits and the spontaneous play of preschool children. *American Journal of Orthopsychiatry*, **46**, 496-502.

Singer, J.L. (1973). *The child's world of make believe*. New York: Academic Press.

Schwartzman, H. (1978). *Transformations: The anthropology of children's play*. New York: Plenum.

Smilansky, S. (1968). *The effects of sociodramatic play on disadvantaged preschool children*. New York: Wiley.

Smith, P.K., & Connolly, K.J. (1980). *The ecology of preschool behavior*. Cambridge: Cambridge University Press.

Sutton-Smith, B. (1967). The role of play in cognitive development. *Young Children*, **6**, 361-370.

Tizard, B., Philips, J., & Plewis, I. (1976). Play in preschool centers II. Effects on play of the child's social class and of the educational orientation of the center. *Journal of Child Psychology and Psychiatry*, **17**, 265-274.

Vygotsky, L.S. (1967). Play and its role in the mental development of the child. *Soviet Psychology*, **5**, 6-18.

Watson, C. (1957). Some personality differences in children related to strict or permissive parental discipline. *Journal of Psychology*, **44**, 227-249.

CHAPTER 9

Travel as Play

Bernard Mergen
George Washington University, Washington, DC

Mindful of Klaus Meier's invective against reinventing the wheel, the title of this essay might more properly be "Some Elements of Play in Four Books of Travel" (Meier, 1983). Even if play has many definitions, some of them paradoxical and self-contradictory, we know that the concept of play is useful for describing certain kinds of behavior and for explaining the probable meaning of those behaviors. Once the specific characteristics of the play under consideration have been identified, it is possible to predict the general development and outcome of a play event. What I am suggesting is that we make a clear distinction between the scientific and phenomenal definitions of play. We need to ask the players, "What do you call x?" And then ask, "How does x differ from y?" We also need to think historically. Does x mean the same thing today that it meant yesterday?

Travel for recreation, as a leisure activity, or for fun obviously has some elements of play. Vacation trips, tourism, and travel for its own sake involve varying amounts of personal freedom and self-definition. For some individuals, travel is a form of play because it offers an escape from the confinement of existing social roles and obligations. For others, travel offers new roles that they are willing to play. "Pleasure is contingent upon their willingness to accept the make-believe, or to half-seriously delude themselves into accepting contrived situations" (Jakle, 1985, p. 4). Both types of travelers may experience frivolity and ecstasy, which Huizinga identifies as elements of play, and passion, idling, inversion, and preparation, characteristics of play noted by Sutton-Smith (Huizinga, 1955; Sutton-Smith, 1980). Moreover, in writing about their experiences, travelers will employ another set of play elements, the literary conventions of humor, fantasy, narrative, and character.

As Bruce Michelson points out in his essay on Mark Twain's *The Innocents Abroad* (1869/1966), it is necessary to consider both the play of the tourist and the play of the narration (Michelson, 1977). In this essay, I want to consider the play of the narration in the context of the play of the traveler who uses a particular kind of transportation. Twain's *Innocents Abroad* will serve nicely as an example of the tourist on a planned, group tour. Joshua Slocum's *Sailing Alone Around the World* (1956), first published in 1900, is the classic of solo, relatively unstructured travel.

Amelia Earhart's autobiographical account of her early years in flying, *The Fun of It*, published in 1932, will serve to illustrate the use of air tavel for individual sport. Finally, Elinor Nickerson, TAASP member and former officer, provides an account of loosely structured family travel in *Kayaks to the Arctic*, published in 1967. These four books provide us with a sample of contrasting travel contexts over a century of time.

Nelson Graburn (1983), drawing on the work of Dean MacCannell, Victor Turner, and others, has recently suggested that tourism should be studied in relation to ritual, play, pilgrimage, class, lifestyle, and cultural change. Reviewing the literature on the anthropology of tourism, Graburn concludes that "tourist behavior and aspirations are direct or indirect indicators of what is significant and meaningful in peoples' lives, of their self-perceptions, their class or group identity, and their social aspirations" (p. 29). Graburn defines a tourist as a "temporarily leisured person who voluntarily visits a place away from home for the purpose of experiencing a change" (p. 11). He further distinguishes between periodic or annual vacations, paralleling cyclical rites of intensification, and arduous, self-testing tourism, paralleling rites of passage.

Tourism, defined in this way, seems too narrow to analyze the books and experiences of Twain, Slocum, Earhart, and Nickerson. None of this group is taking an annual vacation, and although there are elements of self-testing in Twain, Slocum, and Nickerson, none seems to be consciously seeking a significant change. Perhaps it would be useful to distinguish tourism from travel, in which the goal is to maintain a relatively normal existence while seeing new places and meeting unfamiliar people. A more fruitful approach, however, is to consider all definitions partial and to look at books describing travel for pleasure as expressions of feelings about pleasure, passion, idling, inversion, and even, perhaps, preparation.

This would partially satisfy the research methodology of several approaches to the study of the relationships among tourism, travel, and play. Graburn urges developmental or biographical studies that would "expose the relationships between world view and touristic experiences within the individual's socio-psychological life cycle" (Graburn, 1983, p. 28). MacCannell (1976) suggests focusing on the tourist/sight/marker relationship. Travel books, in addition to describing those relationships, are themselves markers in MacCannell's sense because they may be used by later travelers. Because the traveler who writes about his or her experiences is at least partially familiar with literary conventions, he or she can be expected to make the book as instructive, amusing, and entertaining as possible. The selection of incident and character, the choice of words and images, reveals much about the writer's attitudes toward his or her culture's concepts of travel and play. This is nowhere better illustrated than in *Innocents Abroad*.

When Mark Twain booked passage on the steamship *Quaker City* for a five-month tour of Europe and the Holy Land in 1867, he was known as a minor regional humorist. His short stories and stage performances had provided him with just enough public acclaim that he was expected to provide a humorous commentary on the trip, a trip that he described as "a pleasure trip," a "picnic on a gigantic scale" (Twain, 1966, pp. 15, 17). Every incident of the trip, every place visited, every fellow passenger, native guide, and person encountered is used humorously to develop the sense of fun that Samuel Clemens the tourist and Mark Twain the writer are seeking. From the time the ship leaves the dock, Twain recognizes the opportunity the setting provides for fun. "Playing whist by the cabin lamp when it is storming outside is pleasant; walking on the quarterdeck in the moonlight is pleasant; smoking in the breezy foretop is pleasant when one is not afraid to go up there; but these are all feeble and commonplace compared with the joy of seeing people suffering the miseries of seasickness" (p. 29).

This typical passage reveals Twain's ironic humor. Finding pleasure in the discomfort of others involves a certain amount of inversion of the normal order, but more importantly it requires the ability to invent and elaborate a make-believe world where each passenger cries "Oh, my" while rushing past the author to empty his or her stomach over the rail of the ship. As Michelson makes clear in his perceptive essay, Twain is frequently bored with those he calls "pilgrims" on the tour and is sometimes bored by the trip itself, but he invents imaginary travels that enrich the pleasures of the real voyage with those of the make-believe (Michelson, 1977). Thus although *Innocents Abroad* is a catalogue of amusing incidents now familiar to anyone who has traveled abroad—problems with foreign language, confusions with money exchange, the embarrassment of discovering that the person in a foreign crowd whom you have been discussing speaks English—it is also a subtle commentary on the nature of fantasy play and its relation to travel. In one long chapter inspired by his first visit to Rome, Twain first fantasizes a report by a Roman on life in the United States, making invidious comparisons between life in Italy and America; then he invents a playbill and a newspaper review of a gladiatorial contest in the coliseum. The reasons for all this fantasy are given at the beginning of the chapter:

> What is it that confers the noblest delight? What is that which swells a man's breast with pride above that which any other experience can bring to him? Discovery! To know that you are walking where none others have walked, that you are beholding what human eye has not seen before, that you are breathing a virgin atmosphere . . . To do something, say something, see something, before *anybody* else—these are the things that confer a pleasure compared with which other pleasures are tame and commonplace, other ecstasies cheap and trivial . . .

> What is there in Rome for me to see that others have not seen before me? . . . What can I discover? Nothing. Nothing whatsoever. One charm of travel dies here. But if I could be gifted with modern Roman sloth, modern Roman superstition, and modern Roman boundlessness of ignorance, what bewildering worlds of unsuspected wonders I would discover. (pp. 190-191)

For Twain the fun of travel, the elements of play, are a combination of masquerade and mockery, fantasy and memory. He set the standards by which subsequent travel books are judged, so it is not surprising to find these same elements in later accounts of travel. What is unexpected is how the familiar literary devices can be reworked by skillful writers to produce narratives that are fresh and original. Joshua Slocum's *Sailing Alone Around the World* presents his 3-year voyage as having "been to me like reading a book" (Slocum, 1900, p. 276). By this he means that he set out to circumnavigate the world with little idea of what he would encounter. Each day, each port of call was a new adventure, often comic. Certainly Slocum's narrative is artful and humorous. Near the beginning of his trip, Slocum bought a tin clock, "the only timepiece [he] carried on the whole voyage" (p. 22), a useful device not only for navigating, but for framing his narrative, since his story is both fantasy play and a game with time limits. Since Slocum and his readers knew that the cruise took 3 years and 2 months, it was not inappropriate to call attention to the dimension of time. As an element of play, the references to time help to create that sense of separateness that play usually requires. Rather than losing track of time, Slocum is aware that his fun will eventually come to an end. Like children at recess who have a heightened sense of pleasure knowing the bell will ring any minute, Slocum played with time, extending his cruise when he felt like it, but without abandoning his ultimate goal.

Slocum also enjoys playing a kind of stage Yankee. Two weeks out of Nova Scotia he overtakes the bark *Java* bound for Ireland. The wind is too light for the larger ship, whose captain asks how long it has been calm. Slocum's answer is a bit of vaudeville:

> "Dunno, cap'n" I shouted back as loud as I could bawl. "I haven't been here long." At this the mate on the forecastle wore a broad grin. "I left Cape Sable fourteen days ago," I added. (I was now well across toward the Azores.) "Mate," he roared to his chief officer—"mate, come here and listen to the Yankee's yarn. Haul down the flag, mate, haul down the flag!" In the best of humor, after all, the *Java* surrendered to the *Spray*. (p. 31)

Like Twain, Slocum finds humor in Americans he meets in foreign ports, in masquerading, and in trying to speak a foreign language. His word play is as sophisticated as Twain's. When he becomes delirious after eating some cheese he bought in the Azores, he imagines the pilot of the *Pinta* is in his cabin. " 'You did wrong, captain, to mix cheese with plums,' says the pilot of Columbus's ship. 'White cheese is never safe unless you know whence it comes. *Quien sabe*, it may have been from *leche de Capra* and becoming capricious' " (p. 41).

Slocum creates amusing imaginary dialogues, embellishing his narrative with stories about people and places he visits. The lengthiest of these stories concerns Alexander Hare, an English sailor, who in 1815 claimed one of the Keeling islands in the Indian Ocean and established "a seraglio of Malay women in which he moved over from the coast of Africa" (p. 213). A year later the neighboring islands were settled by a Captain

John Clunis-Ross who brought his family and eight sailor-artisans. A conflict between the two widely different colonies was inevitable, and, as Slocum slyly adds, "the channel between the islands was narrow, the water was not deep, and the eight Scotch sailors wore long boots" (p. 214). Hare was driven from his paradise and the descendants of the Malay women and the Scotch sailors inhabit the islands to this day. The 50-year-old Slocum was much franker in his admiration for native women than the 32-year-old Twain. Perhaps the fact that he had already been married twice and raised a family allowed Slocum to flout Victorian standards, or perhaps it was the result of the 30 years that separate the two cruises. Since Slocum traveled alone he may have felt freer from social standards. As he concludes, "It is not necessary, in order to realize the utmost enjoyment of going around the globe, to sail alone, yet for once and the first time there was a great deal of fun in it" (p. 291).

"Fun in it." Whatever it is that makes travel fun and the traveler and travel writer playful seems to originate in the imagination. *The Fun of it*, Amelia Earhart's autobiogaphy subtitled *Random Records of My Own Flying and of Women in Aviation*, suggests some interesting connections between childhood play and adult fun. Describing her youth in Atchinson, Kansas City, and Des Moines, Earhart emphasizes her reading of Scott, Dickens, George Eliot, Thackery, *Harper's Magazine for Young People*, and the *Youth's Companion*. Her father made up western stories and played Indians with her and her friends on Saturdays. In Atchinson she explored the bluffs of the Missouri and their sandstone caves. "One of the particularly entrancing made-up games," she recalls, "was called Bogie. It was played in my grandmother's barn and consisted of taking imaginary journeys in an old abandoned carriage. Fortunately next door lived two understanding cousins who were always bursting with ideas. Together we traveled far and wide through hair-raising adventures without ever leaving the barn" (Earhart, 1932, p. 15).

In 1920, at age 23, Earhart took her first airplane ride and found her career. A year later she made her first solo flight and the following year she bought her first plane in which she set altitude records and performed at air shows. In explaining stunt flying she writes, "I had fun trying to do [stunts], anyway. So much so, in fact, I have sometimes thought that transport companies would do well to have a 'recreation airplane' for their pilots who don't have any chance to play in the big transports or while on duty. If a little stunt ship were available, the men could go up 5,000 feet and 'turn it inside out' to relieve the monotony of hours of straight flying" (p. 37). One of her chapters is called "Joy Hopping," and elements of play are present throughout her narrative. Although Earhart's flying was often done for commercial reasons, she conveys the feeling that even within the limitations of early flight there was ample room for play. She was not a skillful writer and she does not play in her books as much as Twain and Slocum, but she does share their sense of dual identity, as traveler and narrator. After her 1928 flight across the Atlantic with Bill Stultz and Lou Gordon, she describes herself as feeling like a character from *Winnie the Pooh* or *Alice in Wonderland,* catapulted to fame beyond reality. She could only describe the experience of flying and the status it conferred by reference to fantasy.

The travels of Twain, Slocum, and Earhart are all unusual in some way. The journey taken by Elinor Nickerson and her family in the summer of 1966, while longer and more arduous than most family camping trips, was essentially a familiar one. Nickerson, her husband, and three sons aged 19, 12, and 10 flew from California to Northwest Canada and paddled up the Mackenzie River to the Beaufort Sea. Although the length of the summer and the course of the river limited their travel, the Nickersons were more like Slocum than Twain in the freedom they enjoyed to set their own itinerary. Like Slocum, Elinor Nickerson plays in her narration with the humorous behavior of her family and others. She is amused to look through her binoculars at a tugboat and see the crew looking back through their binoculars. The tug "looked like a grand way to spend a summer, combining work and adventure and leisure in sensible proportions" (p. 62). The contrast of work and play is stronger in Nickerson than in the other travel writers discussed. As mother, Nickerson did most of the cooking, and observes that, "camping, even at its best is a lot of hard work" (p. 111). What made the work bearable, even pleasurable, was the opportunity to watch her sons play and to join in their games and fantasies. As with Twain and Slocum, much of the play involved language.

Early in the trip, her 12-year-old causes amusement when he mistakes Martin I. for Martini, a kind of middle-class joke that sets the tone for much that follows. Plagued by biting deer flies, the Nickersons invent a game they call "Deer Fly Lacrosse" as they attempt to kill the flies with their kayak paddles. In the evenings, they play more conventional games with the same enthusiasm. "Never," she writes, "have I had so much fun sharing a crossword puzzle! The tent jumped with our raucous laughter as we invented words and finally deduced the correct ones" (p. 66). Other elements of play include fantasy—the boys pretend to be the Spumoni brothers, famous fallen log walkers; danger—crossing the river where it enters the Arctic Sea; and observing the passage of her oldest son from dependent child to independent adult. "It was fun," she writes, "to see Dev being a boy again, or at least acting the counselor's role with his brothers as he had the previous summer with other children at a private camp" (p. 135). Yet in a final scene, the crossing of the river in rough weather, she acknowledges Devon's coming of age as he makes decisions for the family.

It is clear from the beginning that Elinor Nickerson intends her narrative to be more than a travelogue. She tells us that the kayak trip is a 25th wedding anniversary gift for the family to share. Memories of her own childhood intrude during the trip when she loses the plastic canister used for mixing juice. This canister was called "Orphan Annie" after a shake-up mug obtained from Ovaltine, the sponsor of the "Little Orphan Annie" radio show, when she was a child in the 1930s (p. 142). She is also concerned with maintaining a "normal" family routine during the trip and comparing their life in California with the lives of families they meet in Canada. *Kayaks to the Arctic* domesticates travel and shows that such travel can still be playful.

Despite their obvious differences, these four books exhibit striking similarities in their treatment of the playful aspects of travel. Some of the similarities are superficial and the result of the structure of the experience. In almost all travel books there is a period of preparation, an inventory of equipment, that provides an opportunity for the travel writer to depict himself or herself as innocent or fun seeker, philosopher or reporter. The journey itself provides the setting for personality change, masquerade, comments on food and health, and encounters with people and places. The opportunities to enjoy normally forbidden pleasures during travel are well known. As early as 1928, two psychologists at Howard University used anecdotes of Pullman car travel to illustrate escapism, vanity, identity crisis, hysteria, phobias, exhibitionism, homosexuality, prostitution, kleptomania, megalomania, and compulsion neuroses. Their conclusion that the "desire to show off is as true of the porter as of the passenger" (Swift & Boyd, 1928, p. 416) points to another dimension of travel as play. Finally, at the conclusion of the journey the experience becomes memory and, as Mark Twain observes, the bad memories fade, leaving pleasant experiences to recall and record.

The books by Twain, Slocum, Earhart, and Nickerson point to three specific conclusions. First, although not all journeys are like a book, Slocum's metaphor is appropriate in the sense that both the play of the traveler and the play of the travel writer are structured by the clear boundaries of the beginning and end of a trip. There is an outline of a plot in the travel and tourist experience. The traveler and the travel writer construct their narratives with knowledge of the dimensions of time and space. This, perhaps more than anything else, gives travel its ritualistic aspect. If travel is play because it offers a special time for a pleasurable experience, it is paradoxical that that experience is often mundane in the sense that the traveler is pleased less by escape from the normal than by recreating the familiar.

My second conclusion is that all four writers, quite unexpectedly, emphasize that they are not getting away from it all so much as intensifying what they already do. Twain travels as a reporter, Slocum claims the *Spray* is home, Earhart flys for fun and profit, Nickerson finds the essence of her family in the wilderness. Clearly there are travelers who seek physical escape, but I think Graburn and others overemphasize this aspect of travel. Escape for the travelers I have discussed comes in the form of heightened imagination and make-believe and in the opportunity to observe without deep involvement.

This brings me to my final conclusion, the close link between creativity, discovery, and play in travel. All travelers seem to want to experience something new, whether in the actual discovery of new places or in the creation of new thoughts and feelings about them. It is this desire that tells us most about the individual traveler and his or her culture. Twain was happy to be a member of one of the first organized tours of Europe and the Holy Land. An outsider struggling to get in, Twain is representative of Americans in the 1860s in finding pleasure in group experience.

A loner by temperament, he nonetheless was a member of a culture in which identity was bestowed by the group. In a revealing comment in *Innocents Abroad* he says, "When we went to call on our American Consul General [in Tangier] I noticed that all possible games for parlor amusement seemed to be represented on his center tables. I thought that hinted at lonesomeness" (p. 66). The lone traveler, Slocum, was never lonely. Accustomed to the crowded society of shipboard life, he may have sought escape by sailing alone, but the attention he gives to his ship suggests another motive. Building and sailing the *Spray* alone was more an act of identity creation than mere escape. Like Thoreau, Slocum used the experience to define himself, to recreate in the truest sense.

A generation later, Earhart's more technologically complex society demanded technological answers to the problems raised for individual freedom. Like the thousands of Americans who were using the automobile to discover new places, Earhart chose a mechanical means to a human end. To play in the sky was to make it safe, to domesticate it for future travelers. As Earhart helped to close the air frontier, Nickerson's generation needed to find space for its discoveries and play in remote places and within. Material abundance and urbanization seem to require leisure activities that allow for individual autonomy, an autonomy that can only partially be supplied by travel itself. The autonomy that many people find in play is illustrated in Nickerson's book. Here the family that plays as it travels and travels as it plays makes unexpected discoveries about itself, the places it visits, and its attitudes toward both.

Travel literature offers a rich field for students of play, a field in which the elusive definition of play may finally be captured by a tourist's snapshot and mailed home.

References

Earhart, A. (1932). *The fun of it: Random records of my own flying and of women in aviation.* New York: Harcourt Brace Jovanovich.

Graburn, N.H. (1983). The anthropology of tourism. *Annals of Tourism Research,* **10**(1), 9-33.

Huizinga, J. (1955). *Homo ludens: A study of the play element in culture.* Boston: Beacon Press.

Jakle, J.A. (1985). *The tourist: Travel in twentieth-century North America.* Lincoln: University of Nebraska Press.

MacCannell, D. (1976). *The tourist: A new theory of the leisure class.* New York: Schocken Books.

Meier, K.V. (1983). On the assiduous re-invention of the wheel. *The Association for the Anthropological Study of Play Newsletter,* **10**(1), 11-23.

Michelson, B. (1977). Mark Twain the tourist: The form of *The Innocents Abroad. American Literature,* **49**(3), 385-398.

Nickerson, E. (1967). *Kayaks to the Arctic*. Berkeley, CA: Howell-North Books.

Slocum, J. (1956). *Sailing alone around the world*. New York: Dover Books. (Original work published 1900)

Sutton-Smith, B. (1980). The playground as zoo. *The Association for the Anthropological Study of Play Newsletter, 7*(1), 4-7.

Swift, E.M., & Boyd, C.S. (1928). The Pullman porter looks at life. *Psychoanalytic Review, 15*, 393-416.

Twain, M. (S.L. Clemens). (1966). *The innocents abroad: Or the new pilgrims progress*. New York: Signet Classic. (Original work published 1869)

PART III

Games

The six papers in this part all suggest, in one way or another, that games have extrinsic as well as intrinsic value. Ten years of definition and discussion at the annual meetings of The Association for the Anthropological Study of Play have confirmed the significance of games, have helped to clarify the differences among play, sport, and games, and have revealed a persistent tendency to place games in the service of other activities. These papers continue those trends. All assume that games are a form of play characterized by rules, competition, and one or more of the elements of physical skill, strategy, chance, and make-believe.

De Koven, in his Keynote Address to TAASP at its Tenth Annual Meeting in 1984, illustrated the potential of video games to lead the player to a higher level of game complexity, freed from the constraints of natural laws. In his paper, De Koven provides a glimpse of a future in which individuals distant from each other in space (and perhaps in time) will contest through and with their machines. But the purpose of video game playing is not merely fun, not even the fun of beating an opponent; it is a way of learning to survive in the "virtual" world of high-tech communication and calculation. If De Koven is correct, the video game may unmake the rules and diffuse the competition of game playing.

A more likely outcome of increasingly complex technology in game playing is illustrated by Lonergan's paper on games in a Sard village. In the village studied by Lonergan, factory workers bet on soccer pools, play card games and bocce, and occasionally go hunting. Pastoralists hold horse races and play a guessing game called *la morra*. The games and the manner in which they are played serve to confirm the social class differences between the wage workers and the pastoralists. It is possible to foresee a time when one class of workers in the United States will play video games exclusively, whereas other classes will cling to bowling, softball, and poker. Lonergan's paper also raises the issue of games as a product of leisure and leisure as a product of industrialization. As the factory clock has heightened our awareness of the separation of work and play, we have become increasingly concerned about our performance in both spheres. We need to prepare ourselves to work productively and to play fully (or to work playfully).

The papers of Christie and Noyce, Yawkey, Lytle, and Blair all address this need. Christie and Noyce explore some of the links between play and writing. By encouraging dramatic play, the authors found they could improve the children's writing skills. Although their research leaves many

113

unanswered questions, Christie and Noyce open new vistas on both literacy and play. To what extent can dramatic play be organized, game-like, to enhance a child's writing ability? Do the skills of sustained discourse, narrative, perspective taking, and ideational fluency develop differently in group play and solitary writing?

Yawkey offers a much more highly structured experiment in game playing for improved work performance. By teaching Hispanic parents how to play with their children in specified ways, Yawkey and his associates were able to improve the feelings of the parents toward their children. As in the experiment by Christie and Noyce, dramatic play was organized in a game-like manner to enhance a nonplay performance.

Lytle used organized games to improve the self-image of college students and to make them more cooperative in their work and play. In Lytle's example the intrinsic and extrinsic functions of play are very similar and suggest that the application of game playing to nonplay situations may not be as artificial as it first appears.

Blair's paper on the game she calls "Cubal Analysis" is difficult to categorize, but her approach to the use of games to develop self-awareness and raise consciousness is one of the most ambitious I have encountered. For those who enjoy the challenge of integrating the many dimensions of life into a single system, Cubal Analysis offers fun and rewards. Students of games and those who apply games to education, therapy, and other activities also provide an important link between the study of play and the study of sport. To them we can only say, "play on."

Bernard Mergen

CHAPTER 10

Video Games: At Play in the Virtual World

Bernard De Koven
Playworks Incorporated, California

We are participating in a culture that is undergoing profound and fundamental changes in response to equally profound and fundamental changes in its environment. We can best understand and perhaps even better serve this culture by taking careful note of the changing role and forms of play. The environment to which this new culture is adapting itself is not natural: It is artificial, technological, and manmade. It is a real and vital and evolving environment that is in the process of formation and is itself undergoing explosive change.

This environment is purely technological—produced, maintained, and inhabited by those who have mastered the necessary technological skills. It relates to the natural environment the way an interstate highway relates to the deer trail upon which it was built. It is a "virtual" reality, a technical illusion with real-world power that is produced by an ever more powerful synthesis of new technologies: video, microprocessor, computer science, laser, telecommunications, satellite communication, and space technology. The new culture has produced and, in many ways, become dependent upon forms and expressions of play that are truly unique.

Virtual Pinball

I have chosen Pinball Construction Set, a video simulation of a pinball game, as a case in point, as artifact and evidence of the reality of the virtual world and the nature of play within it. Pinball is a game between a person and a contrivance. It is a game of skill and chance, the nature of which can be easily related to the earlier and mechanically far less sophisticated game of skittles.

In the game of skittles, the player sends a spinning top into an open wooden box. There are partitions and small wooden bowling pins at central positions in the box. As the top caroms off the walls and partitions it may happen to collide with and topple one or more of the wooden pins. Depending on which pin, the player adds points to or subtracts points from his or her score.

The correspondences between pinball and skittles are obvious, and therein lies evidence of a well-established, culturally transmitted game form. Both are essentially solitaire games played between a person and an artifact, both center around the violent gyrations of a rapidly moving object in an unyielding environment. The correspondences between the electro-mechanical pinball table and the computer-generated pinball game are even more admirably and numerously self-evident. The differences, however, are worthy of deliciously profound speculation. Pinball Construction Set is an artifact of a dramatically more solitary and intimate relationship between the player and the machineries of play.

In skittles, once the top is launched there is no legal force that the player can use to influence the outcome of the launch. Since a string-wound top is used, there is room for much deep talk about the best way to wind and pull the string. Once the string is pulled, however, the rest is predetermined. Though the player cheers and jeers, there remains nothing for the player to do but watch his or her fate unwind.

Pinball uses a ball instead of a top, bumpers instead of wooden pins. There is even a spring-loaded launcher that allows somewhat of the same subtle feel that a skittles player might find in a more or less forceful string-pull. Electronics and mechanics are used to throw the ball about with the force and suddenness of a skittles top and to add excitement and information by giving visual and auditory clues and keeping score, but, all in all, the pinball we have so far described is really little more than a fancier skittles.

The truly distinguishing factor is the mechanism that allows the player to maintain influence over the path of the ball, even though the ball has already been launched. Whereas in skittles all that remains after the launch is hope, in pinball there is the flipper. Two flippers, in fact. Furthermore, in addition to the well-timed flip, the tilt mechanism encourages the player to make use of the well-placed nudge. Though the control is insufficient and the jazzed-up dance of the ball remains tantalizingly out of logic's reach, the player has in fact entered a very different mode of play from that provided by skittles. The pinball player does not relinquish control. Though the control is imprecise, though success remains unpredictable regardless of the physical skills mastered, the player has entered into an active, game-spanning relationship with the play machine.

The computer version of pinball as implemented with the Pinball Construction Set is noteworthy because of the thoroughness of its simulation of the "real" game. Though the feel of the table has been reduced to a joystick and the extravagance of pinballish sights and sounds confined to a single screen, the logic and mechanics of pinball are reproduced with admirable accuracy. The score changes and the ball bounces and caroms off of bumpers and gets flipped exactly the way one would expect a pinball should. The pinball machine depicted on the computer screen can never be anything more than a simulation. What appears on the computer screen is a "virtual" pinball machine, whereas the "real" pinball machine is really subject to physical laws.

The term "virtual reality" is not mine. Computer users and software developers need that term to distinguish between two very different, but equally "real" worlds: the virtual world that exists via computer, and the world that comprises everything else. It can be rightly argued that all forms of play create some sort of virtual reality. Maintaining the separation and connection between the two realities is the central theme among players of games and sports. But the virtual reality of computer pinball is far more thorough in its virtuality than its real-world counterpart. The player maintains the same role and task, but the play machine has been changed for one that is even more private (the personal computer) and less bound by the arbitrariness of natural law.

The conceptual evolution from skittles to pinball hints at a cultural shift in the relation of the individual to the machine. The cultural leap represented by Pinball Construction Set moves the player from a position of power within a machine to one of power over that machine.

Pinball Construction Set is, as its name implies, a kind of meta-pinball game—one that not only allows the player to engage in accurate simulations of a pinball game, but also provides the player with the tools to construct yet more computer pinball games. The player can change the shape and location of several different kinds of bumpers, add or remove special targets, and add more flippers and more balls until the game is as complex or as straightforward as desired. The player can go deeper into the mechanism of the machine and tinker with the scoring system, setting up special bonuses for particularly difficult combinations of caroms. The player can go even further than that, delving into the physics of the simulation and, by toying with the effects of gravity or increasing the elasticity of the ball, completely transform the nature of the game.

With Pinball Construction Set, the relationship between the player and the game machine is freed of the vestigial constraints of natural law. The machine can be made impossible—utterly virtual. The machine can be *made*. In fact, the making of the machine is really the best part. Though it is clearly the goal to make a game machine that is truly worth playing, getting to play with the machinery of the game proves to be even more alluring than playing the games the machinery can produce.

The path from skittles to Pinball Construction Set is clearly marked. It delineates a unidirectional evolution in the relationship of power between the player and a play machine. An evolution that parallels that path is occurring within our culture as it embraces and is embraced by the virtual world.

Virtual Culture

Compare the share of time an individual in our culture devotes to the virtual world to the share that individual gives to the natural world. How much time is spent in front of a television, on a telephone, or with a computer? Clearly the share is disproportionate, and clearly it is growing more so in favor of the virtual world. The delineation between virtual and natural world is, however, also growing more difficult to draw. The worlds interpenetrate. There are whole societies that meet and grow in the virtual world of a computer network. The computer network is yet another synthesis of technologies, combining telecommunications with microprocessor and data storage technologies. By dialing a special number, the individual is able to link a home computer to the communications and storage capabilities of a central mainframe computer. Thousands of individual computer-users can share the same host computer and use the facilities to leave private or public messages.

The host computer offers the user access to many different public message centers. The different message centers are identified by interest areas varying from ecology to technology, games to education. In most cases, anyone who visits one of these centers can become a member, reading and leaving messages at will.

Inevitably, each of these message boards becomes the residence of a virtual community. The members of this community engage in a variety of conservations and, in so doing, bargain and make trades, sell and seek help, teach and carry on most of the functions of a human culture. This culture, however, exists wholly within the virtual world. There is no geographic center, no common housing. The individuals within the culture are themselves virtual individuals.

Because the communication that maintains the community is entirely confined to print, the members of the community must establish and maintain their relationships without any clues about the physical nature of the communicants. Neither sex nor age, race nor weight need to be revealed. The identity of a participant is the identity that participant has defined for himself or herself or itself.

There are enviable powers in the virtual world. As it can give the player power over the machineries of play, it can also give the person power over the workings of personal appearance. The result is the creation of a culture whose members can conduct their affairs outside the limits of prejudice. This kind of virtual world empowerment is remarkably akin to the kind of empowerment children and actors gain through episodes of dramatic play. The participants can clearly step outside the sway of appearance, give themselves new names, don masks, and become totally other.

And Now This

Because of play, because of a lifelong, ever-deepening fascination with play, because of those vitalizing and transforming and world-making episodes of sheer play, mere play, each of us in The Association for the Anthropological Study of Play has come to the largely unsupported belief that the study of play is central to the evolution of both culture and career.

What I wish to point out is the possibility that the knowledge we have gained in the pursuit of play has become more useful than we guessed. As students of play we are uniquely aware of the laws that govern the virtual world. We are relatively at ease with the interpenetration of reality and fantasy. The culture that has developed these world-shaping technologies must renew its understanding of the real-world roles of play. The culture that once suppressed play must adapt to a virtual environment in which play is virtually central to survival.

The heroes of the personal computer world have publicly endorsed the notion of a possible synthesis between play and productivity. The most innovative and creative of programmers speak of episodes of play that were vital to the creation of their programs. And they do mean play—real play, world-stopping, flow-embracing, personally potentiating play.

I have had the good fortune to become a professional player in this virtual reality and have designed at least a half dozen more-or-less commercial computer games. I have moved to Silicon Valley to gain real-time, warmware access to heroes of a truly virtual community. As a participant in this high-tech culture, I have become firmly convinced that the role of play is even more vital than we have guessed. I have observed that the virtual worlds we are creating with our computers are conducive to radically different kinds of play than those we found in Pinball and Space Invaders and Pac Man and, yes, even Donkey Kong; but nevertheless these new virtual worlds are worlds of play. As fun as it is to play video games, the virtual universe is yet more varied and at least as rich as we can collectively imagine it to be. Though we are vitally linked to the natural world, at play in the virtual world we are freed from constraints we didn't know we had. We become artists and musicians and players of profound purport; we play with words and ideas, symbols and patterns. As players in the virtual world, we are home.

CHAPTER 11

Games in a Changing Sard Village

David F. Lonergan
Pennsylvania State University

This paper describes the game-playing behavior of men in a central Sardinian village, and relates both the choices of games and the contexts in which they are played to socioeconomic conditions that characterize the players.

Bidda (a pseudonym) is a village with more than 2,000 residents located in Nuoro, one of Sardinia's four provinces. The region known as the Marghine, in which Bidda is included, traditionally had an economic base of agriculture and pastoralism. The last several decades, however, have seen a shift from farming to wage labor as Bidda's economic mainstay, due to agricultural competition from North America and from The Common Market.

The Italian government, through its Fund for the South (*Cassa per il Mezzogiorno*), has brought a number of factories and other businesses to Sardinia by providing loans, grants, and other incentives (King, 1975, 1977). Two of these factories are within commuting distance of Bidda; these, and various bureaus of the government, are the largest employers of village residents.

About 10% of the households in Bidda are supported by pastoralism, which exploits virtually all of the countryside surrounding the nucleated village. The animals raised, in the order of their importance, are sheep, cattle, and pigs. Pastoralists (*pastori*, singular *pastore*, in Italian) are generally looked down upon by the nonpastori majority. This is due to the physical labor they must perform, their out-of-doors work and its long hours, and the threatening aura of violence that surrounds them. Regardless of the species of animal a pastore raises, he must be alert for theft or mutilation of his stock; willingness to use covert violence in reprisal is a prerequisite of successful pastoralism in Sardinia.

The vast majority of Bidda's residents are descended from the farmer-herdsmen of a generation or two past. Now, however, there is a considerable degree of socioeconomic differentiation between these descendants, based on both income and way of making a living. White-collar employment is most highly valued, though a few blue-collar laborers may in fact earn more than some of the white-collar workers.

121

The pastori are most accurately described as a separate, parallel social system that interacts with the nonpastori as infrequently and briefly as possible. Pastori rarely congregate in the village's public squares or in the several bars, but do most of their socializing in one another's homes.

Games and Pastimes

The men of Bidda take part in a variety of games and competitions in a number of contexts. The traditional shepherds' contest of improvised verse has been described by Mathias (1976); it is no longer practiced in Bidda or surrounding villages, which is not altogether surprising, given the generally low status of pastoralism and anything that pertains to it. The availability of recorded music has made musical performance in Bidda extremely rare (Harris, 1974).

As is the case in other aspects of social life in Bidda, pastori and non-pastori take part in games separately and with different frequencies. Indeed, there are several activities in which only one or the other group ever takes part. When both pastori and nonpastori participate in a game, the contexts, styles, and results are usually different.

Though it is only in a marginal sense a game, this discussion will begin with the state-controlled soccer pool. During the soccer season virtually every nonpastori man encountered in Bidda took part in this contest, which is played throughout Italy. One attempts to predict which of Italy's top-level soccer teams will win each game the following Sunday. There are normally 13 matches weekly, and pool winners share a part of the money collected by the state in entry fees. The betting pool is not particularly important, and most men have rarely, if ever, done better than 9 or 10 right of 13, according to informants. But the context of the game is of interest. Men pick up wagering forms in the bars and discuss the merits of rival teams while drinking companionably. Knowledge of players and coaches from Rome or Naples or Venice is commonplace. In most cases, friends submit very similar forms, often even to the extent of choosing the same point-spread (a game option). Soccer matches are watched on television or listened to on the radio.

Among the pastori no participation in this game was observed; it is certainly an atypical activity for a pastore, if any do indeed take part. Some pastori are not certain precisely which cities have teams of major importance. Younger pastori were observed listening to radio broadcasts of games between minor teams, games held on the island at Cagliari or Sassari, but these are not part of the betting pool system.

Another game, or rather series of games, that has importance in the social life of men in bars is competition at cards. Card games played by men in bars are varied, but most are games of luck, like the contemporary American game "slapjack," rather than games of skill, such as cribbage. This feature usually prohibits any very great imbalance of scores between players over the course of an afternoon's play. The bar as an arena for card playing is usually exploited by older men with time to kill; younger men, below retirement age, are more likely to play games of skill in their own or in friends' homes. Poker and several varieties of gin-like games are occasionally played, the latter sometimes by married couples during family visits.

Outdoor Sports

A few older men occasionally take part in bocce, or lawn bowling. The weather does not often permit participation in any comfort, but when it does, active retired men sometimes play bocce. The game is apparently not of interest to pastori. Men well advanced into middle age whose schedules permit free time during midday may also compete at bocce on occasion.

Bidda fields its own soccer team for games against other Sard villages; the team members are unpaid, but are very popular and well known. Residents of Bidda vary tremendously with regard to their support of the team, some traveling to all away games and some rarely attending even home games. Nonpastori make up virtually all of the audience, and young unmarried men and women are probably the most common categories of person in attendance.

Spectators are both vocal and active in support of their team during a game. Players, according to their team membership, are cheered or hissed, referees only the latter. Waving and clapping are frequent, as is display of pennants with the village colors. On an average Sunday, drinkingduring the game is moderate, but on a patron saint's day the wine is likely to flow freely during and after the match. As far as was observed, home and visiting spectators are well behaved throughout; there is a strong norm against overt conflict in one's village, although several informants mentioned getting into fights with strangers in larger towns, where anonymity reigns.

Hunting is neither precisely a game nor an overt competition, yet a consideration of the sport would seem to add to this discussion. Throughout Sardinia there are state lands that are off-limits to hunting for reasons of game conservation, and there are animal species that are protected wherever they may be encountered. The majority of the island is open to hunting, which may legally be done only on Sundays and Thursdays. No property outside the village may be declared off-limits to hunters, except with governmental permission, though hunters are liable for any hurt they may do to domesticated animals.

Birds, foxes, and hares are the chief targets, although wild boar are encountered on extremely rare occasions. The sole legal hunting weapon is the shotgun, loaded with shot only. Even with these provisions, hunting in rocky and brush-filled land too often leads to shooting accidents. Most men in Bidda possess some form of firearm, a shotgun or a pistol of some kind.

Hunting is done almost exclusively by nonpastori, in and around Bidda at least. The pastori occasionally take their half-starved dogs with them on their daily rounds, hoping to catch a hare, but this seems almost never to happen. Some of the younger, unemployed nonpastori hunt on occasion, usually during regular working hours when their favorite companions are otherwise occupied. Wild game, like the wild mushrooms that may be freely foraged on hunting trips, forms a special and beloved part of local cuisine and so allows an unemployed man to turn his excess free time into a benefit through hunting.

For the most part, however, hunting is engaged in by successful older men, who often possess (and willingly display) expensive automatic shotguns. Though some of them may hunt relatively rarely, their freedom to do so is one of several recognized signs of success. No one would hunt of whom it might be alleged that the food collected was a welcome addition for nutritional reasons; it is rather for reasons of gastronomic appreciation that one seeks wild game.

Pastori Pastimes

Horses were once of great significance in Bidda as a sign of economic success. At present many pastori continue to maintain horses, at some expense, that are used only once or twice in most years. There is no precise correlation between income and horse ownership among pastori, though only well-to-do pastori have the resources to maintain one or more horses. Some pastori, especially older ones, do not bother to do so, and no nonpastori were ever observed to own animals, aside from a very few household pets. One cannot say that horse ownership is a sure diagnostic sign of economic success among pastori, as it once was, but it is at least one of several ways to demonstrate wealth. Horses are the only animals owned by pastori that are incapable of being economically exploited and are in fact a considerable burden. Their ancestries, aptitudes, and personalities become significant topics of discussion as the annual horse-oriented festivals draw near; horses that have not been ridden or even given adequate exercise for months are suddenly exercised and brushed daily and become reaccustomed to being ridden.

Men exhibit their horses and horsemanship in the *ardia*, the form of which varies from village to village and even from holiday to holiday within the same village. In one village near Bidda, a kind of joust was until recently an integral part of the ardia; informants from Bidda said that that particular ardia was not considered "proper" until blood had been spilled, and it had finally been altered by legislation to avoid further injury to horses and riders.

A more common form of the ardia is a long horse race over rough ground, the winner of which is given a cash prize. The ardia honoring Bidda's patron saint takes this form and occasions participation by pastori from neighboring villages as well. An informant said that such festivals were virtually the only acceptable excuse for going to another village where one could, with luck, encounter pastori with whom to make friends. These "friends" are the individuals whom one asks in to commit large-scale thefts against enemies in one's village or by whom one is invited to take part in "foreign" stock thefts. Pastori also like to cultivate acquaintances in other villages to act as listening posts; one can check with one's contacts in several neighboring villages to discover whether anyone was involved in transporting large numbers of sheep at about the time that one's own flock was taken.

A much shorter and less publicized ardia takes place on Bidda's lesser patron saint's day. A few local pastori, normally no more than a dozen, ride their horses in a number of short races, two horses at a time. The object appears to be more to enjoy the proceedings than to attempt to win. No prize is awarded, and only a few relatives are present as spectators. A great deal of wine is consumed both between heats and after the ardia is completed. The riders, usually young unmarried pastori, canter from house to house across the village after the race, stopping and demanding wine at the homes of their families and close relatives. The riders encourage one another to perform acts of daring on horseback, all the while becoming more intoxicated. Men do headstands on their saddles, stand on the backs of cantering horses, force their horses to climb concrete steps, and finally invade the courtyards and homes of their relatives and friends on horseback. At this point no further escalation is possible and the postardia celebration quickly comes to an end.

La Morra

Following major ardias, which are usually dominated by the younger pastori, these men often gather in bars or in their homes. Riders from other villages are invited along, and men drink and celebrate for hours. A favorite recreation at such a time is *la morra*, a guessing game played throughout Italy. It is played by two teams of two each, who stand together in the middle of a room surrounded by seated spectators. The two men on a team stand side by side, facing the opposing team. One man from each team competes at a time, waving his right hand at the opposing player and shouting a number between 0 and 10. Each player will expose from none to all five digits on the right hand, and the object of the game is to guess how many fingers will be exposed by both men. The number guessed by any player should never be more than five higher than however many digits he himself has decided to expose.

La morra is played at a rapid pace, the players crouching and shouting loudly, shaking their fists in one another's faces. Often neither player guesses correctly, and the same two may play several rounds in a row. When one finally guesses the right number, he will shout "Mudu!" (mute) to his opponent, and immediately begin play with the other member of the opposing team. It is an exciting and mercurial game, which rouses players' emotions. Spectators shout derisive comments as the game progresses.

Pastori say that a match of *la morra*, amid drinking and fellowship in a rare holiday atmosphere, presents a fine opportunity to ask a neighbor whether he has in fact been responsible for some act of vandalism of which he has long been suspected. By picking a moment when conflict is at a minimum and good feeling is at its highest, a pastore assures his neighbor that he wants to settle the matter finally and amicably. Whatever developments have led to vandalism between them are (ostensibly) relegated to the past. If a pastore can demonstrate his ability to attribute properly the responsibility for past vandalism and boldly confront the other, evidently he feels no further need to prove himself concerning the matter; to have it settled and no longer producing resentment or suspicion is sufficient.

It is illegal to play *la morra* in Sardinia, due to the ease with which the game can become violent. Players face one another, crouching and swinging their right arms down toward one another. They shout and play rapidly, and the potential for cheating, or trying to cheat, is great. One can shout a number and try to quickly perceive how many fingers the opponent is showing, then a split-second later reveal the appropriate number of one's own digits to bring the total to the desired point. The easiest way to cheat seems to be to hide the thumb until the opponent has committed himself, then seem to have already been concealing or revealing the thumb, whichever advances one's position. Playing the game requires great presence of mind, and a certain opportunity to cheat seems to be built into the rules. There is no judge or referee, so if a player fails to be truly simultaneous with his opponent in playing a round, no disinterested party is present to call the foul. All one can do is try to cheat as effectively as one's opponent does; when individuals become frustrated they may strike their opponents almost without thinking, while crouched face-to-face with them.

According to informants, the incidence of violence over *la morra* in Bidda and surrounding villages has generally been low, but the law against playing the game was necessary to control violence in traditional shepherd villages. In Bidda, *la morra* is usually not played in public but instead takes place in private homes. On one occasion a member of the state police was observed at a game and seemed perfectly relaxed at being present during an illegal activity. On important festival days *la morra* is often played in bars, as police will turn a deaf ear to evidence of nonviolent games. The law against *la morra* serves to keep the players discreet rather than to prohibit the game; this seems to be the case concerning many regulations in Bidda.

La morra is one of the few recreations in which both pastori and nonpastori take part. Pastori play the game on rare occasions, usually in the aftermath of some major celebration, and are likely to play it in situations where some of the participants are strangers to the village or to the majority of the pastori present. Nonpastori, on the other hand, are likely to play the game on secular holidays, such as a housewarming party or some other celebration of events in the life cycle. No firm estimate of the incidence of *la morra* playing occasions could be made, but the impression was gained that the game is a relatively rare and special event. Typically, *la morra* takes place at an all-male gathering, after the men have eaten and drunk a great deal. Partners are chosen and a score-keeper appointed, and there are usually many more men watching the game than playing. Some men are unwilling ever to play *la morra* or will only play briefly and with reluctance, because they are unable to relax sufficiently in front of so many spectators. Effective play requires impressive self-possession, particularly considering the pointed catcalls from the spectators. Teams that lose stand down and are as quickly replaced by new players.

La morra among nonpastori almost never becomes violent, but this is not due to any scruples about cheating. In fact, it might be argued that to win at *la morra* virtually requires cheating. Nonpastori men feel free to dispute the claims of victory their opponents make or to suggest with facial expression and bodily posturing that they are amazed at the wicked play of their cheating opponents. When any significant gap exists between two opponents in terms of social importance, however, the more dominant individual almost invariably can both cheat more aggressively and succeed in making his claims to victory stick. No one could cheat on every turn, and likewise a player or a duo that always won would quickly lose popularity, but men of Bidda can be said to reflect in their play the social realities of dominance and relative importance in everyday life.

Conclusions

The manner in which the pastori and nonpastori men of Bidda segregate their recreations from one another both reflects and maintains the social boundaries existing within the village. The two groups hold differing attitudes regarding the natural environment: to one an opportunity for sport, to the other a workplace. Social differentiation largely denies the pastori use of public places in the village, either for game and sport purposes or for the purpose of social interaction.

The ardia is the only public ceremony in Bidda over which the pastori exert control, due to their local monopoly on horses. Pastori enjoy the ardia and the ensuing matches of *la morra*, but are quick to point out the utilitarian nature of the latter in regard to their pastoralist life-style.

The nonpastori have developed a way of life with considerable emphasis on games, both as pastimes and as indices of social position. The utter exclusion of pastori from the others' activities illustrates this in an extreme form. Nonpastori are free to indulge in game playing, without ulterior motives, in a way that their peasant ancestors and pastori neighbors could never afford.

References

Harris, C. (1974). *Hennage*. New York: Holt, Rinehart & Winston.

King, R. (1975). Ottana. *Geography*, **60**, 218-222.

King, R. (1977). Recent industrialisation in Sardinia. *Erdkunde*, **31**, 87-102.

Mathias, E. (1976). La gara poetica. *Ethos*, **4**, 483-507.

CHAPTER 12

Play and Writing: Possible Connections

James F. Christie
Ruth M. Noyce
University of Kansas

Students in traditional writing classes seldom consider written composition to be "child's play." Because the primary emphasis has been on generating a finished product for the teacher to scrutinize and criticize, students have tended to regard writing as hard work. Current "process" approaches to writing instruction, such as the Bay Area National Writing Project, however, are promoting play-like prewriting and composing activities, raising the possibility that certain types of play may contribute to the development of writing abilities.

Our interest in examining relationships between play and writing stems from a classroom observation in which a National Writing Project teacher/consultant demonstrated the value of role playing as a prewriting activity to prepare students to write from various points of view. Research has shown that speech play makes important contributions to children's oral language development (Chukovsky, 1971; Weir, 1962) and that training in dramatic play can result in gains in verbal fluency (Lovinger, 1974; Smilansky, 1968) and aural comprehension (Pellegrini & Galda, 1982). Given these links between play and language, it seemed likely that certain forms of play, such as the prewriting activity that we had observed, might facilitate children's learning to write.

As a result of examining the literature in both areas, we found several links between play and writing. These connections involve (a) sustained discourse, (b) narrative skills, (c) perspective taking, and (d) ideational fluency. Our purpose here is to describe these links and to suggest some directions for future research.

Sustained Discourse

The ability to sustain discourse by engaging in monologues of considerable length is an important prewriting skill. Oral monologues are an early step toward the "closed schema" needed to complete a story or composition, that is, input from an audience is not necessary as it is in "open" oral dialogue (Bereiter & Scardamalia, 1982). Moffett (1983) explains the importance of sustained discourse in learning to write:

> The first step toward writing is made when a speaker takes over a conversation and sustains some subject alone. He has started to create a solo discourse that while intended to communicate to others is less collaborative, less prompted, and less corrected by feedback than dialogue. He bears more of the responsibility for effective communication. He has moved away from drama toward narrative, exposition, and theory—the domains of writing. (p. 85)

Vygotsky (1962) has emphasized the importance of children's conversations with themselves during solitary play in the learning of sustained discourse. Rubin and Dyck (1980) found that two types of play encourage this type of activity: (a) solitary constructive play, in which a child uses objects to build something, and (b) solitary dramatic play, in which the child takes on a role and uses make-believe transformations, for example, adopting the role of a doctor and pretending to take a doll's temperature with a pencil. Children engaged in more monologues with themselves during these two types of play than during other forms of play. Both solitary constructive and solitary dramatic play appear to be contexts in which children can develop skill in sustained discourse.

Narrative Skills

Among the skills needed by the writer of a narrative are the ability to generate enough writing to produce a complete story, the ability to integrate and connect story events in a logical manner, and the ability to communicate with the reader using explicit words. We found links between each of these three skills—writing fluency, story organization, and use of precise vocabulary—and play.

Writing Fluency

When children engage in dramatic play, they learn to extend their play episodes by adding new events that are related to the story line. For example, if children have adopted roles as family members preparing a meal, they might extend the dramatization by deciding to go to the store to get some food. Children's ability to sustain dramatic play eposides in this manner increases between the ages of 4 and 5 (Iwanaga, 1973).

Research supports the possibility that experience in extending story lines gained through dramatic play may transfer to children's storytelling skills. Correlational studies have revealed significant relationships between group dramatic play and children's oral and written story fluency. Children who regularly engage in group dramatic play tend to tell and write longer stories than other children (Johnson, 1976; Pellegrini, 1980).

It has been demonstrated that play-like experiences with language structures can produce similar gains in older children's writing fluency. Noyce and Christie (1983) compared an integrated sentence-modeling curriculum, which included oral language games and humorous writing activities (e.g., writing cartoon conversations), with a curriculum that involved drill-like exercises in which students wrote sentences imitating a model pattern. Results showed that third graders receiving the play-oriented curriculum wrote significantly longer stories than students who received the pattern drill. Perhaps the motivational power of play was responsible for this gain in writing fluency. If play-like activities make the act of writing more enjoyable for children, they may put more effort and energy into their written compositions.

Story Organization

When children engage in group dramatic play, they must make cooperative decisions about story sequence. For example, children enacting a hospital scene might decide on the following sequence: first, the doctor will take the patient's temperature; then, the nurse will administer an injection; and finally, the doctor will perform an operation. This experience with planning story lines may promote children's story organization skills. Saltz and Johnson (1974) found that preschoolers who received dramatic play training were more successful than others at connecting and integrating story events.

Caster and Pellegrini (1984) found evidence that constructive play also contributes to children's story organization skills. They examined the "narrative-like" structure of preschoolers' play in dramatic and constructive play contexts. The children's play was rated on a scale ranging from simple actions to contoured episodes, which consisted of two or more connected series of actions. For example, in a birthday party dramatization, a child might act out a series of events needed to prepare food for the party and then enact a string of actions connected with serving the make-believe food to the party guests. The investigators found that 4-year-olds used more of these contoured episodes in constructive play, whereas 5-year-olds used more in dramatic play. Both types of play appear to give children valuable experience with narrative organization.

Precise Vocabulary

Observational research by Garvey (1977) and others has revealed that group dramatic play places heavy linguistic demands on children. In order for this type of play to be successful, players must clearly designate the roles to be adopted and the make-believe identities of objects, actions, and situations. Otherwise, ambiguity and confusion will ensue (Pellegrini, DeStefano, & Thompson, 1983). For example, if one player decides that a block of wood will be used as a make-believe hamburger, this must be communicated to the other players so that they will also treat the piece of wood as if it were a sandwich. Because clarity of expression is required, dramatic play encourages children to use precise vocabulary.

This link between group dramatic play and precise language has been strengthened in recent studies by Pellegrini. He found that preschoolers used more explicit language in dramatic play settings than in constructive play settings (Pellegrini, 1982). It should be noted, however, that this study involved only 4 subjects. In a study with a considerably larger sample size, Pellegrini (1984) reported that primary grade children used more explicit language during dramatic enactments of stories than during other forms of story reconstruction, suggesting that dramatic play prewriting activities might lead students to use more precise vocabulary in their writing.

Perspective Taking

The ability to view the world from another person's perspective is an important prerequisite to writing. In order to communicate effectively, a writer must be able to imagine the reader's point of view. Story writers must also be able to enter into the roles of the characters that they have created and write from these characters' perspectives. The importance of this skill to writing was demonstrated in the 1974 National Assessment of Educational Progress (Atwater, 1981), which evaluated students' ability to enter into and elaborate on a role through an exercise in which they pretended to be a pair of tennis shoes. Role-taking and role-elaboration skills were considered to be a "primary trait" of a good writer.

A growing body of research supports the possibility that dramatic play contributes to children's perspective-taking abilities. When children engage in dramatic play, they act out a variety of roles. A child might, on various occasions, take on the role of a parent, baby, grandparent, grocer, and firefighter. In order to accurately portray such characters, children must mentally put themselves in other people's places and experience the world from their points of view. Rubin and Maioni (1975) found a significant correlation between the frequency with which children engaged in group dramatic play and their perspective-taking skills. Other researchers have reported that training in dramatic play resulted in gains in preschool, kindergarten, and third grade students' cognitive role-taking abilities (Burns & Brainerd, 1979; Iannotti, 1978; Rosen, 1974). Unfortunately, many of the assessment instruments used in these studies suffer from limited reliability and/or validity (Johnsen & Christie, 1984), making it difficult to draw any firm conclusions about the relationship between play and perspective taking.

The above research generally supports Atwater's (1981) contention that dramatic play experiences during the preschool and kindergarten years promote children's readiness for all types of writing by enhancing their role-taking skills. It is also possible that using dramatic play as a prewriting activity will help elementary grade students incorporate perspective taking into their writing. As was mentioned earlier, teachers in National Writing Project workshops are using dramatic play activities for this purpose.

Ideational Fluency

The problem of deciding what to write about makes writing a difficult task for many children. Current approaches to writing instruction, which focus attention on each phase of the composition process, point out the importance of prewriting experiences for promoting ideational fluency, the ability to generate a large number of ideas. Sutton-Smith (1971) has argued that make-believe play has a key role in the development of this important aspect of creativity. If play does promote ideational fluency, then dramatic play prewriting activities might be an effective way to stimulate ideas for later writing.

A series of studies by Dansky supports the connection between dramatic play and mental fluency. Dansky and Silverman (1975) found that when preschoolers were given opportunities to play with objects they later generated more uses for similar objects than children who did not engage in play. In a later study, Dansky (1980) found that gains in associative fluency occurred only for children who engaged in dramatic play with the objects, a finding that suggests that make-believe, rather than the mere opportunity for free play, was responsible for the increases in fluency. Dansky hypothesized that the free symbolic transformations that occur in dramatic play loosen old mental associations, making ideational fluency possible.

Mills (1983) used a combination of constructive and dramatic play prewriting activities to stimulate the writing of intermediate grade students. The children first planned and built a miniature replica of a small town. They then created imaginary characters who lived in the town and described these characters in writing. They also engaged in dramatic play, acting out the characters they had created. The students wrote letters from their imaginary characters to characters that others were enacting, and they set up and wrote a town newspaper. Mills reported that the children responded very positively to these play-related writing activities and that they exhibited high levels of imagination and creativity in their writing. Unfortunately, no control group was used, so it is not known if these changes in attitude and writing quality were caused solely by the play experiences.

Summary and Recommendations for Future Research

Results of the studies reviewed above suggest that play may make important contributions to young children's *readiness* to write. Dramatic play has been found to facilitate the development of solitary discourse, several narrative skills, perspective taking, and ideational fluency. Constructive play has also been linked with the growth of solitary discourse, story organization, and creativity. Unfortunately, problems with sampling, assessment instruments, and experimental designs color some of these findings. So, while there do appear to be links between certain types of play and skills that are involved in learning to write, further research is needed to confirm these relationships.

We were able to find little evidence directly relating play and actual *writing*. The skills mentioned in the preceding paragraph involved oral language or performance on an assessment instrument (e.g., a perspective-taking test). The only link between play and children's writing ability involved writing fluency. Kindergartners' levels of dramatic play were found to be related to the number of words that they wrote (Pellegrini, 1980), and play-like prewriting activities appeared to increase the length of third-graders' written compositions (Noyce & Christie, 1983).

Future research should focus on direct links between play and writing. Correlational studies, using a longitudinal design, could examine the relationship between children's play patterns in preschool and/or kindergarten and the characteristics of their writing during the primary grades. It would be interesting to determine if children who engaged in high levels of dramatic play during early childhood later wrote stories that were better organized and more creative than those written by children who rarely engaged in this type of play. Causality, of course, could not be inferred, and such studies would have to be carefully controlled for differences in intelligence.

There is also a need for experimental studies to determine the impact of dramatic play prewriting activities on primary and intermediate grade students' writing. One could, for example, investigate the effects of prewriting dramatizations on children's ability to enter into and elaborate on different types of roles in their writing. A variation of Atwater's (1981) "Tennis Shoe" primary trait procedure could be used to assess this skill. Children's writing could also be examined to determine if dramatic play activities had effects on story length and organization, the use of precise vocabulary, and aspects of creativity such as originality and imagination. The instrument developed by May (1967) for determining the degree of originality and vocabulary skill in a child's writing would be appropriate for use in such studies. The reported effectiveness of Mills' (1983) constructive and dramatic play activities in building positive attitudes toward writing suggests that possible relationships between both types of play and writing attitudes should also be explored.

In conclusion, our review has uncovered several promising links between play and writing. More research is needed, however, before any definite conclusions can be drawn. Such research will add to our understanding of play's role in literacy development and may ultimately result in the creation of more effective procedures for helping children learn how to write.

References

Atwater, J.D. (1981). *Better testing, better writing: A report to the Ford Foundation*. New York: Ford Foundation.

Bereiter, C., & Scardamalia, M. (1982). From conversation to composition: The role of instruction in a developmental process. In R. Glaser (Ed.), *Advances in instructional psychology* (Vol. 2). Hillsdale, NJ: Erlbaum.

Burns, S.M., & Brainerd, C.J. (1979). Effects of constructive and dramatic play on perspective taking in very young children. *Developmental Psychology, 15*, 512-521.

Caster, T.R., & Pellegrini, A.D. (1984, March). *The development of children's narrative-like play behaviors.* Paper presented at the meeting of The Association for the Anthropological Study of Play, Clemson University.

Chukovsky, K. (1971). *From two to five.* Los Angeles: University of California Press.

Dansky, J.L. (1980). Make-believe: A mediator of the relationship between play and associative fluency. *Child Development, 51*, 576-579.

Dansky, J.L., & Silverman, I.W. (1975). Play: A general facilitator of associative fluency. *Developmental Psychology, 11*, 104.

Garvey, C. (1977). *Play.* Cambridge, MA: Harvard University Press.

Iannotti, R.J. (1978). Effect of role-taking experiences on role taking, empathy, altruism, and aggression. *Developmental Psychology, 14*, 119-124.

Iwanaga, M. (1973). Development of interpersonal play structure in three, four, and five-year-old children. *Journal of Research and Development in Education, 6*, 71-82.

Johnsen, E.P., & Christie, J.F. (1984). Play and social cognition. In B. Sutton-Smith & D. Kelley-Byrne (Eds.), *The masks of play.* Champaign, IL: Leisure Press.

Johnson, J.E. (1976). Relations of divergent thinking and intelligence test scores with social and nonsocial make-believe play of preschool children. *Child Development, 47*, 1200-1203.

Lovinger, S.L. (1974). Socio-dramatic play and language development in preschool disadvantaged children. *Psychology in the Schools, 11*, 313-320.

May, F.B. (1967). *Teaching language as communication to children.* Columbus, OH: Charles E. Merrill.

Mills, B.S. (1983). Imagination: The connection between writing and play. *Educational Leadership, 40*, 50-53.

Moffett, J. (1983). *Teaching the universe of discourse.* Boston: Houghton Mifflin.

Noyce, R.M., & Christie, J.F. (1983). Effects of an integrated approach to grammar instruction on third graders' reading and writing. *Elementary School Journal, 84*, 63-69.

Pellegrini, A.D. (1980). The relationship between kindergartners' play and achievement in prereading, language, and writing. *Psychology in the Schools, 17*, 530-535.

Pellegrini, A.D. (1982). The construction of cohesive text by preschoolers in two play contexts. *Discourse Processes, 5,* 101-108.

Pellegrini, A.D. (1984). The effect of dramatic play on children's generation of cohesive text. *Discourse Processes.*

Pellegrini, A.D., DeStefano, J.S., & Thompson, D.L. (1983). Saying what you mean: Using play to teach "literate language." *Language Arts, 60,* 380-384.

Pellegrini, A.D., & Galda, L. (1982). The effects of thematic-fantasy play training on the development of children's story comprehension. *American Educational Research Journal, 19,* 443-452.

Rosen, C.E. (1974). The effects of sociodramatic play on problem-solving behavior among culturally disadvantaged preschool children. *Child Development, 45,* 920-927.

Rubin, K.H., & Dyck, L. (1980). Preschoolers' private speech in a play setting. *Merrill-Palmer Quarterly, 26,* 219-229.

Rubin, K., & Maioni, T. (1975). Play preference and its relationship to egocentrism, popularity, and classification skills in preschoolers. *Merrill-Palmer Quarterly, 21,* 171-179.

Saltz, E., & Johnson, J.E. (1974). Training for thematic-fantasy play in culturally disadvantaged children: Preliminary results. *Journal of Educational Psychology, 66,* 623-630.

Smilansky, S. (1968). *The effects of sociodramatic play on disadvantaged preschool children.* New York: Wiley.

Sutton-Smith, B. (1971). The role of play in cognitive development. In R.E. Herron & B. Sutton-Smith (Eds.), *Child's play.* New York: Wiley.

Vygotsky, L.S. (1962). *Thought and language.* Cambridge, MA: Massachusetts Institute of Technology.

Weir, R. (1962). *Language in the crib.* The Hague: Mouton.

CHAPTER 13

Effects of Dramatic Play as a Basis of a Parent Instructional Model for Home Intervention Programming for Hispanic Parents of Preschool Children

Thomas D. Yawkey
Pennsylvania State University

This study examines the effects of training Hispanic parents of children enrolled in Project PIAGET to develop, use, and practice various dramatic play activities and games with their youngsters in home settings. Project PIAGET stands for Promoting Intellectual Adaptation Given Experiential Transforming and is a Title VII federally funded demonstration project for Hispanic preschoolers with limited English proficiency (LEP) and their parents.

These Hispanic parents were trained to use systematically an adult/child Play Mastery Cycle with their youngsters in home settings. The study examines the effects of using the Play Mastery Cycle on parents' feelings about their children, uses of play activities and games with their youngsters at home, and perceptions of their children's growth. We predicted that Hispanic parents in the experimental group who were trained to use the Play Mastery Cycle would at posttest trial (a) have greater positive feelings toward their children, (b) use more play activities and games with their children in the home and home-related settings, and (c) have higher perceptions of their children's growth and development than Hispanic parents in the comparison group, who did not receive this training. We will discuss our findings after an introductory review of the literature on child and parent/child play training and an overview of Project PIAGET.

Child and Parent/Child Training

Since the publication of Piaget's book *Play, Dreams and Imitation in Childhood* (1962), play has generally been considered a dynamic and necessary structure of cognitive growth. With the assumptions that play and its various forms (e.g., dramatic, sociodramatic, and functional play) are significant for cognitive growth and that children of lower socioeconomic status (SES) tend to show a marked paucity of play compared to other groups of children, an increasing number of investigators have attempted to increase play and examine its effect on various cognitive and cognitive-related skills (see Bruner, Jolly, & Sylva, 1976; Christie & Johnsen, 1983). Whether play in lower SES children should be considered from deficit (e.g., Saltz, Dixon, & Johnson, 1977) or difference perspectives (e.g., Schwartzman, 1979, 1984) are points for discussion, further debate, and empirical research (Lacy & Tindall, 1976; Loy, 1982).

These "play tutoring" studies focusing on children have shown generally that dramatic and sociodramatic play, by permitting youngsters to transform objects and situations and at the same time note their initial identities and states (i.e., decenter), could encourage a variety of cognitive, social, and language skills and performances. For example, play tutoring studies have trained children in dramatic and/or sociodramatic play and noted increases in problem solving (e.g., Sylva, Bruner, & Genova, 1976), language (e.g., Smilansky, 1968), associative fluency (e.g., Pellegrini, 1981), reading growth (Yawkey, 1980) and affective-perspective taking (Saltz, Dixon, & Johnson, 1977). Methodological problems inherent in these "play tutoring" studies have been noted and detailed elsewhere (see Christie & Johnsen, 1983).

"Play training" or "tutoring" has also centered on parents as recipients who in turn are taught to use varied roles to guide the dramatic play, games, and playful acts of their children in home settings. Assuming that reciprocal interactions between parent and child are critical to and form the basis for intellectual and emotional stimulation of young children (Bee, Van Engeren, Streissguth, Nyman, & Lechie, 1975; Bronfenbrenner, 1975) and that the reciprocal interplay occurring between parent and child can be symbolized as play, games, and playful acts (Gordon, 1970; Piers & Landau, 1980; Pulaski, 1980), play tutoring of parents (where parents are shown how to use play as they guide their children in home settings) has provided the foundation for parent education, training, and development progams (see Day & Parker, 1972).

Parent play tutoring programs where parents are systematically trained to use play and varied roles in guiding their child's play as a basis for reciprocal interaction should, at maximum, affect (a) the child's cognitive, language, and/or social growth (e.g., Madden, Levenstein, & Levenstein, 1976; Schaefer, 1972) and (b) the parents' own self-perceptions of their roles as parents and care-givers (Gordon, 1969; Yawkey, 1982b).

Examples of parent-play and parent-play tutoring programs include Levenstein's (1971) Verbal Interaction Project, Gordon's (1969) Florida Parent Education Infant and Toddler Programs, and Nimnicht, Arango, and Adcock's (1971) Parent Child Toy Library Program. In the Verbal Interaction Project (Levenstein, 1971), home visitors called "Toy Demonstrators" modeled for lower SES parents the uses of toys (e.g., hammer and pegs, mailbox, hand puppets) and interaction modes with their youngsters as they played with these objects. Using a variety of standardized tests on the children (Cattell Intelligence Scale for Infants,

Stanford-Benet Intelligence Scale for preschoolers ages 3 and 4, Peabody Picture Vocabulary Test for all ages), Levenstein's findings showed that the children enrolled in the parent-play program made significant IQ gains at the end of 1 or 2 years of participation and those who had participated for 2 full years retained or increased their IQ gains into kindergarten and second grade. For the parents in Levenstein's program, results showed that mothers significantly increased their parenting skills and verbal-cognitive interactions as measured by the Parent and Child Together (PACT) instrument and that both the children's scores on the Child Behavior Traits scale and those of their parents on the PACT correlated with the children's IQ scores (Levenstein, 1971). This suggests a triadic relationship among the child's behaviors, mother's parenting skills, and child's cognitive development.

In Gordon's (1969) Florida model, lower and middle SES parents were trained by home visitors (parent educators or paraprofessionals) to use dramatic play and play activities for stimulation in weekly visits lasting 30 to 60 minutes. The results indicated that preschoolers enrolled in the Florida programs for all 3 years, the first 2 consecutive years, only the first year, or only the third year yielded higher IQ scores (on the Stanford-Binet) than those in the control groups. Using a self-concept scale, interviews, and home observation reports of mother/child interaction, findings showed the trained parents had significantly more positive views of themselves and their parenting roles (Gordon, 1969). In addition, the parents trained by the home visitors significantly increased their social family activities and community involvement (Gordon, 1969).

Nimnicht, Arango, and Adcock's (1971) Parent-Child Toy Library Program was aimed at showing parents of young children, ages 3 to 8, how to encourage cognitive development and self-concept through parent/child dramatic play in home settings. This program focused on a set of toys and games (e.g., sound cans, color lotto, stacking squares) and lasted 8 consecutive weeks. The parents were shown and practiced specific behaviors with these toys, role-played with other adults to learn how to use the toys and games, and were encouraged to use these objects and activities in the home with their children. Based on self-reports, interviews, and discussions with the parents, the findings showed that the parents trained to use the toys and games reported increased gains in their children's language development, reading, pattern recognition, and simple mathematical skills (Nimnicht, Arango, & Adcock, 1971). Finally, the parents reported greater feelings of competence in working with their children in home settings (Nimnicht, Arango, & Adcock, 1971).

Overview of Project PIAGET

Project PIAGET was funded for the 3-year period from 1981 through 1984 and was sponsored by the Bethlehem, Pennsylvania Area School District with The Pennsylvania State University, University Park. Project PIAGET was aimed at teaching English language (oral and written) to 5-year-old Spanish-dominant Puerto Rican children in center/classroom programs, and concerned with showing their parents how to work with their own children in home programs. The programs for Hispanic bilingual populations are based principally on Jean Piaget's views of growth, development, and cognitive competencies with modifications made on the model to provide a "goodness of fit" with objectives of both cognition and social-cognitive communication.

The overall goals of Project PIAGET were as follows (Yawkey, 1982a, 1984):

- To develop the proficiency of bilingual children in the English language while supporting growth and usage of their Spanish language.
- To take advantage of the young child's major formative and developmental years to help the child learn the English language and acquire concept growth that will enable him or her to succeed in formal public schooling—beginning in grade 1 in the Commonwealth of Pennsylvania.
- To capitalize on the significant contributions that the immediate and extended families and Hispanic sociocultural milieu can make in cooperatively working as an integral unit in the PIAGET programs to arrest the limited language proficiency of these bilingual children from lower socioeconomic status.
- To recognize and understand that schooling of children and families is imperative if the Spanish-speaking populations are to lift themselves from their lower socioeconomic levels.
- To educate the whole child by recognizing that language systems are interrelated with other major areas of cognition, social/emotional growth, self-identity growth, and progress in the kindergarten curriculum areas of reading, mathematics, social studies, science, the arts, and physical recreation.

These goals were implemented in two components of Project PIAGET, the Home Program and Center/Classroom Program.

PIAGET Home Program

The Home Program enrolled Hispanic parents of the children in the Center/Classroom Program. These bilingual parents were trained in their homes by Project PIAGET home visitors or paraprofessionals. The goals implemented by the home visitors with the parents included the following (Yawkey, 1982b, 1984):

- Training parents in the use of the adult/child Play Mastery Cycle.
- Demonstrating the use of the Play Mastery Cycle with play activities that could be used by parents with children in the home settings.
- Helping parents recognize the valuable contributions that home and school make to the development and education of their children's intellectual, communication, social, physical, and emotional growth.
- Expanding positive attitudes of the parents concerning their contributions to their children's development and the Hispanic community.

- Teaching parents to use their own homes and Hispanic community as learning centers to enhance their youngster's learning and development.

Four home visitors were employed in Project PIAGET to implement these five goals. Half of their time was spent in the homes working with the parents and the other half was focused on the Center/Classroom Program. The home visitors trained the parents to use the Play Mastery Cycle in 1-hour sessions each week throughout the academic school year. Spanish was the language of instruction in the Home Program. The parent/child Play Mastery Cycle was the core of the home intervention and the parents were shown and role-played the use of dramatic play, play activities, and playful actions. In turn, these parents used elements of the Play Mastery Cycle with their own children in home settings. The Play Mastery Cycle is explained in detail later in this paper.

Briefly, the Play Mastery Cycle was developed to increase dramatic play, play activities, and playful acts between parent and child. It was developed, piloted, and field-tested under a grant from the Margaret M. Patton Foundation (Yawkey, 1982a) prior to its use in Project PIAGET. The target population for the field-testing was bilingual and monolingual Head Start parents from lower income levels. The results at the end of a 6-month period showed that parents using the Play Mastery Cycle compared to those not receiving the model (a) used a significantly greater number of play activities with their children in home settings on the Parent-Child Play Preferences' Inventory and (b) had a significantly greater capacity to take the perspective or role of their child in various situations using the Parent Scale of the Parent-Child Perspective Taking instrument (Yawkey, 1982a).

PIAGET Center/Classroom Program

This component program enrolled bilingual 5-year-olds and was located in kindergarten classrooms of four elementary schools in Bethlehem. The goals of the program included the following (Yawkey, 1982b, 1984):

- Nurturing the child's intelligence in language and cognition using assumptions of development and growth taken and modified from Piaget's theory of intelligence.
- Providing concrete and sequenced series of language/cognitive concepts to construct knowledge concepts using teacher-guided Piagetian-derived experiential techniques.
- Focusing on the child's self-regulation of his or her growth and learning.
- Using language/cognitive concepts throughout the four baseline knowledge systems that served the center/classroom program as the primary curricular base: social knowledge, representation, logico-mathematical and physical knowledge, and self- and social identity.

The program teaching staff consisted of two bilingual teachers, one full-time and one half-time. The children in the Center/Classroom Program received half-day instruction 5 days a week throughout the academic year. Paraprofessionals also worked with the children in the Center/Classroom Program. The program evolved around the four knowledge domains identified in the goals listed above and consisted of 38 performance objectives that were phased in and terminated as the youngsters mastered them. In order to implement these performance objectives with the children in the Center/Classroom Program, the bilingual staff employed 18 Piagetian-derived instructional strategies. The performance objectives and the instructional strategies are explained in detail elsewhere (see Yawkey, 1982b, 1984 for a review). Since the focus of this paper is on the Home Program with its use of the parent/child Play Mastery Cycle, the results of the children's acquisition of language/cognitive competencies in the Center/Classroom Programs are found elsewhere (see Yawkey, 1982b, 1984 for a description).

Project Years 1981-1982 and 1982-1983

The parent/child Play Mastery Cycle was the foundation of the experimental treatment for Project PIAGET's Home Component during 1981-1983. The Play Mastery Cycle was not used in the comparison group of Hispanic parents during that time period. Different groups of Hispanic parents were enrolled in the experimental and comparison groups in 1981-1982 and 1982-1983. Similar procedures were used with parents in 1981-1982 and were replicated with different parents and at different locations.

First, the procedures and materials used with Hispanic parents in the experimental and comparison groups across both project years are outlined briefly below. Second, the number of parent participants, dependent measures, and results for each project year are described and discussed. The focus of the study is on the effects of the parent/child Play Mastery Cycle on parents' feelings toward their children, use of dramatic play activities in home and home-related situations, and perceptions of their children's growth and development.

In the experimental groups and across the project years 1981-1982 and 1982-1983, the Play Mastery Cycle, used by the Hispanic parents, was the foundation for the Project PIAGET Home Program. In operationalizing the Play Mastery Cycle, a trained home visitor worked with each of the parents in their homes for 1 hour per week while the children were enrolled in Project PIAGET's Center/Classroom Program. The role of the PIAGET home visitor was to train the parent to use the parent/child Play Mastery Cycle with the child in home and home-related settings.

The PIAGET home visitors were trained in two ways. First, the four home visitors working in the PIAGET Home Program received 8 hours of training in the Play Mastery Cycle using videotaping and receiving feedback on response criteria. Second, each home visitor was observed by a Project PIAGET graduate assistant on an ongoing basis at minimum once a month as she used the Play Mastery Cycle with a parent in the home setting. In both forms of training, the home visitor's roles and action routines in the Play Mastery Cycle were assessed and critiqued.

The Play Mastery Cycle consists of five content components that were hierarchically ordered and presented in linear fashion beginning with the first and terminating with the fifth component. The components, together with maximum duration of each component in minutes, are (a) Summarizing and Reporting from the Previous Week (5 minutes), (b) Explaining the Current Session's Play Action Plan (10 minutes), (c) Modeling the Play Action Plan for the Parent (15 minutes), (d) Modeling of the Play Action Plan by the Parent (15 minutes), and (e) Extending the Play Action Plan from Home to Home-Related Settings (10 minutes). Each of the Play Mastery Components is briefly described below. More detailed descriptions are found elsewhere (Yawkey, 1982b, 1984). The Play Mastery Cycle emphasized the following roles of the parent in dramatic play and play activities: present and unengaged, attentive and uninvolved, modeler, and engaged and responsive with the child (see McCune-Nicholich & Fenson, 1984; Yawkey & Cornelius, 1984 for reviews of parent roles in dramatic play activities).

Component 1: Summarizing and reporting from the previous week (5 minutes).   The Play Mastery Cycle began with the parent orally reporting to the home visitor concerning the settings in which play was used and how it was used in them. This component provided the parent with the opportunity to review the previous week's use of the Play Mastery Cycle and to ask questions that arose about its use in home and home-related settings. In addition, the home visitor was able to see whether the parent used the Play Mastery Cycle, determine whether it was used properly, and see the settings in which it was employed.

Component 2: Explaining the current session's play action plan (10 minutes).   The home visitor, in this component of the Play Mastery Cycle, explained and described to the parent the action plan to be used with her child this particular week. Each play action plan was phrased in specific behavioral terms and identified the set of behavioral routines that the parent was to use with her child and the toys and/or play materials needed to carry out the plan. Each play action plan provided the parents with specific roles and actions to be used with their children. The number of play action plans introduced by the home visitor each week varied from one to three. The toy objects and play materials used in play action plans were common and easily found in the homes.

Two examples of play action plans describing parents' routines follow (Yawkey, 1982b, 1984):

1. Parents join and help their children play
   (a) by asking them open-ended questions as they play with objects or at situations, and
   (b) by waiting for answers to their questions.

2. Parents join in and help their children play
   (a) by adding another toy object to their play activity that is related to and consistent with their original play theme, and
   (b) by waiting and observing them as they make decisions on its use in their play.

Component 3: Modeling the play action plan for the parent (15 minutes). In this component, the home visitor modeled the play action plan (described in Component 2) for the parents and demonstrated the "whats" and "hows" of this plan. The parent observed the home visitor while the play action plan was modeled. The home visitor again repeated the modeling of the play action plan for the parents and they were also urged to repeat it several times with their child depending on his or her interests and attention.

Component 4: Modeling of the play action plan by the parent (15 minutes). After observing the modeling of the play action plan, the parent was encouraged to imitate the same routines and use the same toys and play materials in similar ways as the home visitor. The parent practiced the plan based on the modeling without the child present, and the home visitor determined how effectively the parent matched the criterion episode and operationalized the play action plan. The parent's errors and misunderstandings in performing the routines in the play action play were corrected, appropriate ones reinforced, and questions about the routines answered.

Component 5: Extending the play action plan from home to home-related settings (10 minutes). The play action plan explained, modeled, and practiced in Components 2 through 4 of the Play Mastery Cycle used situations in the home setting. Component 5 attempted to show parents how the play action plan could be used with children in other situations outside the home setting. The home visitor guided the parent in selecting, at minimum, one home-related setting in which the particular play action plan was to be used during the week.

Examples of home-related settings and different situations where the play action plan might be utilized included at a relative or friend's house, at a grocery store, in the car, or walking down the street. In these settings, the parent used the play action plan where applicable and picked up on the youngster's incidental activities and actions outside the home. In extending the play action plan from home to home-related settings, the parents learned that it was usable, generalizable, and transportable.

The Hispanic parents enrolled in the comparison groups across project years 1981-1982 and 1982-1983 also had children enrolled in bilingual kindergarten programs and received support services in their homes. In the comparison groups, these home services varied between project years 1981-1982 and 1982-1983 because two different school districts, or local education agencies (LEAs), administered the services to the parents. For this reason, the procedures in the comparison groups for 1981-1982 and 1982-1983 are described separately.

In the comparison group project years 1981-1982, the Hispanic parents were now shown how to work systematically with their children in home settings. The home visitor in the bilingual kindergarten program made four visits to the Hispanic parents in the comparison group during the 1981-1982 project year. All visits lasted approximately 30 minutes. The first and fourth visits were similar in that they provided information to the parents about the bilingual program in which their children were enrolled. In addition, the parents were asked during the first visit to complete a questionnaire about dual language use in the home. This fourth visit focused largely on supplementing information about the performance of the child in the classroom.

The second and third visits emphasized parent/community relations and the roles parents might play in strengthening this relationship through appropriate parent/teacher associations and committees. Since the Hispanic parents in these comparison groups received no direct instruction on ways of working with their kindergartners in home settings, it might be assumed that they did what they regularly do with their children in home settings.

In the project years 1982-1983, the comparison group of Hispanic parents with youngsters enrolled in kindergarten bilingual programs received support services on a regular basis. The home visitor made visits to each of these parents twice a month. The home visitor also made additional visits to these parents when invited or when problems arose concerning the youngster's behavior in the classroom. The focus of this home program was on showing these bilingual parents how to reinforce in the home skills the children learned in the classroom. Generally the home visitor showed the parents specific skill activities that the children were performing in the classroom. The activities dealt largely with skills of the three Rs—reading, 'riting, and 'rithmetic. The home visitor showed the parents how to reinforce and practice these skills with the youngsters. In addition, the home visitor left worksheets for the parent and child to complete and activities that they might do together in the home (e.g., finger play games).

Methods for Project Years: 1981-1982

The Hispanic parents with preschoolers in Project PIAGET constituting the experimental group received the Play Mastery Cycle treatment in the Home program. The Hispanic parents with preschoolers enrolled in bilingual kindergarten education programs constituted the comparison groups.

All groups were pretested in January 1982 and posttested in June 1982, with approximately 6 months of treatment intervening between testings.

Subjects.   The experimental and comparison groups each contained 40 bilingual parents. Of the 40 families in the Project PIAGET Home Program, 29 were single-parent families and 11 were dual-parent families.

In the comparison group, 25 were single-parent families and 15 were dual-parent families. Since the mother was the primary head-of-household and chief care-giver for the majority of families, she was designated as the target recipient of the intervention across groups.

All parents were Puerto Rican and came from the lower income populations and agricultural region of Central Puerto Rico. The experimental group had resided in Bethlehem from 1 to 5 years; the comparison group parents had resided in a nearby city from 2 to 6 years.

The experimental site in Bethlehem is 150 miles from the comparison site. Families had moved to their respective cities for employment reasons and to escape the ghetto-like environments of Philadelphia, New York, and Newark. The size of both cities ranged between 70,000 and 80,000 people and parents from both groups were members of lower-income populations, as indicated by economic recessions, unemployment, enrollment in federal assistance programs, and blue-collar occupations for those employed (Warner, Meeker, & Eels, 1960).

Dependent measures.   The investigation examined parents' feelings about their children, use of play activities and actions with their youngsters in home and home-related settings, and perceptions of their youngsters' growth and development. The Hispanic parents in the experimental and comparison groups were individually administered three instruments in Spanish by a trained home visitor: (a) Parent Attitude Amplification Test: Parent Form (PAAP), (b) Test for Parental Utilization of Play Activities with Their Children (TPUP), and (c) Alpern-Boll Developmental Profile (ABDP). A brief description of each instrument follows and more detailed explanations are found elsewhere (Yawkey, 1982b, 1984).

The PAAP assessed parents' feelings and attitudes about their youngsters relative to various situations or tasks found in home settings. An example of an item from the PAAP is, "Your child is happy doing things at home." Using a Likert form, the parent chose whether she "strongly agrees," "agrees," "disagrees," or "strongly disagrees" with the descriptive statement. The PAAP consisted of 50 questions with a scoring range of 1 (for "strongly disagrees") to 4 (for "strongly agrees") and the absolute range per parent was 50 to 200 points. Total testing time per individual was 60 minutes; the reliability was .91 (Yawkey, 1982b, 1984).

The TPUP evaluated the quantity and quality of parental use of play and play-related activities with their children in home settings. One example of an item from the TPUP is, "You read your child story books at home." The parent responded whether she performed this activity/action with her child: "always," "regularly," "sometimes," or "never." With a Likert scoring range of 1 point (for "never") to 4 (for "always"), the absolute range per individual across its 50 questions was 50 to 200 points. The total testing time for each parent was 60 minutes, and the test reliability was .94 (Yawkey, 1982b, 1984).

The ABDP, a normed developmental profile, assessed parents' perceptions of their youngster's growth and development. The questions are grouped into five growth areas: physical age, self-help age, social age, academic age, and communication age. A total "growth equivalency age" and mean monthly growth age were obtained as per directions in the administration manual. Behavioral statements for each growth area were read and the parent indicated whether or not the youngster had mastered each action. If the parent perceived that the youngster could perform the behavioral action (e.g., "can tie his/her shoelaces"), he or she was credited with "passing" that item. If the parent perceived that the youngster couldn't perform the behavior, the child "failed" and no growth points were awarded for that action or item. Each of the items that were "passed" were worth from two to four "growth months." Growth months were summed within each area to indicate the parent's perceptions of her child (in that growth area) converted to years and months. Total administration time per parent was 120 minutes.

Results and discussion.   The data were analyzed using a 2 (groups: experimental and comparison) × 2 (trials: pre and post) analysis of variance with repeated measures (ANOVR) on factor B-trials. The 2 × 2 ANOVR was run separately for the PAAP, TPUP, and total and subgrowth areas of the ABDP.

First, for the PAAP, parents in the experimental group at posttest trial had significantly greater feelings about their children than the comparison group parents at the posttest trial ($F = 6.87$, $df = 1,78$, $p = .01$). Second, the results on the TPUP showed similar results. Experimental group parents at posttest trial performed a significantly greater number of play activities and actions with their children in home and home-related settings than comparison group parents ($F = 5.40$, $df = 1,78$, $p = .05$). Finally, experimental group parents at posttest trial had significantly higher perceptions of their child's physical age ($F = 9.48$, $df = 1,78$, $p = .05$) and academic age ($F = 4.46$, $df = 1,78$, $p = .03$) than comparison group parents at posttest trial. In addition, experimental group parents at posttest trial had higher mean monthly growth perceptions ($F = 5.30$, $df = 1,78$, $p = .02$) and greater total perceptions across all five growth areas ($F = 4.52$, $df = 1,78$, $p = .05$) for their children than did comparison parents at posttest trial. No significant effects were noted for ABDP subgrowth areas of self-help age ($F = 2.99$, $df = 1,78$, $p = .10$), social age ($F = .05$, $df = 1,78$, $p = .80$), or communication age ($F = .68$, $df = 1,78$, $p = .46$).

Methods for Project Years: 1982-1983

Another group of Hispanic parents having children enrolled in Project PIAGET comprised the experimental group for project years 1982-1983. A different group of Hispanic parents with children in bilingual kindergarten programs constituted the comparison group. Both groups of parents were pretested in September 1982 and posttested in May 1983 with 9 months between testings.

Subjects.   The experimental and comparison groups each had 44 parents. In the experimental group there were 24 dual- and 20 single-parent families; there were 23 dual- and 21 single-parent families in the comparison group. The mother was again designated as the target recipient across intervention groups.

This group of parents had demographic characteristics similar to those of the parents in project years 1981-1982: (a) all were Puerto Rican, (b) the participants came from Central Puerto Rico and to their respective cities in Pennsylvania for similar reasons, and (c) the families represented lower income populations. The experimental group had resided in Bethlehem from 1 to 4 years and those in the comparison group resided in a nearby city from 2 to 4 years.

The city serving as a comparison site for 1982-1983 was 200 miles from Bethlehem. The two cities had population ranges from 70,000 to 87,000 and had comparable economic bases.

Dependent measures. The study again assessed parents' feelings about their children (with the PAAP), use of play activities with their youngsters (using the TPUP), and perceptions of their youngsters' growth (with the ABDP).

The three instruments, PAAP, TPUP, and ABDP, have already been described. They were administered in the same manner, in Spanish, and were scored in the same way as in 1981-1982.

Results and discussion. A 2 (groups: experimental and comparison) × 2 (trials: pre and post) analysis of variance with repeated measures on factor B was separately run on the PAAP, TPUP, and total and subgrowth areas of the ABDP.

First, on the PAAP, experimental group parents at posttest trial had significantly greater and more positive feelings about their youngsters than those in the comparison group at posttest trial ($F = 4.59$, $df = 1,86$, $p = .05$). Second, parents in the experimental group at posttest trial yielded significantly higher numbers of play activities in home settings than those in the comparison group at posttest trial on the TPUP ($F = 4.50$, $df = 1,86$, $p = .05$). Third, on the ABDP, experimental group parents had significantly higher perceptions of their child's academic age ($F = 7.37$, $df = 1,86$, $p = .008$), self-help age ($F = 6.60$, $df = 1,86$, $p = .01$), and communication age ($F = 4.00$, $df = 1,86$, $p = .05$). Also, the experimental parents at posttest trial had significantly higher monthly growth perceptions of their child than those in the comparison group ($F = 12.66$, $df = 1,86$, $p = .001$). No significant effects were noted between groups at posttest trials for total ABDP perceptions ($F = 2.37$, $df = 1,86$, $p = .13$) or for ABDP subgrowth areas of social age ($F = .61$, $df = 1,86$, $p = .44$) and physical age ($F = 2.58$, $df = 1,86$, $p = .11$).

General Discussion

The results of the use of the parent/child Play Mastery Cycle reported here provide some indication of the utility of the model to improve parents' feelings toward their children, use of dramatic play and play activities in home settings, and perceptions of their youngsters' growth and development. The findings for project years 1981-1982 and 1982-1983 show that the Play Mastery Cycle, which emphasized dramatic play and play activities with parents, appeared to encourage more positive attitudes and feelings of parents toward their children. With the Play Mastery Cycle, parents at the end of the intervention were using significantly more dramatic play and play activities in the home than those parents in the comparison groups at the end of the same time period. In addition, parents in the intervention group had higher perceptions of their children's growth in various developmental areas (e.g., academic age, self-help age), mean monthly growth, and total overall development age (in project year 1981-1982).

A parent "play tutoring" program appears to be an effective form of intervention in increasing Hispanic parents' positive feelings about their roles as parents and developing ways of working with their children through forms of parent/child play. However, the problems (e.g., more time spent by parents in experimental vis-à-vis comparison groups) inherent in research on play tutoring with either children or parents as clients are evident (for reviews, see Christie & Johnsen, 1983). The research outcomes of project year 1983-1984, as a third-year replication, should provide further insight into the use of the Play Mastery Cycle with parents and assist in refining this model.

Acknowledgments

The authors' research and writings on cognitivist play, communication, and cognition in minority and handicapped children and their parents is supported, in part, by grants from the United States Department of Education (USDE), Office of Bilingual Education and Minority Languages Affairs (OBEMLA). The writers also express their appreciation to Dr. Mary J. Mahony and Ms. Cindy L. Ryan, OBEMLA staff members, for their continued guidance and support. The paper's narrative, data results, and interpretation represent those of the authors and not USDE and OBEMLA.

References

Bee, H.L., Van Engeren, L.F., Streissguth, A.F., Nyman, A.P., & Lechie, M.S. (1975). In U. Bronfenbrenner & M.A. Mahoney (Eds.), *Influences in human development*. Hinsdale, IL: Dryden.

Bronfenbrenner, U. (1975). Is early intervention effective? In U. Bronfenbrenner & M.A. Mahoney (Eds.), *Influences in human development*. Hinsdale, IL: Dryden.

Bruner, J., Jolly, A., & Sylva, K. (Eds.). (1976). *Play*. New York: Basic Books.

Christie, J.F., & Johnsen, E.P. (1983). The role of play in social-intellectual development. *Review of Educational Research*, **53**(1), 93-115.

Day, M.C., & Parker, R.K. (Eds.). (1972). *The preschool in action: Exploring early childhood programs* (2nd ed.). Boston: Allyn & Bacon.

Gordon, I.J. (Ed.). (1969). *Early stimulation through parent education* (Final technical report submitted to the Children's Bureau, Office of Child Development, United States Department of Health, Education and Welfare). Gainesville, FL: Institute for Development of Human Resources.

Gordon, I.J. (1970). *Baby learning through baby play*. New York: St. Martin's Press.

Lacy, D.F., & Tindall, B.A. (Eds.). (1976). *The anthropological study of play: Problems and prospects*. Champaign, IL: Leisure Press.

Levenstein, P. (1971). *Verbal Interaction Project: 1967-1980* (Final Technical Report submitted to the Children's Bureau, Office of Child Development, United States Department of Health, Education and Welfare). Freeport, NY: Verbal Interaction Project.

Loy, J. (Ed.). (1982). *The paradoxes of play*. Champaign, IL: Leisure Press.

Madden, J., Levenstein, P., & Levenstein, S. (1976). Longitudinal IQ outcomes of the mother-child home program. *Child Development, 47*, 1015-1025.

McCune-Nicholich, L., & Fenson, L. (1984). Methodological issues in studying early pretend play. In T.D. Yawkey & A.D. Pellegrini (Eds.), *Child's play: Developmental and applied*. Hillsdale, NJ: Erlbaum.

Nimnicht, G., Arango, M., & Adcock, D. (1971). *A report on the evaluation of the Parent/Child Toy-Lending Library Program*. San Francisco: Far West Laboratory for Educational Research and Development.

Pellegrini, A. (1981). Speech play and language development in young children. *Journal of Research and Development in Education, 14*, 73-80.

Piaget, J. (1962). *Play, dreams and imitation in childhood*. New York: W.W. Norton.

Piers, M.W., & Landau, G.M. (1980). *The gift of play*. New York: W.W. Norton.

Pulaski, M.A. (1980). *Understanding Piaget*. New York: Harper & Row.

Saltz, E., Dixon, B., & Johnson, J. (1977). Training disadvantaged preschoolers on various fantasy activities: Effects on cognition, functioning and impulse control. *Child Development, 48*, 367-380.

Schaefer, E.S. (1972). Parents as educators: Evidence from cross-sectional longitudinal and intervention research. In W.W. Hartup (Ed.), *On the young child: Reviews of research* (Vol. 2). Washington, DC: National Association for Young Children.

Schwartzman, H.B. (1979). The sociocultural context of play. In B. Sutton-Smith (Ed.), *Play and learning*. New York: Gardner Press.

Schwartzman, H.B. (1984). Imaginative play: Deficit or difference? In T.D. Yawkey & A.D. Pellegrini (Eds.), *Child's play: Developmental and applied*. Hillsdale, NJ: Erlbaum.

Smilansky, S. (1968). *The effects of sociodramatic play on disadvantaged pre-school children.* New York: Wiley.

Sylva, K., Bruner, J., & Genova, P. (1976). The role of play in problem solving of children 3-5 years old. In J. Bruner, A. Jolly, & K. Sylva (Eds.), *Play.* New York: Basic Books.

Warner, W., Meeker, M., & Eels, K. (1960). *Social class in America.* New York: Harper & Row.

Yawkey, T.D. (1980). Effects of social relationships' curricula and sex differences on reading and imaginativeness in young children. *Alberta Journal of Educational Research, 26*(3), 159-168.

Yawkey, T.D. (1982a). Effects of parents' play routines on imaginative play in their developmentally delayed preschoolers. *The Journal of Current Topics in Early Childhood and Special Education, 18*(8), 66-75.

Yawkey, T.D. (1982b). *Project PIAGET: Bilingual-Hispanic Title VII Demonstration Kindergarten Model—Results of the First Project Year, 1981-1982* (Vol. 1) (Final Technical Report Number 135 submitted to the Office of Bilingual Education and Minority Languages Affairs, United States Department of Education). University Park: Pennsylvania State University.

Yawkey, T.D. (1984). *Project PIAGET: Bilingual-Hispanic Title VII Demonstration Kindergarten Model—Results for the Second Project Year, 1983-1984* (Vol. 1) (Final Technical Report Number 165 submitted to the Office of Bilingual Education and Minority Languages Affairs, United States Department of Education). University Park: Pennsylvania State University.

Yawkey, T.D., & Cornelius, G.M. (1984). Imaginativeness in preschoolers from single parent families. University Park: Pennsylvania State University.

CHAPTER 14

Interpersonal Relations Within the Adult Social Recreational Play World

Donald E. Lytle
California State University, Chico

Many popular outdoor education programs and community recreational offerings employ cooperative games and challenge activities. Project Adventure, Outward Bound, Inter-Action, and New Game festivals are four examples that have grown significantly within recent years. The popularity of such programs and their growing pervasiveness have contributed to the inclusion of social recreational activities within public and private educational institutions. Social recreational play experiences allow groups to form naturally, and the impact of this gaming experience is enhanced by its novelty, enjoyability, immediacy, and sociability. However, there is a paucity of controlled study of the effects of these programs upon interpersonal relations, particularly among adult populations.

From their early work in group dynamics, Bennis and Shepard (1956) referred to "authority relations and personal relations" as central to the formation and development of any group. Similarly, many others have written about interpersonal relations involving power and status (Corsini & Rosenberg, 1955; Swanson, 1951; Varon, 1953). Nyberg (1981) wrote of power as being a fundamental category of all human behavior. Schutz (1958) labeled these predominant interpersonal processes within groups as control and inclusion. To account for close and intimate interaction between two individuals, he added the third category of affection. The interpersonal behaviors of control, inclusion, and affection relate to Horney's (1945) socio-emotional relationships of "moving against people," "moving away from people," and "moving toward people."

People Games

This paper is based on a year's study of college students engaged in a social recreational games class at a Northern California state university (Lytle, 1985). The games class, entitled People Games, has been taught over the past 10 years with an enrollment range of 46 to 89 students per semester. Slightly more women than men have enrolled in the class over the years. The class met twice a week in the mornings for a total of 30 sessions every semester. Social recreational games and activities were enjoyed for an average of 35 minutes every class period.

The games played have been referred to in the outdoor education, recreation, and play literature as mixers, icebreakers, socializers, diversions, group challenge, initiative activities, and family or parlor games. Physical educators have referred to them as lead-up games, noncompetitive games, games of low organization, relays, rainy day activities, informal dance and rhythms, self-testing activities, and contests. Traditional sport equipment was used sparingly and students participated in many activities each class meeting.

Most of the time play took place outdoors on a large grassy field. Other areas used less frequently were a blacktop area, tennis courts, and an indoor multipurpose room used during inclement weather. Typical play attire was casual and included running or tennis shoes, shorts, T-shirts, and sweat suits. Most students elected to take the course on a credit/no credit grading basis, which was strongly advocated. The primary criteria for credit were attendance, participation, and preparation and presentation of a teaching assignment that consisted of leading the class in a day of activities. This was done with a partner or with three people.

The Study

The problem in this study was to determine the effect of the social recreational gaming experiences upon the participants' interpersonal relations relative to control and inclusion. Affection was not considered an appropriate dimension to study, as this category applied to dyads and not groups. Schutz's theory (1958) of interpersonal relations and the accompanying test instrument, the FIRO-B, were selected to evaluate individuals in the categories of control and inclusion. FIRO-B is an acronym meaning Fundamental Interpersonal Relations Orientation-Behavior, and the test has demonstrated validity in contexts such as therapy, education, counseling, friendship, and courtship (Schutz, 1978). The FIRO-B inventory scores each of the three interpersonal relation categories on both behavior expressed and behavior wanted from others.

Each subscale of the test instrument consists of nine single-statement items, each of which is answered on a six-alternative Guttman-type scale (Guttman, 1950). An example for the category of expressed inclusion states, "I try to be with people." Of the 54-item questionnaire, 30 items are arranged with answer alternatives on a continuum from "never" to "usually." The remaining 24 items allow responses that range from "nobody" to "most people." The scores on each subscale—inclusion, expressed and wanted; control, expressed and wanted; and affection, expressed and wanted—range from a low of 0 to a high of 9.

A quasi-experimental study was conducted with two People Games classes resulting in 57 usable subjects who completed a FIRO-B pretest during the first week of the semester and a posttest during the last week of the semester. This constituted the experimental group to be compared with a nonequivalent control group of students who had enrolled in one of two lower division political science classes. The control group also completed FIRO-B pre- and posttests. There were 27 males and 30 females in the experimental group and 20 males and 27 females in the control group who had enrolled in either Introduction to Political Science or California Local and State Government. Students from every academic school within the university were represented in both the control and experimental groups, as were all class levels. However, the control group was composed primarily of freshmen and sophomores, whereas the experimental group students were mainly juniors and seniors. Unlike most of the People Games students, the political science undergraduates elected to take the class for a letter grade.

It was predicted that after participating in the social recreational games class, students would feel more comfortable with themselves and others. Thus expressed inclusion scores would increase significantly over the course of the semester. In the area of control, it was hypothesized that the games class students would gain in personal power and confidence, and desire less control from others. Initial scores of expressed control would increase and scores of control wanted from others would decrease after experiencing the social recreational play activities.

Furthermore, it was predicted that compared to the nonequivalent control group, students in the games class would score significantly higher in posttest expressed inclusion and expressed control. All of the hypotheses were predicated upon the condition that there would be no significant differences between the two groups on pretest measures. A correlated t-test was used to compare pretests between the groups, an uncorrelated t-test was used to compare pretests and posttests scores within groups, and a one-way analysis of variance was used to compare the experimental and control group's posttest scores.

Data Analysis

Analysis of the pretest scores for the control and experimental groups revealed no significant differences between them relative to control or inclusion scores. The scores were fairly homogenous except that the games group scored much higher on inclusion wanted from others ($p = .069$). From the pretest comparisons it was ascertained that the two groups were not significantly different at the outset of the experiment.

The games group scores on expressed inclusion increased from a mean of 5.40 to 5.86 by the conclusion of the class. The resultant t-test value translated into a significant difference at the .01 level. Scores of inclusion wanted from others increased very slightly from pre- to posttest for the People Games group. Similarly, wanted control scores changed very little from the beginning of the games class to the end. Scores of expressed control, however, increased significantly from pretest to posttest as hypothesized. This change was significant at the .02 level.

Comparing the posttest mean scores of the experimental and the control groups using a one-way analysis of variance, there were no significant differences in any of the four areas compared. In all cases the experimental group had higher mean scores than the control group. Expressed inclusion mean scores for the experimental group were in the predicted direction with the largest difference of all posttest comparisons. This was a nonsignificant probability of .128. Wanted inclusion mean scores being higher for the experimental than the control group was not in the predicted direction; however, on the pretest comparisons the experimental group approached a significant difference compared to the control group on inclusion wanted from others.

In that expressed and wanted affection scales were part of the FIRO-B, ex post facto comparisons were made. Using an uncorrelated t-test, pretest affection scores of the experimental and control groups were compared. The experimental group scored significantly higher than the control group on both expressed and wanted affection. Both were at the .05 level of confidence. When comparing expressed and wanted affection pretest to posttest mean scores in the experimental group, neither difference was significant. However, the greatly increased scores from pre- to posttest for the experimental group on expressed affection approached significance with a probability of .107.

Descriptive statistical analyses were generated for all male and female subjects, because a nonstated hypothesis predicted that men compared to women would be significantly different on expressed control and expressed inclusion. When all male subjects were compared to all female subjects, the expressed inclusion mean scores yielded the only significant difference. Males, as other FIRO-B studies with college populations (Schutz, 1978) have shown, had higher expressed inclusion scores than females. That was significant at the .02 level. What is interesting is that males from the games class were the primary contributors to this result. Surprisingly, there was not a significant difference between men and women on expressed control, contrary to findings of many earlier studies with collegiate populations (Schutz, 1978).

There were no significant changes between pretests and posttests for female and male students in the control group. However, women in the experimental group significantly increased their pretest mean scores on expressed control. This was significant at the .036 level. Whereas the women in the games group changed very little in expressed inclusion from pre- to posttest, the men showed a most significant change, raising their pretest mean scores from 5.11 to 6.11. This change was significant at the .001 level. The only other significant semester change registered for the men in the experimental group was on expressed control. This was significant at the .05 level.

Summing the results for men and women in the experimental group, the men increased their mean scores over the course of the games class in all six FIRO-B areas, and the women increased in three: expressed control, expressed affection, and wanted affection. The only significant change for the women was for expressed control. The men changed significantly in expressed inclusion and wanted inclusion from pretest to posttest.

Conclusions and Discussion

Many conclusions can be extracted from this study. First, the students entering the games class portrayed significantly different affection behavior than collegiate peers who enrolled in the political science classes. It is to be remembered that the affection category refers to dyad intimacy and not group feelings (Schutz, 1958).

There are at least two explanations for the affection behavior of those choosing the play class. There may have been a compelling need to seek and promote close relations with others, and the opportunity to play socially with one's peers may have been perceived as a viable vehicle toward that end. The novel People Games class may have represented a social and institutionally sanctioned opportunity for individuals to work on their anxiety about being lovable and liked by others.

The other explanation, which is my preference, holds that these individuals were active, healthy seekers of relationships, having established intimate, satisfying relations with others and desiring to continue in this regard. After all, the students in the games class were older than those in the control group. Gard (1964) studied psychopathological personalities of individuals and their characteristic orientations toward other people. He found that the higher the affection score on the FIRO-B, the more mentally and socially healthy the individual. I believe the members of the play class were more willing to risk personal involvement in play activities that often involved holding hands, hugging, and other interpersonal contact than were their peers.

The playing of social recreational games purportedly caused change in the participants' interpersonal orientations to others. Specifically, two behaviors, expressed inclusion and expressed control, changed dramatically. The expression of inclusion relates to one's self-concept and has to do with identity, individuality, understanding, interest, commitment, and participation (Schutz, 1966). Playing allowed group members to show themselves, and their humanness was reaffirmed by one another. Thus initiating and establishing satisfying relations was a natural by-product of the gaming experience.

Self-confidence also relates to the expression of control, which Schutz (1966) said "is exhibited through the group task" (p. 23). At the core of expressed control is the desire to control one's future. Not only are power and influence part of this behavior, but also feelings of accomplishment and independence. These manifestations are readily influenced by physically active, enjoyable, trust-filled, socially interactive play experiences.

Inclusion behavior involves interaction and association over time with others, but what is important is the quality of time spent with others.

During the course of playing games and participating in fun activities there was only a modicum of exclusion or elimination of individuals from the games. For the play to continue, which was desired by most, other participants must be accepted and quality time was ensured for the most part by the nature of playing games. The players are viewed as necessary for the pleasurable phenomenon to continue. Furthermore, the types of activities and gaming involved the entire group in active and dynamic interaction. Thus the cooperative nature of the activities helped participants gain mutual trust. Frost, Stimpson, and Maughan (1978) studied seven interpersonal relation groups of male and female undergraduates. They found that trusted individuals have high self-esteem and are highly influential, although they express little need to control others.

A composite portrait of the students who played in the games class emerges. These students became more easily the initiators and originators of action, particularly interaction with others, compared to their nonplaying peers. They were able to exert influence over each other in a trusting environment. These individuals most probably gained in self-confidence and feelings of self-esteem and gained and/or were reinforced in the ability to lead others while securing independence.

They did not need to be influenced by others nor desire others to include them. They were generally balanced in sense of self and were able to interact with others evenly and in a healthy manner. From what they learned of self and others in enjoyable, largely cooperative game play, they emerged as independent, highly interactive and healthy individuals who exhibited positive control in relation to others and in directing their own future.

Men who experienced the cooperative games and activities changed considerably in their desire to interact with others. Undoubtedly they felt very secure in their interactions with other participants and confident in initiating and maintaining associations with other people. They also had a strong desire for others to include them as active, reliable, confident members of a dyad or group. That the physical and strategic skills were not difficult or threatening in most of the playful activities may have had a primary influence on the men.

Women within the games class became much more confident in controlling their lives. They became more independent and less dependent upon control from others. Thus they were able to influence other people in healthy and positive ways and were less influenced by others after having participated in the games class. Generalization of these inferences is to be restricted, for the women who entered the play group were not highly confident in controlling others nor themselves.

The results of this study lead one to speculate upon their implications. For instance, nontraditional games and cooperative play activities purportedly caused young male adults to change in desiring much more interaction with others. Would similar play experiences initiated earlier in life aid the individual in balancing his life in terms of subsequent relations? Would more cooperative play experiences with the opposite sex over a long period of time, or during a critical age period, have a

deleterious or salubrious effect on one's feelings, motivations, and behaviors? The questions are plentiful and the explanations are few and
debatable at best.

The environment, game selection, and leadership are of singular importance to promote positive change in interpersonal behavior. It is suggested
that the leader(s) participate with the entire group and that personal safety
of the participants be carefully supervised. Additionally, the style of
leadership should be positive and joyful, yet professional in the planning
and presentation of activities. Furthermore, experience in leading social,
physical games and activities is imperative. For instance, timing as to
when to move from one activity to the next and game/activity selection
and progression are critical factors in setting the stage for healthy change.
Flexibility and creative adaptation of games to given populations and situations would be most helpful. Ideas from group members and their presen-
tations would be important in weaning the group from the teacher/leader
and confirming group independence from dependent beginnings.

This type of play experience is not only valuable for personal and social
reasons but may also be important for professional teaching/leading preparation. If this type of experience allows prospective educators, recreational
leaders, and others in the helping professions to feel more confident, then
it can serve their students and clientele toward that end. Curricular
relevance is indicated with this type of experience, and training in its
execution for students in specified degree programs would be desirable.

This study has served as a preliminary attempt to investigate interpersonal needs of college men and women within a positive play milieu. To
better study these conditions it is suggested that the age of the participants
be examined. A truer experimental design would also aid the interpretation of future results. Additionally, longitudinal studies are necessary to
determine both the long-term effects of these gaming experiences and
to understand more fully possible gender differences, critical periods, and
conditions of playful social interaction.

However limited the current understanding of play and its consequences, the power of play is again exposed with the conclusions drawn
from the present study. As individuals are allowed to and learn to move
and play with others under positive, joyful, cooperative conditions, they
feel good about themselves and reaffirm their personal power. They can
accept their flaws more readily and they can accept other humans un-
conditionally. Physical educators, recreational specialists, and others need
not be apologetic in advocating and planning social play experiences for
children and adults, for it is decidedly important to provide play space,
acceptance, variability, and opportunity for everyone to play.

References

Bennis, W., & Shepard, H.A. (1956). A theory of group development.
Human Relations, 9, 415-437.

Corsini, R., & Rosenberg, B. (1955). Mechanisms of groups psycho-therapy: Processes and dynamics. *Journal of Abnormal and Social Psychology*, **51**, 191-198.

Frost, T., Stimpson, D.V., & Maughan, M.R. (1978). Some correlates of trust. *Journal of Psychology*, **99**, 103-108.

Gard, J. (1964). Interpersonal orientations in clinical groups. *Journal of Abnormal and Social Psychology*, **69**, 516-521.

Guttman, L. (1950). The basis for scalogram analysis. In S. Stouffer (Ed.), *Measurement and prediction*. Princeton, NJ: Princeton University Press.

Horney, K. (1945). *Our inner conflicts*. New York: Norton.

Lytle, Donald E. (1985). *Changes in interpersonal relations of college students as a result of social-recreational play*. Unpublished doctoral dissertation, United States International University, San Diego, CA.

Nyberg, D. (1981). *Power over power*. Ithaca, NY: Cornell University Press.

Schutz, W. (1958). *FIRO. A three-dimensional theory of interpersonal behavior*. New York: Holt, Rinehart & Winston.

Schutz, W. (1966). *The interpersonal underworld*. Palo Alto, CA: California Science and Behavior Books.

Schutz, W. (1978). *The FIRO awareness scales manual*. Palo Alto, CA: Consulting Psychologists Press.

Swanson, G. (1951). Some effects of member object-relationships on small groups. *Human Relations*, **4**, 355-380.

Varon, E. (1953). Recurrent phenomena in group psychotherapy. *International Journal of Group Psychotherapy*, **3**, 49-58.

CHAPTER 15
Cubal Analysis: A Game Matrix

Karin Blair
École Supérieur de Commerce de Genève, Switzerland

Cubal Analysis is the name I have given to a series of concepts that constitutes a postsexist and postethnocentric conceptual model of the psyche. These cubal concepts can be incorporated into a game matrix centered around an octahedronal die. Basically, both the model and the games embodying it assume simply that people can be understood as living somewhere within a three-dimensional coordinate system that can be conceptualized as a cube, that is, arrayed in relation to three primary axes of existence: time, space, and value. Living is most immediately conditioned by one's passage through time, or aging, by one's passage through space in a body that is sexually differentiated, and by one's passage through a culture that allots everything a place on a scale of good and bad.

This cubal model invites us to become conscious of our states of being in relation to this framework, where mathematical symmetry replaces the more arbitrary and skewed conceptions we encounter in everyday life. Cultural loading is obvious in all individual lives. Each of us is born into a family already marked by a certain status that is commonly defined in terms of money, privileges, and prestige. The culture into which we are born inevitably colors our perceptions of age and sexuality as well, making us feel all the more constrained because these areas of our lives seem natural rather than cultural. The cube, by representing free access to all the possible distributions and combinations of age, sex, and value, permits the individual equal access to an imaginative encounter with all possible dimensions of these axes and of individual lives.

In contemplating a geometrical cube, one finds six sides, each representing one alternative on the three basic axes: good opposite bad, young/new opposite old, masculine opposite feminine. The eight apexes, each one formed by the coming together of three adjoining planes, locate eight character types defined by all the possible combinations of the basic poles. For example, there is the good old man and the bad old man, the good old woman and the bad old woman, the good young man and the bad young man, and the good young woman and the bad young woman. Thus the eight apexes offer personified images for these polarities. As a three-dimensional object, the cube when rolled as a die could only offer one face: one term of each of the three pairs involved in elaborating the cube as an analytical tool. The octahedron, however, offers eight surfaces that correspond to the apexes of the cube. Hence one roll of my octahedronal die identifies a single character type.

At first glance the cube functions in terms of mutually exclusive opposites: one cannot be both masculine and feminine, young and old, or good and bad at the same time. And at first there are advantages to this: one can use the cube to locate oneself in terms of oppositions seen as mutually exclusive—I can know who I am because of who or what I am not. Although this is a necessary first step, there is an equally important second step. Attempts to know oneself solely through mutually exclusive oppositions usually come to grief or to painful isolation. On a second level of reflection one sees that the cubal model is more concerned with balance and the relative weighing of oppositions. Since two poles are needed to structure an axis, one is led to see that both terms of an opposition are equally necessary. I call Cubal Analysis a postsexist and postethnocentric model for this reason: we can no longer define, for example, evil as the absence of good, or the feminine as the absence of the masculine, or peace as the absence of war. Each term of an opposing pair needs its complementary opposite even as I cannot move toward one thing without moving away from another—and what I move away from today I may move toward tomorrow. So to sum up, there is a first use of the cube for reflection or identity by distinction and a second for movement. Both are necessary: thought precedes action.

In my book *Cubal Analysis* (1983) I describe one arrangement of the cube for reflection. Imagine yourself sitting in the cube. Under you is yellow, the rising explorative energy of the new, above you blue, the codified structures of experience and age; before you is black, unrelenting limitation, behind you white, the supportive presence of the good; to the right is green, receptive feminine energy, and to the left red, assertive masculine energy. This is a perfect arrangement for reflection, with all movement held in balance, everything encouraging your stillness in the center.

In terms of movement, however, this arrangement needs to be reversed. The first motion of an infant is to push, but this presumes support, which needs to be found physically in the ground and in being centered, and mentally in thought, in knowing who and where one is. Thus the black as a limit needs to be behind to push against. Similarly, the blue needs to be on the ground because we need habits, patterns of response, and knowledge to push off from and balance out explorations into the unknown. If we are right-handed, we need the assertive energy on the right and the receptive on the left. The good in front of us, like the youthful energy above us, can stimulate us to reach out to explore and eventually to pull ourselves toward that which we want, or to pull it to us. The initial attempt to know who and where I am needs stasis and solitude, the second step involves balance and relationship, even as physical motion, walking, is a function of balance and relationship.

One of the pleasures of games and play is the opportunity to be aware of dichotomies that are necessary for consciousness without the double binds they are often linked to in everyday life. Not only are our real-life possibilities skewed by cultural biases, but the institutions that stand to gain by the skew often use the double bind to maintain power. Whereas a dichotomy can function to increase awareness by creating psychic space within which to move between its poles, a double bind immobilizes one. In cubal terms this situation invites a reflective orientation of the cube. In this context, then, I would like to define a play space as that field of tension between the poles of a dichotomy, not a double bind.

Before playing with cubal games let us look at Cubal Analysis in terms of what it can contribute to an understanding of games and play space. First of all, how would boredom and anxiety, the boundaries of flow Csikszentmihalyi has established as parameters of play, fit on the cube? In terms of character types I have used the terms *role-retainer* and *shape-shifter* to elaborate possible meanings for the value axis, the role retainer being the good person and the shape-shifter the bad one. In looking at these character types one can see that although the role-retainer is the good person who is reliable and who does what he or she should, such a person can become a bore. He or she can be too predictable and become uninteresting. On the other hand, the shape-shifter is probably considered bad precisely because he or she is a source of anxiety. One cannot predict that character type's behavior easily enough, though boredom is never a risk. From here we can make the jump to placing boredom and anxiety on opposite poles of the value axis. The intermediary of the character types lets us see how both the "good" and "bad" poles have their limits, although our usual tendency would be to see the good as infinitely attractive and the bad as infinitely repulsive. By looking through the cube we can see how good and bad, boredom and anxiety mark out the limits of our competence on opposite sides. Reflecting on the sources of our anxiety can lead to self-knowledge, which through taking action can lead to increased competence.

If boredom and anxiety mark one set of parameters in game playing, how can the other dimensions of the cube help us to find other parameters? The space axis is differentiated into the masculine and the feminine, which are often described in terms of assertiveness and receptivity. Just as the cube encourages us to find a balance between our masculine and feminine sides, so it can foster consciously finding a balance between assertiveness and receptivity. Turn-taking and "fair play" could be seen as examples of such balance, obvious to us, perhaps, but not to all ages and cultures.

The final axis is that of time, which can easily be translated into the young and the old or the new and the old. By implication, there needs to be a balance between what is familiar and what is not, between what can be codified and what remains elusive. This dimension surfaces in sports, where good performance is a function of both rigorous practice and openness to favorable conjunctions of inner psychic state and configurations in the playing field. In terms of board or role-playing games, the cubal die can be taken as an index to one's inner state at any given time, thereby "psychifying" the game in terms of performance. Here the use of chance can be a way of creating space for the new and unexpected even in a game that has become familiar through replaying. Insofar as my presence is not irrelevant to my situation I can be seen as psychifying my surroundings; in this perspective the throw of a die can be seen as a kind of index to myself at a given time and place and an invitation to participate in what might otherwise seem closed.

I could deal with Cubal Analysis next in terms of gender, but the issues of war and peace are perhaps just as relevant and perhaps more global. In our usual ways of thinking, games are commonly associated with war rather than with peace. There is the obvious common element of competition between two sides, one of which will be eliminated from the "game." When the game space is a sports field of some sort, elimination is not annihilation. When the game board is another's living space, however, whether we interpret that as one's body or as the larger environment in which one feels at home, severe destruction of identity is the result.

Gandhi and others have pointed out that damage to another reverberates on the doer, and nuclear war insofar as we can conceive of it dramatizes the issue. War has been an inseparable part of human history, dramatizing social issues and identity. "Which side are you on?" can at least in wartime be asked without fear of being intrusive and be answered simply, because a clearly dichotomized world resolves into winners and losers. As in games, traditionally war has been thought of in terms of winners and losers who are clearly and mutually defining. Winners are automatically presumed to be good and losers bad, unless losers want to think of themselves as winners in some ultimate or heavenly tally sheet. Nuclear arms, however, by threatening mass annihilation, have made war a no-win situation that has perhaps already begun to poison the atmosphere with double binds. If we win we are destroyed, if we lose we are destroyed. Therefore I want to move out of the domain of no-win double binds now associated with war, be it cold or hot, psychological or material, into that of games as peace activities. Having mutually respectful winners and losers is an advance over the no-win situation because in staying alive and conscious to take turns, today's loser can be tomorrow's winner. Restructuring games in a cooperative perspective is an even greater advance, since the symbiotic relationship of all parties is stressed.

First of all, what does peace usually mean besides the absence of war? Can we imagine it, enjoy it outside the context of having fought and obviously survived? Is peace simply recuperation time before the next war? Let us start with the idea of recuperation as a reestablishment of inner balance. During war we must remain focused on the enemy as if caught in the mind set of identity by distinction. During peace we can attend to ourselves and our needs; we feel justified in concentrating on inner balance. What I am going to suggest in this context is that we consciously attend to inner balance so that we will no longer need some form of violence to do this for us. Just as reflection precedes action, self-control should precede if not replace controlling others. By focusing on inner balance I can be confident my feelings will not sweep me away, which is perhaps one of the elements needed to break out of no-win double binds.

Running in mental circles is accompanied by anxiety, as if an emotional abyss surrounded the mental circle. By delimiting a model of psychic space that, unlike the circle or sphere, permits clear orientation, I can explore myself with more confidence. I can see that the distinctions I make in any given situation are limited, even though my need to make them seems unlimited or essential to any sense of self: Double binds and running in circles are ineffective because they interfere with clear distinctions. That I make distinctions can be seen through the cube as independent of how I make them; therefore how I make them in any given time and place can move more easily and take into account the symbiotic relationship between opposing elements in any situation, both or all of which have something to contribute, just as all the apexes of the cube are needed to keep the space intact.

References

Blair, K. (1983). *Cubal Analysis*. Weston, CT: Magic Circle Press.

Czikszentmihalyi, M. (1975). *Beyond boredom and anxiety: The experience of play in work and games*. San Francisco, CA: Jossey-Bass.

PART IV

Sport

Sport is an ambiguous term standing between work and leisure and partaking of both. This is true even with regard to preadolescent baseball, as Gary Alan Fine's paper clearly indicates. Perhaps, as Fine, quoting Piaget, notes, the concept of winning does not truly emerge until the child has reached the age of 7 or 8. As long as preadolescent informal baseball is "organized" by the children themselves, Fine points out, their game is slanted more toward play than toward work. But it is not long before adult-sponsored and organized baseball pulls the children into a world that mimics if it does not duplicate adult behavior. The desire to win, however, may be even deeper than, and conceptually distinct from, the springs of both work and leisure: it may reflect a survival trait rooted deep in the human genetic and behavioral make-up. Whatever it is, it soon emerges in human development and influences both work and play.

Oliver's paper on the cultural implications of the soccer phenomenon in America provides evidence for weighing the comparative attraction of different sports in America. Already, in some fashionable private Eastern schools, the percentage of students "trying out" for football has plummeted whereas the percentage going out for soccer has risen spectacularly. While football is alive and well, indeed dominant in such places as Nebraska and Texas, the move in Texas to qualify the passion for football with the requirement of academic achievement signals a shift in the national mood. Strange that soccer—a sport that, as David Reisman once told me in a private conversation, is retrograde in terms of human development because it disallows the use of hands, the feature that distinguishes man most clearly from the animals—should now be increasing its attraction and dominance among large segments of the world's population.

Perhaps the surge in popularity of soccer so carefully described by Oliver reflects a sociobiological response to the carrying to extremes of the specialization characteristic of American football. The vast majority of humans cannot compete with 300-pound tackles or 4.4 sprint-speed wide receivers. But the vast majority of humans, despite their lack of size, speed, or height, can compete successfully on the soccer field. In our cooperative age, perhaps this trend is an example of how the mass of humanity is evolving. Even the two sexes can compete successfully on the soccer field, at least until puberty. "The implications of this massive entry of girls directly into male team sports have yet to be examined," Oliver notes, "but it is an area ripe for research." The fact that the coach

167

is less dominant and controlling in soccer than in football and baseball is another reflection of the antispecialized character of the sport.

Yet the soccer violence at the European Cup soccer final in Brussels in May 1985, in which 38 spectators were killed, as well as other instances of hooliganism in the British soccer tradition and in that of other countries, has caused soul-searching among commentators throughout the world. Is there something wrong with the sport? The players? The linkage between the game and the spectators is indirect and any direct causal relationship between player activity and spectator violence can be doubted. Spectators, whether from deprived or enriched backgrounds, can participate in the spectacle they are watching only vicariously, and it is a truism that those outside the main arena of competition, whether in war or in sport, often reflect the dehumanizing rather than humanizing character of those activities.

The soccer violence at Brussels is more analogous to events such as the Paxton Boys' massacre of harmless Indians in Pennsylvania in the 18th century or to other instances in which a scapegoat must be found upon which a mob unable or unwilling to confront the real "enemy" can vent its fury. The problem, whether it is an attack by the fans of one team on those of another or (as Oliver describes) the browbeating of an official by the father of one of the players, is not the fault of the game or of the players but of those watching the game. The rules of the game provide sufficient control for the players; what may need to be altered are the rules governing the conduct of the spectators.

James and Joan Weatherly discuss the perversion of the play impulse, primarily in terms of the visions of George Orwell and Neil Postman, but whether the viciousness of children, either self-directed or controlled by their adult superiors, is characteristic of "sport" as opposed to "play" is doubtful. The individual child or adult at play can move in the paths of perversion. Group play, and more particularly organized sports, do have their perversions; however, because these activities take place in front of thousands, because the rules governing the activities are known to all, and because athletic merit is easily recognized by all, such activities do not equal the viciousness of play attributed to some individuals functioning without control in corrupt political societies.

Sport is an important activity in the United States, with both redeeming and perverse features. The conflicts inherent in sports may be over such mundane matters (as Wilma Harrington points out) as who controls the gymnasium in a school in which teachers and athletic staff both claim preeminence. But few, except for some of the more traditional academic intellectuals, refuse to concede that sport is as vital a human activity as any other engaged in by mankind.

Wilcomb E. Washburn

CHAPTER 16

Physical Education Versus Athletics: A Teacher's Perception of Who Controls the Gymnasium

Wilma M. Harrington
University of Georgia

This paper concerns the influence of an athletic program on the physical education program in a high school in the rural south. Locke and Massengale's (1978) work on teacher/coach role conflict addressed the issues surrounding the individual occupying two professional roles. There appears to be another conflict in schools where some individuals are teachers and others are teacher/coaches. I have called this status conflict; it focuses on the control that accompanies the status associated with a specific role. The impact of status conflict is important because what exists is a disparity between program priorities. When the athletic program has priority over the physical education program, the instructional program can be perceived as unimportant and secondary. The instructional program intended to serve all students becomes subsidiary to the extracurricular athletic program that is designed to serve an elite few.

The observations presented here are based on ethnographic field work conducted over a 3-month period in a predominantly black rural high school in northeastern Georgia. The focus of the observation was to describe and define the instuctional environment within which one female physical educator worked. As the observation progressed it became apparent that one facet of the situation that influenced how the teacher acted and reacted was her perception of the status of her work as compared to that of the athletic staff, whom she referred to as the "cooches."

Over the 3 months of observation a series of situations occurred that consistently indicated a pattern of conflict between the physical educator and the athletic staff. The conflict involved several categories of control. I have labeled these categories facilities/instructional setting and organization responsibilities. Had either of these situations existed exclusive of the other, the status confict would not have been as powerful or obvious. However, the combination served to create a teacher perception that the role of physical education in the total school program was a minor one when compared to the major emphasis given athletics.

Facilities/Instructional Setting

In *Schoolteacher: A Sociological Study*, Lortie (1975) discusses the bounded nature of the classroom. Teachers perceive their classrooms as their domain or territory and readily resent intrusions by other staff, administrators, and parents. For the physical educator the question of who dominates the gymnasium and locker room areas can become an issue when outsiders continually disrupt and infringe on class time and facilities. In the setting observed there were definite sources for conflict of this nature.

The gymnasium was also the varsity basketball court and it was basketball season. Every time there was a home game at least two periods were lost on the day of the game and the day after so the floor and locker rooms could be cleaned. The schedule was never predetermined. The custodial staff would simply appear and begin work. Therefore, the teaching schedule was continually disrupted with no forewarning other than knowing it was home game day.

Because of the floor composition, several conditions had to be met for class. Students were not permitted to wear any but white-soled shoes because dark-soled shoes scuffed the floor. The principal also requested the teacher to sweep the floor between classes. He suggested that a student who did not take physical education be assigned this task and be given a physical education grade for the effort.

The gym was large enough to accommodate two classes. A curtain partition was used to separate the two halves. This was operated by a motor located in the athletic director's office, which was locked at all times. The physical education teacher did not have a key to the area and was therefore dependent on the athletic director to remember to lower the partition. She also had to depend on him to remember to return the bleachers to a closed position in order to have full use of her half of the gymnasium. When the bleachers were out, at least one third of the teaching area was unavailable. The athletic director taught in another area of the building and was not easily accessible when the curtain had not been lowered or the bleachers moved. The custodians of course had keys to these areas, but they were even less accessible than the athletic director.

Two of the classes observed were coeducational. The boys were to be assigned lockers in the boys' locker room by the male teacher conducting the adjacent class. He did not bother to make locker assignments because he "had too much on him." The boys dressed in the bathroom or the unoccupied half of the girls' locker room. What did he mean by having too much on him? This teacher/coach kept the statistics for the basketball games, and because it was the competitive season, his time was devoted to that. The male students generally dressed somewhere in private and then carried their clothes and books into the gym. On a number of occasions the boys' locker room was locked so they could not get into the bathroom to change. All of this combined to make students late for class or unable to take class.

The lack of control over the facility often resulted in last-minute changes or loss of class time. The teacher felt that physical education had a low priority and athletics had a high priority. This feeling was further confirmed when she discovered that the building wing where the gym and health classrooms were located was to be identified as the athletics wing. Why this was being done and who authorized it is illuminating.

The assistant principal and the principal did not know anything about it. The art teacher who was painting the sign did not know who authorized it. When it was determined that the curriculum director for the district was responsible, she indicated that it was to be done because that was what was on the architect's plan. It is interesting to note that according to the physical educator the curriculum director's main responsibilities were encouraging school spirit and advising the cheerleaders at the high school. Her husband was an assistant football coach and head baseball coach. She also kept the school scoreboard, which was located on the side of a store downtown, up-to-date on the win and loss records of the athletic teams.

The outcome of the wing dispute was a positive one. The area was designated for health and physical education. On the surface, the mislabeling of the wing appears to be a misunderstanding that could occur at any time. However, the fact that the principal was not consulted or aware of what was going on belies the fact that it never occurred to the individual responsible that athletics is an after-school program like band, not an academic area like math or science.

One further incident involving the control of facilities should serve to support the view that the athletic director assumed he had a great deal of control in this setting. The high school was a new facility that had opened at the beginning of the school year. A new weight room was included. When the physical educator requested a mezzanine area above the gym for classroom activities, she discovered that the athletic director had decided to annex the area for another weight room. He had already ordered equipment. He revealed all of this when he found out the area was for physical education use. This was brought to the principal's attention. His reaction was to go to the superintendent and inform him that the area was a physical education facility and that he did not believe athletics should have it. What this was, of course, was a confrontation between the school administrator and the athletic director. The principal won.

What is interesting and revealing about this particular situation is the extent to which the athletic program exerted influence. The principal did not tell the athletic director what would happen, he went to the superintendent, his superior, to resolve the problem. The mezzanine area is now a physical education classroom, but the athletic director is still trying to get it for a weight room. However, the conflict created by the situation served to support the teacher's belief that the priority program was not hers. It is also interesting to note that the superior who wanted the teacher to give a grade for floor sweeping seemed willing to take up her cause.

The teacher's belief was that this was not the case, but that what ensued was a facet of a power struggle between the principal and the athletic director.

The notion that teachers view their classrooms as their territory is accompanied by a definite feeling of autonomy of action. The situations cited present a lack of control and autonomy in the use of the gymnasium during the time designated for instruction. They also indicate that this lack of control provides a source of conflict. The naming of the wing and the classroom designation situation present two very overt instances of differing values that contributed to the physical educator's belief that the program she was involved with had to fight for visibility and facility space.

Organization/Responsibilities

The organizational scheme for the school provides another source of conflict or disparity between programs. The other academic areas such as mathematics, science, and English were organized into departments with a designated head. Budget requests as well as curricular decisions were made through these structures. The athletic director was responsible for the athletic programs. There was no physical education department. No one was in charge. There was no organized communication among the five individuals who taught physical education. Any requests for equipment were made through the science department.

The athletic director met with his staff and they were viewed as a unit just as mathematics, science, and English were. The individual coaches who taught one or two physical education classes consulted with one another on content. There were no meetings or agreements among the five teachers regarding what the curriculum in physical education would be. Everybody did his or her own thing. I once asked the teacher I observed what went on in the other classes and she did not know beyond what we saw in the adjacent area.

The absence of any identity within the organizational structure contributed to the perception that physical education was a low priority area, especially given the fact that the athletic staff were afforded organizational visibility.

Let me also point out that the female observed was the only female physical education teacher. There were no female coaches. The only coeducational classes were taught by the teacher I observed. She taught four coeducational classes and two girls' classes. The only other all-girl class was taught by a male who only had one physical education assignment. The other classes were all taught by male teacher/coaches. One male teacher/coach taught physical education full-time. He did not have coeducational classes because he did not want to teach girls. The principal had attempted to fire this individual because of poor teaching, but the athletic director wanted him retained as assistant football coach. He therefore remained on the faculty and was assigned physical education classes.

It is difficult to believe that programs have status when there is not a commitment to quality. The lack of a unit for planning and decision making does allow for a degree of autonomy in terms of content selection and teaching. On the other hand, the absence of any form of recogition serves to perpetuate the idea that the program is not very important. The retention of a poor teacher so he can coach also emphasizes what is valued and what is not.

Conclusion

The question of who controls the gymnasium is a crucial one for physical education. Lortie's (1975) findings that the role of the teacher is strongly affected by classroom phenomena may be translated to the gymnasium. Teachers assume autonomy over their classes and evaluate their roles based on the degree of control they have over their territory.

The preceding has been an analysis of the factors influencing one teacher's perceptions of the degree of control and autonomy she exerted over her territory. The competition for control was most definitely the athletic program. The extent to which this situation prevails in other settings must be addressed. This has a direct implication for professional preparation and role explication. Teacher/coach role conflict and the resolution of that conflict has a direct bearing on the status conflict between physical education and athletics. It would appear that the rewards and status reside with athletics. A situation in which an extracurricular program has the ability to influence the conduct of a curricular area should be a source of concern. The values established for a particular school program can be inferred from the status and influence exerted by members of the group providing the program. Individuals who occupy inferior roles readily determine this by assessing their control over facilities, their instructional settings, their place in the organizational structure, and the job responsibilities of those occupying similar roles.

References

Locke, L.F., & Massengale, J.D. (1978). Role conflict in teacher/coaches. *Research Quarterly*, **49**(2), 162-174.

Lortie, D.C. (1975). *School teacher: A sociological study*. Chicago: University of Chicago Press.

CHAPTER 17

Organized Baseball and Its Folk Equivalents: The Transition From Informal to Formal Control

Gary Alan Fine
University of Minnesota

What connection does folklore have with the national pastime of a post-industrial society? For a century baseball has been recognized as the national pastime of the United States (e.g., Gomme, 1898/1964). There can be no doubt, particularly with the economic changes that have rocked baseball during the past century, that baseball is a business—and a big and profitable business at that. Contracts, unions, free agents, labor/management negotiation, and lockouts may seem more directly relevant to the way in which baseball is enacted in the United States during the 1980s than do play, tradition, relaxation, and fun. Yet, despite this commercialization and commodification of baseball, there are several ways in which baseball is still a folk game.

First, despite the legends about baseball being an autochthonous American game, springing like Athene full-blown from the brow of Abner Doubleday, the game of baseball is recognized to have developed from the English game of rounders (Gomme, 1898/1964) and to have been played in New England as "Town Ball" (Coffin, 1971). Thus baseball springs, like so many other sports, from folk roots. Second, these origin legends about the founding and the development of baseball, its heroes and great moments, themselves constitute a folk tradition (Moe, 1982). Although this folk tradition merges with an extensive written tradition, the legends of baseball are still passed on from father to son, with the written accounts merely supplementing this process (Coffin, 1971). Third, baseball players share the folk characteristics of any occupation, including a robust occupational folklore (Reese, 1975). Baseball has developed a folk speech (Fine, 1979a; Scholl, 1977), ritual rhymes and cheers (Larson, 1980; Weeks, 1906), and a set of superstitions and taboos (Gmelch, 1971). For all of these reasons baseball may properly be considered to be a folk game. However, none of these features shall concern us in this chapter. Instead, it is my intention to depict the folkloristic characteristics of baseball by describing how baseball games, as they are played, resemble folk games. This analysis will touch on the other ways of understanding the folklore of baseball through a concern with how a generally nonfolk activity is transformed to folk play. I shall focus for most of my examples on preadolescents, both in informal games and in Little League baseball, based on 3 years of participant observation in New England and Minnesota (Fine, in press).

Rules

One way that a formal game can be differentiated from a folk game is by the codification, inflexibility, and enforcement of rules. Little League baseball is an example of this, as of course is professional baseball. In the Little League setting rules are a given; they represent how the game is to be directed, and most participants agree that any deviation from these rules is a failure—the game has come apart. Rules in Little League baseball play a very important role. Local Little Leagues are expected to follow the rules provided by the national organization, and coaches and umpires are supposed to be knowledgeable about these rules and enforce them without exception. Players, although not expected to memorize the rules, must be generally aware of what they are allowed and required to do; they must follow the directions of their coaches who do know the rules.

Each year the national organization provides an updated rule book to each local league. For a game as simple as preadolescent baseball these rules are extensive indeed, running 52 pages in 1977. The rules attempt to cover every contingency that might arise while playing baseball, and provide a basis from which umpires can make decisions without incurring the wrath of coaches.

The fact that rules are deemed necessary reflects the competitive focus of Little League baseball. Winning is deemed to be important. In children's informal games a formal set of rules is not considered necessary. Piaget (1962) notes that in preadolescent marble playing older children are able to negotiate the rules of the game, and this negotiation is seen as developmentally valuable. Devereux (1976) describes informal baseball games among preadolescents similarly:

> Maybe we didn't learn to be expert baseball players, but we did have a lot of fun. Moreover in an indirect and incidental way, we learned a lot of other kinds of things which are probably more important for children between the ages of eight and twelve. Precisely because there was no official rule book and no adult or even other child designated as rule enforcers, we somehow had to improvise the whole thing. . . . We gradually learned to understand the invisible boundary conditions of our relationships to each other. (p. 48)

The contrast between Little League and informal baseball is evident in the rule-governed character of the games. Informal baseball has the characteristics of folk games in which rules are not written. It is important to recognize that all games have rules; preadolescents playing by themselves are not in a benighted, pastoral state of anarchy, the peaceable kingdom.

Instead, the rules that do exist are continually subject to negotiation. Negotiation can occur on any and all "rules"—which are emergent from the particular circumstances of the game: what to do when the old jacket being used as second base slides from its originally designated spot, or is it fair to pitch to 10-year-olds as one pitches to 12-year-olds. Anything is potentially negotiable in a folk game, so long as it is seen as problematic and one of the participants suggests that a change is needed.

Although rules in Little League baseball are not immutable, these disputes are always highly charged in that participants believe in principle that the rules should be unchanged. Deviation from the rules as written and as understood is considered inappropriate. Thus the participants in a Little League baseball game might agree that a particular rule change would increase the satisfaction of participants, but still the rule would not be changed because the sanctity of the rules means more than does the temporary satisfaction of the players. This, of course, contrasts with the orientation of folk games in which the rules provide only for a means of achieving participant satisfaction. As Hughes (1983) notes in her study of the children's game "Four-Square," folk rules provide a structure that can be altered when the participants demand.

Although in formal games it is occasionally possible to change the rules, more common is the subversion of these rules through what Mark Clark calls "strategic rule breaking" (Clark, 1981). Clark found that most coaches (in his study, basketball coaches) teach their players behaviors that technically are considered rule breaking, although they often are legitimate rule breaking (such as deliberately fouling an opposing player in the late moments of a game). A similar attitude is found in an account of the 1954 Little League baseball champions from Schenectady, New York, by Mike Maietta, the manager of that team:

> We're playing this team from Montreal, and the manager obviously has told the kids to wipe us out, physically, you know; they're running into my first baseman and taking out my second baseman, and barreling over my catcher; their pitcher is throwing at my kids' heads. . . . The Canadian kids scared them half to death; it was the first time that any of my kids had seen the bad part of baseball. . . . If you're gonna win in Little League tournaments, you gotta have tough kids, kids who would give it right back, not be scared off. . . . I figured, if somebody from some other team tried some dirty trick, my kids were going to get up and let them have it right back, not come into the dugout and start crying. . . . You have to be ruthless, because the other guys are ruthless, too, and you have to have kids on your team who are tough, fighters, rough-and-ready kids who aren't going to take any bullshit. (Ralbovsky, 1974, p. 240)

Such strategic disregard for the rules is not acceptable in folk games. While it may be tolerated in that nothing is done about it, the perpetrator quickly receives a negative reputation as a person who "cheats" and who plays "dirty." Because informal games are not based on the formal determination of rules, there is no appeal from such an unfavorable reputation. Such a player may find himself or herself excluded from future games. Claims that this sort of behavior is legitimate may be unanswered and such a player might even be correct in terms of the formal game. The rules in informal games are more morally circumscribed but also more flexible if there is consensus.

Consider this example. Although the specific example is hypothetical, it corresponds to many similar situations I have witnessed while watching informal baseball games. There are not enough players to comprise two full teams, so it is agreed that a player on the team that is batting shall be required to be the catcher and must catch to the best of his ability. One inning a batter with two strikes on him swings at a pitch and misses it. However, the ball bounces off the catcher's glove and rolls away. The batter runs to first base, which he reaches safely. The players on the fielding team object to this, both because this rule is rarely used and because the catcher was on the opposing team (although they do not necessarily claim that the catcher deliberately dropped the ball). Although such a situation might be resolved differently on different occasions, most preadolescents will agree to settle the controversy by considering the batter out or perhaps by giving him another swing. In my experience even the batting team would agree that it would be unfair for the batter to take the base, unless this rule had previously been made explicit. However, if the batter decides to argue technically, although he may formally be correct, he may discover that players on both teams will be aligned against him, and he may lose esteem in the eyes of his fellows as a result of the dispute.

So among preadolescents disputes over the rules become a matter of strategic debate. Children must and do learn the rules for arguing—essentially the meta-rules of the game. Some of the informality of children's rules are comically highlighted in this comparison between the Little League rules and how preadolescent informal baseball is actually played:

> PROTESTS—Protests shall be considered only when based on the violation or interpretation of a playing rule or the use of an ineligible player. No protest shall be considered on a decision involving an umpire's judgment.
>
> Protests—A protest was considered only when you were awfully sure you could lick the other guy. There was no umpire, unless some kid was on crutches and couldn't play. Nobody paid any attention to his calls, because he was just another kid.
>
> FIELD DECORUM—The actions of players, managers, coaches, umpires, and League officials must be above reproach.
>
> Field decorum—There were no managers, or coaches, or any of those big people. Only players who swore and spat. Anyone caught being above reproach got clobbered. (Levin, 1969, pp. 4, 6)

Although this satire overemphasizes the aggressive and anarchic components of informal preadolescent games, it does point to the difference between a formal structure and an emergent structure. The rules in informal baseball game are situational, whereas in Little League they are enduring.

Environments of Formal and Informal Play

Little League fields attempt to duplicate the stadia of professional baseball teams. The equipment used in Little League is designed to be a close replica of that used by adult superstars, with the physical safety and ability of Little Leaguers built into the design of the equipment. The closer the Little League equipment and field is to professional baseball, the better it is. In informal folk baseball games, players make a virtue of necessity. Any open space will suffice, even if trees and gulleys are located in the middle of the field. Players alter the rules to meet the problems of the environment. It might be decided that any ball that rolls into the drainage ditch is a ground rule double; any ball that flies into the neighbor's yard is an automatic home run, and the player who hits it must retrieve it. Preadolescents formulate rules to deal with the environment, as opposed to formal games in which the field is laid out to meet the preestablished rules. In folk baseball games, the equipment consists of whatever is available. I have seen jackets, gloves, even rocks used as bases. Typically baseball bats are similar to those used by Little League, although often not officially authorized or broken and taped together. The ball is usually old and worn out, and may in some cases be a softball or a rubber ball. The game is made to fit whatever equipment is available. Martin Levin provides an insightful, if sardonic, perspective on the environment and equipment:

> PLAYING EQUIPMENT—Each team must have at least twelve conventional baseball uniforms. The Official Little League Shoulder Patch must be affixed to the upper left sleeve of the uniform blouse. Games may not be played except in uniforms. These uniforms are the property of the League, and are to be loaned to the players for such period as the League may determine.

> Playing equipment—Each guy came out to the ballfield looking like a bum. Shirts were optional. Patches went on pants because they were torn up sliding. Anybody wearing a clean or neat garment was jumped on, and rubbed around in the dirt.

> EQUIPMENT—The ball shall weigh not less than five ounces or more than five and one-quarter (5-1/4) ounces avoirdupois. It shall measure not less than nine (9) inches nor more than nine and one-quarter (9-1/4) inches in circumference. The bat shall be round and made of wood. It shall not be more than thirty-three (33) inches in length. Bats may be taped for a distance not exceeding sixteen (16) inches from the small end. The first baseman is the only fielder who may wear a mitt. All other fielders must use fielder's gloves.

> Equipment—The ball could be of any weight, and anybody stupid enough to say "avoirdupois" out loud deserved what he got. Circumference of the ball depended on the amount of tape wrapped around it. Sometimes the tape came loose when you hit the ball, and the circumference changed rapidly. Sometimes it was just tape by the time it reached the fielder, and the circumference was zero (0).

> Bats were made of wood and were round unless they had been used for hitting rocks. After bats were broken they were taped for their entire length and it was hard to tell which was the small end. The first baseman was lucky if he got either a mitt or a glove. The only mitt belonged to the fat right fielder, who wore it even when he was at bat. (Levin, 1969, p. 4)

Again, this account gives us the flavor of informal games. Problems are solved as they arise. The only rule is that the game should provide the maximum amount of fun (see Goffman, 1961). Some of the equipment substitutions in informal games are folk artifacts, such as the ball covered with tape or a base that is created by a player with a saw. Sometimes objects are put to uses other than those originally intended to keep the game flowing (such as a jacket or Frisbee used as a base). Although the environment and the equipment are central in formal games, they become decidedly secondary in folk games, where the pragmatics of the game take precedence over official requirements.

Game Organization

Formal games need to be controlled; there is constantly the sense that they are in danger of breaking into anarchy from which they can never recover. This is because they are perceived of as (and sometimes are) forced. That is, participants may wish to do other things if they were allowed to. Thus, Little League adults must attempt to direct preadolescent attention. This they achieve with partial success, but the success that they do achieve is sufficient to allow the game to continue. Consider an atypical example of the organizational difficulties a Little League game might get into:

> In the bottom of the sixth inning the White Sox scored five runs against the Pirates and trailed 6-5, with the bases loaded and two outs. Hence, the next play determined the outcome of the game. On the critical pitch, the ball came across the plate so that the batter had to move in order to avoid getting hit. He moved by sticking his head into the strike zone, rather than away. The pitch hit him in the head (but did not injure him). The White Sox thought that because the batter had been hit by the pitch he would take his base, and the team erupted in jubilant excitement as the game was tied and they stood an excellent chance of winning. The Pirates coach protested, claiming that the batter should not go to first base. Both sets of coaches demanded a decision from Warren Dahlgren, the umpire. Warren threw up his hands, commenting "I don't know what it is, I've never had a kid get hit in the head like that before" and refused to decide. Warren walked in the general direction of Phil Conklin, the Pirates coach, and asked his opinion. Phil asked him some questions about the sequence of events and responded formally and matter-of-factly: "There is two strikes and the batter bats." This decision would, of course, save the day for the Pirates. Bruce Silverstein, the White Sox coach, yelled at Warren "What did you ask him for?"
>
> To complicate matters, in addition to the players being angry and upset, the parents in the stands were also involved in a controversy and were yelling at the umpire. Four young adults were hanging on the backstop and were harassing Dahlgren. While this is happening, Terry Conklin, Phil's son and the assistant coach of the Pirates, walks over to Warren and speaks to him. As Terry walked back to the dugout, Warren yelled a new decision: "The batter's out!", a decision which terminated all chances for the White Sox to win or tie the game. Bruce immediately yelled "What?!" and rushed over

to home plate, where he was met by Phil Conklin and the umpire. They loudly explained that if a batter intentionally puts his head into the strike zone, he is automatically out. The indication was that the batter's act was intentional, since he put his head into the strike zone, rather than pulling it away.

By this time players were rushing onto the field ready for a fight. The boy leading the White Sox was told forcibly by his coach to return to the dugout. Phil Conklin also told his team to return to the dugout, and disaster was averted. (Field Notes)

This situation, of course, is not typical of Little League, but it is a useful example in that it indicates the importance of the adult power structure in organizing the game. The game comes dangerously close to anarchy. The umpire is largely to blame for the situation, because for a while he abdicates his responsibility to make a decision and then seems to accept the pleadings of one team at the expense of their opponents.

In informal "sandlot" games the authority structure operates differently. It is not that there is no authority structure. Instead, the structure works not through role occupancy but by moral suasion. I "umpired" several preadolescent games during the course of studying preadolescent baseball (see Fine & Glassner, 1979). In these games my decisions were occasionally overruled by the preadolescents, as when they felt that I was using an excessively narrow strike zone. In games without umpires that I witnessed, and there are many of these, the natural authority structure of the preadolescent world operates. Those preadolescents who have the most prestige with their peers can suggest directions of group action (see Fine, 1979b; Sherif & Sherif, 1953). Because teams usually are selected to ensure a relatively equal division of skills, often both teams have boys of high esteem. These boys frequently are selected to serve as captains. Since participation in informal baseball games is voluntary, the primary outcome is the generation of fun, and the participants are all friends, the maintenance of social ties is more important than the technical debate over some rule. Consensus outweighs correctness. In one informal game, the best player on one team declared that he was out, even though his teammates were sure that he was safe and the opposing team was not sure what had happened. This high-status player felt that honesty and justice were on this occasion more important than the immediate baseball situation, and of course this "sense of fairness" allowed him to argue vigorously on subsequent plays.

One reason that such strategic noblesse oblige is possible in folk baseball games is that usually the score does not matter. However, the significance of victory and defeat is conditioned on the particular situation, as some folk games (such as games between towns, bars, fathers vs. sons, or students vs. teachers) involve group pride and are hard-fought. Still, there is a sense in most folk baseball, and certainly in informal games, that the outcome of the game does not really matter. Informal games are events in themselves, rather than part of a string of similar events that we call a season. For the Little League game, the outcome of a game has a lasting effect on the rest of the season; informal game outcomes have no effect after their completion. It is readily apparent why players find these losses easier to accept.

Constraints of Preadolescent Baseball

One of the distinguishing factors of any type of voluntary activity is that the constraints and control on a person's activity must ultimately be internal. The person engages in the activity primarily because he wants to and believes that it pays its own way in enjoyment:

> Games can be fun to play, and fun alone is the approved reason for playing them. The individual, in contrast to his treatment of "serious" activity, claims a right to complain about a game that does not pay its way in immediate pleasure and whether the game is pleasurable or not, to plead a slight excuse, such as an indisposition of mood, for not participating. (Goffman, 1961, p. 17)

But Goffman goes beyond this by recognizing that voluntary games can be temporarily ignored while other things are happening. Games are subject to breaks and pleasant diversions, which follow the wanderings of players' attentions and interests, but do not inevitably disrupt a game—although if such interests are shared the game can be suddenly abandoned (Fine, 1983). Side involvements are perfectly possible and legitimate, and can be either collective or personal.

Collective side involvements do threaten the existence of the game, although this is not necessarily a problem. Most informal, voluntary games have no fixed endings. A baseball game can last 3 or 23 innings. It continues as long as the players wish to continue. The game can continue even if individual players decide to leave. However, when the bulk of the players decide to discontinue the activity, it is called off, either immediately or (in the case of finishing an inning for fairness) in short order. Despite formal rules specifying six, seven, or nine innings (depending on the ages of the players), the game can end at any time. Players collectively decide that there are other things that have greater appeal than what is going on in the game (what social psychologists such as Thibault & Kelley, 1959, speak of as comparison level for alternatives):

> Players engaged in an informal game are distracted by the arrival of an ice cream truck. The players run over to the truck, make their purchases, and then sit around on the park grass eating the ice cream. After a while former players drift home and the game doesn't continue. (Field Notes)

Contrast with this the effects of constraints on Little League baseball. For a team to decide that something interests them more than the game would be impossible for the baseball structure to handle and would be subversive of the organization of Little League baseball.[1] Such a decision would no doubt be attributed to the "short attention spans" of children.

The adults who are committed to the efficient completion of the Little League games need to ensure that attention remains on the game. In this way Little League is similar to an industrial organization in which focused action is directed to the assembly line.

In both formal and informal settings short-term disengagements are possible and, as long as they are clearly defined as temporary, do not threaten the game structure. These short-term distractions are perhaps best exemplified by the now-traditional seventh-inning stretch. However, anyone who has observed preadolescent baseball on any level, Little League or informal, realizes that such temporary side involvements are frequent. Even within the formal structure of Little League, players will refocus their attention:

> Carey Kasky is sitting in the Orioles dugout eating a box of Red Hots (cinnamon candy drops). After a while, he begins to throw them at his teammates, while Orioles coaches (including his father) do not complain. Soon most of the players are throwing Red Hots and laughing wildly. Todd Caxton, one of the twelve-year-old stars, throws a Red Hot which hits Carey's father on the back of the neck. The team thinks that this is hilarious. Coach Kasky doesn't become upset at this fooling around. (Field Notes)

Throughout this hilarity, which may seem contrary to the spirit of Little League, there is no doubt that a Little League game is *still* in progress. Although Little League does constrain players, in practice this constraint is applied with a light hand when the threat to the structure of the game is defined as momentary. In informal games temporary disengagements are just part of the fun of the encounter, and it doesn't matter if the temporary disengagement becomes permanent, as long as it is collectively decided.

Individual side involvements also characterize baseball games. Individuals have various interests and attention spans, and sometimes they discover that the game is no longer fun and involving. Recall Goffman's comments about the requirement of the presence of fun in games and that an individual can withdraw if the game is not pleasurable. In these terms Little League baseball is not a game. The individual player is committed to remaining in the scene whether or not he is satisfied. Although I have witnessed a handful of cases in which players expressed the desire not to pitch, and one case in which a player asked not to be placed in the game at all, I never observed a player leaving the playing area unless he was injured and needed medical attention. Little League is in this sense a workplace where one's presence is compulsory.

This contrasts with informal, preadolescent-organized games. On such occasions a player has the "right" to leave when he wishes, although, depending on the player's status and ability, other players may exert social pressure on him or her to remain. Since informal teams are frequently chosen to achieve an equitable balance between the two sides, the absence of a key player may have serious consequences. If a "star" leaves, the players who remain may choose to rearrange themselves to equalize the teams. If poor or unneeded players leave, play can continue as if nothing happened, until a lower limit is reached. Without four players on a team a meaningful game of baseball can hardly be played, although if necessary rules can be altered, such as having everyone other than the batter play in the field. Players may choose to play a baseball-related game (such as "Flies Up" or "Roll-the-Bat," in which a batter hits flies until another player catches the ball or rolls it so it hits the batter's bat on the ground [Sullivan, 1980]).

In both Little League and informal games side involvements that are temporary and that do not cause the player to leave the scene are tolerated, and these activities are vital in preventing boredom from driving players from the game. Baseball is not an engrossing game *at any given moment* for most of the participants. Most of the offensive team merely sit or stand waiting for something to happen in this slow, elegant game; most of the fielders are also waiting for something to happen. It is quite possible for a fielder (particularly an outfielder) not to have a single fielding play during the entire game. The only ones assured of action are the pitcher, catcher, and batter. As a result, it is hardly surprising that the attention of participants wanders. Temporary side involvements include such things as discussions on topics unrelated to the game, drawing in the dirt, playing with sticks, chewing gum, and, where the rules tolerate it, eating ice cream or candy:

> Randy Brosky and Tom Capek of the Pirates are in the dugout playing a ball game which seems to have been initiated by Tom. It consists of bouncing a ball at an angle off the floor and one wall of the dugout so that it lands in the upper rafters of the dugout. There is a small crack where the rafters meet the back wall and the object of the game is to get the ball into one of these cracks. The task was sufficiently challenging that it held their attention and Tom played it for most of the Little League game. (Field Notes)

Coaches must keep a careful eye on their players to ensure that this "fun" does not spread too widely, undermining the game. Side involvements remind us that whatever the task at hand (including work) people try to make the best of things, and do this by finding pleasurable activity to occupy their attention—a fact to which "play during work" testifies (Handelman, 1976; Roy, 1959). Such activities are usually consistent with the continuation of the primary, formal activities.

Developmental Continuities in Preadolescent Baseball

The formal sport of baseball as played today by professionals and by adult-organized Little Leaguers developed from folk baseball. Baseball, in becoming rule-governed, based on written documents, and organized by outside authorities rather than by the participants themselves, has drifted from its folk moorings to something resembling an industrial organization. Although folklorists disagree over the limits to folk activity, there is little question that the formal games of baseball that are played today qualitatively differ in their orientation to the rules and their structured activity from the folk games from which they derived.

The development of organized baseball did not cause folk baseball to disappear—clearly it has not disappeared. However, something interesting has happened in the way players learn about the baseball they play. Just as industrial baseball developed from folk baseball, so now children who learn how to play baseball learn the formal, "industrial" game (at least a form deemed appropriate for their age). Then in their play with peers they transform the game, and their transformations make baseball a folk game once again. By changing the rule of three strikes for a strikeout to allowing a variable number of strikes, they add the flexibility that is characteristic of folk variants. By respecifying ground rules, positions, and equipment as a function of circumstance, they bring the folk emphasis on pragmatic necessity into a game that is formally based on unchanging requirements. Preadolescents have transformed a game created and specified by adults into a game that is appropriate for their preferences, social structure, and environment.

In the "re-folklorizing" of baseball, one traditional folkloric component is lost. Rather than baseball being a ceremony (the pledge of allegiance, the batter in a warm-up circle, the ritualized cheering), baseball has become a folk game. Formal baseball can be described as an industrial work organization that is overlaid with ritual and ceremony (see Goodin, 1980; Lane, 1981). However, the focal activity can hardly be considered a folk game. Preadolescent baseball does not have the ritualistic, ceremonial overlay but does constitute a folk game, because the rules are orally determined and because it is a collection of variants instead of an official version of the game.

Of course, preadolescent baseball does not exist as such. Let us not forget that we are discussing children. The game of "preadolescent baseball" changes as the participants become older and more mature. As Piaget (1962) has noted, the child's conception of rules develops as he or she ages.

Piaget in *The Moral Judgement of the Child* (1962) posits that the practice or application of rules falls into four developmental categories, which are invariant in their sequence. First, there is a stage in which rules have only a motor or idiocentric character. This leads to the formal or ritualized schema and suggests an individual rather than social orientation. Rules, as we commonly think of them, do not exist at this time. "Baseball" does not exist on this level; still, at this age (prior to age 2) the child may play quite happily for extended periods with a ball, bouncing or rolling it.

The second stage, which occurs at ages 2 to 5, is termed the egocentric stage by Piaget. The child now knows of the existence of rules, that is, codifications or requirements of behavior. Although the child attempts to follow these rules, he or she does this imperfectly. The child may play with others without insisting that the rules be uniformly obeyed or even agreed on. Children in this stage play together "on their own." We would still be hard-pressed to claim that baseball occurred at this stage; rather, children may play ball games together at this age, but not in a coordinated way. Furthermore, the child probably doesn't have the motor coordination to perform competently all the tasks necessary for playing baseball.

The third stage of rule practice and application brings us closer to "real" baseball. Piaget calls this stage, which first appears between ages 7 and 8, incipient cooperation. The concept of winning has become important and players become interested in the rules and in controlling other players. The nature of the rules are still only vaguely understood, and players may understand the rules differently. However, this age represents the beginning of baseball recognizable to adults. Depending on the desire to win, sharp and prolonged disputes may occur, as each child wishes to assert the primacy of his or her view of what should be going on in contradiction to partners who have different views. Baseball at this age is a fragile enterprise, both because of the child's relatively short attention span and because disagreements are frequent. This is also the age at which fathers and other adult guardians (gym teachers and coaches) are instructing players in how to play baseball "correctly."

By age 11 or 12, Piaget claims that the fourth and final stage of the codification of rules occur. Piaget claims that every detail of procedure of the game (in his case, marbles) is determined, and these "laws" are known to all children of that age. Although I have argued against the notion of "fixed" and inflexible rules, the idea of rules doesn't fully develop until preadolescence. Whether or not rules are negotiated—and I think they frequently are—there is no question that preadolescents recognize that rules can and do constrain their behavior and that baseball is a game of rules, however flexible they are in practice.

In addition to the practice of rules, Piaget also posits three stages of the consciousness of rules, which run concurrently with the stages of the practice of rules. During the first stage, until approximately age 4, rules are not coercive, either because they are purely motor or because they are seen as nonobligatory. Ball players can do whatever they wish because they don't realize that rules should direct their behavior. During the second stage of the consciousness of rules, from approximately age 4 to 9 or 10 (the end of the egocentric stage and the first half of the cooperating stage), rules are regarded as sacred and untouchable, derived from adults. Any violation of rules seems to the child to be a moral transgression. This is similar to the way in which rules are regarded by *adults* in Little League. Finally, during the third stage, a rule is seen as an agreement arrived at by mutual agreement. Here Piaget admits that rules can be altered if one gains general opinion on one side, and this seems characteristic of the informal baseball games. However, in informal baseball the rules are easily changed and not valued as such. Perhaps becaue Piaget selected an economically based game such as marbles (in which the marbles serve as the mode of exchange and also as a status sign) the rules seem to have particular importance. One suspects that children who play marbles do not have "fun" as their *primary* goal. Marble players are to baseball players as adult poker players are to adults who play darts. In the first activity the outcome has economic or material significance; in the second the outcome is enjoyment and personal satisfaction. The more the activity is connected to material rewards, the more one will need a firmly anchored set of rules.

Let us examine Piaget's dual schemata, tying it to a general conception of preadolescent ball playing. While I have not conducted a systematic examination of children's informal baseball, my 3 years of observation of Little League baseball (Fine, 1980; Fine & Glassner, 1979) suggest some general principles, which are of course subject to additional research.

In the development of children's baseball, which occurs in the broadly defined preadolescent period, there is a shift from unorganized play in which anything can happen and in which rules are almost irrelevant to a game in which rules, though perhaps ambiguously defined, acquire social significance and are treated as being invariant. Finally, by late preadolescence (the period of Little League activity) players remain concerned with rules not as ends in themselves, but as means to other ends, the manufacture of enjoyment. Rules now become more flexible than they had been previously. Children move from unorganized, egocentric control to operating under a set of eternal, fixed rules and then to a final stage in which they can make and alter the rules. One can see in this a parallel to Kohlberg's stages of moral development (Kohlberg & Gilligan, 1972), the preconventional, conventional, and postconventional stages, in which what is at issue is the child's relationship to moral requirements and rules. Sport rules are easily seen as moral rules of proper action.

In this developmental sequence, the amount of social organization necessary to perpetuate the game increases. Preadolescence, when the child becomes attuned to the nature of rules and what can be done with them, represents the period of the rise of team games. This reflects the characterization of preadolescence as "The Gang Age" (Fine, 1980; Furfey, 1927).

Piaget's stages of the consciousness of rules reflect changes in the control system of games. At the earliest stages of play whatever control exists is purely personal; the rules as such have no power. With time, however, children learn the significance of rules and the rules, as well as they are known, have an impersonal compelling power. Finally, in the late preadolescent period the personal and the impersonal control systems merge (Ciuciu, 1974), and we find a guided collectivism. The rules do make a difference; behavior in a late preadolescent baseball game is not random, yet the rules are not so critical that the persons involved can't modify or dispense with them when deemed appropriate. The growth of impersonal rule systems parallels the growth of sophistication in social affairs and the development of impression management skills. Together these forces produce the informal baseball games described earlier in this chapter.

Conclusion

Despite the considerable research on child development, little attention has been given to how children play games, in this case, baseball. I argue that preadolescent informal baseball is a folk game, both because of its oral diffusion and because of its variants. In this, preadolescent informal baseball contrasts with Little League baseball, an adult-sponsored and organized game with roots in that developmental stage in which rules are considered sacred. Although both informal baseball and Little League have components of work and play associated with them, Little League is slanted more to work, whereas informal baseball has more components of play. The significance of rules, the environment, and the legitimacy of side involvements all help to distinguish the structure of informal baseball from that of Little League.

Preadolescent baseball is set within a developmental context. Children go through "stages" (probably less clearly defined and more situational than stage theorists would lead us to believe). Whatever the precise constraining aspects of the stages, they have some validity for allowing adults to understand how children view games. Children's views of games such as baseball change as a consequence of their age. This change influences their orientation to the rules and to each other. While they are learning that rules have and should have constraining power over their own actions, preadolescents are also learning that they have social power in that they can alter these constraints. The transition of preadolescents to "organized" sport carries with it the implication that ultimately they are the organizers. It is the removal of the child's organizing power that some adults (e.g., Devereux, 1976) find most objectionable about adult-dominated, rule-governed Little League baseball.

Note

1. A student once informed me about a problem that Anglo Little League coaches had when they coached Little League teams of Zuni Indian youngsters. The Zuni tribe is known for being publicly uncompetitive. In the middle of the game, even in close, exciting games, these youngsters would simply turn their attention to other activities, leaving the competitive coaches frustrated and fuming.

References

Ciuciu, G. (1974). The socialization process of children by means of extemporized and organized games. *International Review of Sport Sociology*, **9**, 7-22.

Clark, M.W. (1981). *Strategic rule breaking: Existence, function and outcome in American sport*. Paper presented at the North American Society for the Sociology of Sport, Fort Worth, Texas.

Coffin, T.P. (1971). *The old ball game: Baseball in folklore and fiction*. New York: Herder and Herder.

Devereux, E. (1976). Backyard vs. Little League baseball: The impoverishment of children's games. In D. Landers (Ed.), *Social problems in athletics*. Urbana: University of Illinois Press.

Fine, G.A. (1979a). Baseball chatter. *Children's Folklore Newsletter,* 1(2), 2-3.

Fine, G.A. (1979b). Small groups and culture creation: The idioculture of Little League baseball teams. *American Sociological Review,* 44, 733-745.

Fine, G.A. (1980). Cracking diamonds: Observer role in Little League baseball settings and the acquisition of social competence. In W. Shaffir, R. Stebbins, & A. Turowetz (Eds.), *Fieldwork experience.* New York: St. Martin's.

Fine, G.A. (1983). *Shared fantasy: Role-playing games as social worlds.* Chicago: University of Chicago Press.

Fine, G.A. (in press). *With the boys: Little League baseball and preadolescent culture.* Chicago: University of Chicago Press.

Fine, G.A., & Glassner, B. (1979). Participant observation with children: Promise and problems. *Urban Life,* 8, 153-174.

Furfey, P. (1927). *The gang age.* New York: Macmillan.

Gmelch, G.J. (1971). Baseball magic. *Trans-Action,* 8, 39-41, 54.

Goffman, E. (1961). *Encounters.* Indianapolis: Bobbs-Merrill.

Gomme, A.B. (1964). *The traditional games of England, Scotland, and Ireland* (Vol. 2). New York: Dover. (Original work published 1898)

Goodin, R.E. (1980). *Manipulatory politics.* New Haven, CT: Yale University Press.

Handelman, D. (1976). Re-thinking "Banana time": Symbolic integration in a work setting. *Urban Life,* 4, 433-448.

Hughes, L. (1983). Beyond the rules of the game: Why are Rooie rules nice? In F. Manning (Ed.) *The world of play* (pp. 183-199). Champaign, IL: Leisure Press.

Kohlberg, L., & Gilligan, C. (1972). The adolescent as a philosopher: The discovery of the self in a post-conventional world. In J. Kagan & R. Coles (Eds.), *12 to 16: Early adolescence.* New York: W.W. Norton.

Lane, C. (1981). *The rites of rulers.* Cambridge: Cambridge University Press.

Larson, K. (1980). *Keep up the chatter: Ritual communications in American summer softball.* Paper presented at the annual meeting of the American Anthropological Association, Washington, DC.

Levin, M. (1969, June 21). Tell it like it was. *Saturday Review,* pp. 4, 6.

Moe, J.F. (1982). *Some who made it: Traditional sports narratives about regional baseball.* Paper presented at the American Folklore Society, Minneapolis, MN.

Piaget, J. (1962). *The moral judgement of the child.* New York: Collier.

Ralbovsky, M. (1974). *Destiny's darlings.* New York: Hawthorne.

Reese, G.P. (1975). *The baseball story: A motif index derived from stories found in books written by baseball players and managers between 1946-1973.* Unpublished master's thesis, State University of New York College at Oneonta.

Roy, D.F. (1959). "Banana time": Job satisfaction and informal interaction. *Human Organization, 18*, 158-168.

Scholl, R. (1977). *Running Press glossary of baseball language.* Philadelphia: Running Press.

Sherif, M., & Sherif, C. (1953). *Groups in harmony and tension.* New York: Harper.

Sullivan III, C.W. (1980, Summer-Fall). Roll-the-Bat. *Southwest Folklore, 4*, 84-86.

Thibault, J.W., & Kelley, H.H. (1959). *The social psychology of groups.* New York: John Wiley & Sons.

Weeks, L.T. (1906). Ball-lore. *Journal of American Folklore, 19*, 350.

CHAPTER 18

Cultural Implications of the Soccer Phenomenon in America

Leonard P. Oliver
Oliver Associates, Washington, DC

The rapid growth of soccer in America, particularly at the youth level, is a cultural phenomenon—an exceptional and significant occurrence that is only now being recognized, analyzed, and interpreted by those who follow sport. Soccer holds promise of affecting our characters, our families, our communities, our country, and perhaps one day, our international relations. "The game that never sleeps" is here, and my purpose is to examine its implications for our culture, just as it influences cultures around the world.

The statistics are staggering. The United States Soccer Federation (USSF) formally registered its one millionth youngster in 1983. It is estimated that 8 million Americans play soccer at all levels, with 3 million youngsters under 10 playing competitively. The YMCA reports soccer as its largest team sport, with 400,000 boys and girls participating through 900 YMCAs. In the metropolitan Washington, DC, area, 75,000 boys and girls are on organized teams, the Long Island Soccer League has 62,000 youngsters registered, Illinois reported 9,000 registered young players in 1977 and 46,000 in 1983, and high schools like Centerville in Ohio regularly draw 4,000 fans to a game. The President's Council on Physical Fitness and Sport reports that soccer is the fastest growing high school sport in the nation. There are 532 colleges with intercollegiate varsity soccer (502 colleges field football teams) and leading soccer schools like the University of San Francisco, Indiana University, and Penn State University attract 7,000 to 10,000 spectators at home games.

Unfortunately, this growth and participation are often ignored or overshadowed by the media's barometer of the value of a sport in our country, the strength of the professional franchises, and here we are hurting. The North American Soccer League (NASL), now defunct, lost 20 to 25 million dollars in its last year of operation. Still, in spite of the NASL's woes, there are 36 indoor and outdoor professional soccer franchises in our country.

Beyond the statistics and the poor-cousin image portrayed by the media, I look at another national barometer—Madison Avenue. We see Ricky

Davis, formerly with the Cosmos, bathing with Ivory Soap after performing an acrobatic bicycle kick, Prudential advertising family protection with a distinctive soccer ball on the front lawn (the black and white ball arrived in 1964—the "TV ball"—invented in Germany and giving soccer its identifying trademark), soccer players downing Pepsi after a workout, and little tykes clambering into a Peugeot after a game—all 14! Even if the media sports desks do not know where the fans are, you can bet Madison Avenue's market surveys do.

I grew up with soccer in the streets of Philadelphia, taught by an immigrant Scottish father, and I can remember endless conversations beginning, "So you're a soccer player—how is it played?" and ending, "But it's still a foreign sport!" Standing outside a São Paulo stadium signing autographs at the Pan Am Games in 1963, or being greeted by the town's youngsters after a game with my Bavarian town team, Bad Aibling, during service days, or seeing Pele make his debut at the World Cup in Sweden in 1958—I always felt more at home abroad as a soccer player. That has changed in just a generation. Now everybody talks soccer, coaches, or has a kid playing in towns where some people have never seen a professional game or kicked a ball themselves.

Unfortunately, all of this soccer interest and participation has not translated into recognition for soccer nationally, into fan support for the outdoor professional teams, or into a truly competitive international U.S. team. One of the reasons, for example, that the governing board of the Fédération Internationale de Football Association (FIFA) rejected the United States' bid to host the 1986 World Cup was the perceived lack of commitment to the sport by the American public and those who ran the professional teams.

One unanswered question, therefore, is when (and if—if you listen to the cynics) the mass participation of young people in soccer will produce the fans for the professional teams. Beyond this obvious question, there are many more subtle issues related to the constraints on the growth of soccer in America, factors fueling the surge, and the potential influence of soccer on our culture.

Because there are few rigorous, analytical studies of soccer in America, with most books written by coaches stressing how to play or by feature writers unfamiliar with the nuances of the game, I will attempt a thoughtful, albeit intuitive analysis of some issues related to soccer in America.

Soccer and Culture

A Brief History

Many newcomers to soccer attribute its kickoff in America to Pele's signing with the Cosmos for 3 years and $3.5 million in 1975—admittedly a dramatic event that captured the attention of the world's sporting community. Others go back to 1966, when the heart-throbbing World Cup final of England versus West Germany was telecast live to the United

States from London, an event that aroused the interest of the business community because of the unexpectedly high Nielsen rating. Some old-timers go back to 1950, when the United States National Team, composed mainly of amateurs, upset England 1 to 0 in a game still referred to as "the biggest upset in soccer history." But soccer has been around in America for over 200 years. It was brought over by English colonists, played more formally and rather brutally by colleges starting in the mid-1800s (Princeton and Rutgers played an inaugural intercollegiate match in 1869), and then given strong impetus, at least in our northeastern urban areas, by the waves of immigrants who brought their culture, including soccer, with them. Factory teams and local amateur teams, primarily associated with ethnic clubs in the cities, flourished through the 1930s. For example, I spent 5 years playing top-class amateur soccer with the Kensington Blue Bells in Philadelphia, a club founded in the early 1900s by Scottish immigrants.

So there is a history of soccer in America, one that is interconnected with the lives of working-class people, but it remains for the most part undocumented. With the new interest in social and working-class history, perhaps soccer's link with its ethnic roots will unfold.

The history of soccer itself has been the subject of long debate. As a boy, I used to hear folklore stories from my father of English workmen in the 11th century digging in an old battlefield and uncovering the skull of a Danish soldier. Since the Danish had recently occupied England, the workers vented their feelings by kicking the skull around—the first soccer ball.

Actually, football games (as soccer is known in the rest of the world) have been documented in the writings of the Chinese as early as 80 B.C., and soccer-like games have been appearing in literature ever since. The game was often banned in England for its violence, as whole towns in the Middle Ages occasionally went at it with a large ball. But it was in the 1860s in England that the "kicking game" was separated from the "game with hands," with rugby and soccer emerging from the same egg.

The Football Association was formed in England in 1863 (the world *soccer* comes from an abbreviation for "association") and codified the rules of the game, thus beginning the modern era of soccer. British sailors, merchants, factory workers, and schoolboys subsequently carried soccer to Brazil, Russia, Germany, the United States, and other nations as the Empire expanded, although it did not catch on in major English territories such as Canada, Australia, and India. Once introduced in most countries, however, soccer developed rapidly until today there are 175 soccer-playing nations, more than are in the United Nations, each with its distinct approach to the game.

The International Culture of Soccer

Soccer in many countries cannot be understood apart from the country's culture, traditions, class structure, geography, and values. Soccer reflects a nation's culture because it permeates all levels of a society. There are probably climatic reasons why South Americans in their warm climate play at a different pace than the English, who play right through the winter and have to keep running to combat the cold. Brazilian soccer, so well documented by Janet Lever (1983) in *Soccer Madness*, is "alegre," soccer to a Samba beat—joyous, unpredictable, spontaneous, "poetry and motion." (A São Paulo psychologist once observed that Brazilians have lost their self-esteem, and "soccer comes in as a saving element—the sensation of taking part in a collective undertaking . . . rich in emotions" [Hoge, 1982, p. A-2].)

England's "Dunkirk style" is tenacious, with hard tackling, fairness, and a "let's-get-the-job-done" attitude. West Germany's highly disciplined, mechanistic, orderly "systems soccer" was called by Pele on TV in 1982 "ten robots alongside Rummenigge" (Europe's "player of the year"). The superbly conditioned Soviets engage in "technical soccer," by the book, but often fail against the flamboyant South Americans and the gritty, determined English. Italians may learn acting before soccer, treating the sport (as in most Latin-language countries) as a matter of life and death. In fact, one Italian coach was overheard to remark that "some say football is a matter of life and death. Well it isn't—it's more important than that!" Giovanni Arpino (1982), an Italian novelist, describes why the Italians won the World Cup in 1982:

> They won because they knew what Italians abroad must do, . . . like the people from Calabria, from Basilicata, like the Venetians, the Piedmontese who had to face the unknown awaiting them in New York, in the Pampas, in the steppes, in deserts, or when they had to build a dam or a bridge. . . . In their veins and brains they found the winning spur before feeling it in their muscles. (p. 2)

Culture and Soccer in the United States

The idea of soccer being a national cultural phenomenon in the United States is only now creeping into our collective psyche as soccer spreads into our middle-class structure and into our playing fields that just a few years ago exhibited football goal posts. Until the early 1970s, soccer had been the province of ethnic groups, with the St. Louis CYOs, some prep schools, urban high schools, and colleges displaying home-grown talent. Today, soccer is rapidly becoming white, middle-class, suburban, and small town, if we look at the areas of most dramatic growth. The *Milwaukee Sentinel* (November 9, 1983), for example, recently reported that "soccer is in vogue for youngsters. It has the station wagon, hand-knit sweater sort of panache usually associated with polo."

Given our nation's multicultural mix, it would be interesting to analyze our distinct approach to soccer, our "American style," and entertain some speculations on what style of international soccer we can look forward to once we become truly competitive with other nations. Just as soccer has permeated other cultures, it holds the potential of affecting ours, although there are some deeply ingrained constraints to its growth in our country.

Constraints on Soccer's Growth

Lack of a Recognized, Americanized Professional League

Kids need heroes—we all know this from our own childhoods. And my heroes were professional athletes in soccer and baseball. Similarly, communities need identification with their professional franchises if they hope to attract sustained fan support. American kids need American heroes. We have them in baseball, football, and basketball, but not yet in soccer.

Since 1968, when the NASL was founded, professional soccer owners and coaches have emphasized foreign talent—overaged, often slow, uninspiring, ex-internationals with no stake in the American game or building community loyalties. As a token to young American players, the NASL required 2 or 3 Americans on the field at all times, and former and foreign coaches complained that they could not field their best 11 players. Entertainment was placed by the owners before building the sport, and city by city, foreign stars are still being signed for the Major Indoor Soccer League (MISL).

Because of the chaos in the NASL and professional soccer in general, we are a soccer yearling, a failure in the world's eyes as evidenced by our ill-fated bid for the 1986 World Cup. Our "American delegation" included Kissinger, Pele, and Beckenbauer—no local officials who could talk about the growth of soccer in their communities, no youth leaders—and we were rejected. Soccer is also a failure in the media's all-encompassing perspective, particularly television's, but it extends to print journalism also. Because of the media's influence on the public, general public perception—outside of soccer players, promoters, and administrators—is that soccer has not yet permeated our society and perhaps never will. We are in a Catch-22: the media do not promote soccer, the fans don't come out, and the media can claim it was doomed.

In the meantime, we have tampered with the rules to "Americanize" soccer (the NASL initiated a 35-yard line for offsides and "shootouts" to satisfy the so-called American penchant for scoring and results—we would widen the goals if we could), just to be brought up short by FIFA sanctions. The only professional soccer franchises making it are the indoor teams in the MISL. Indoor soccer is a mutation of soccer, with human "pinballs," hockey's dasher boards and plays, football's razzmatazz, Star Wars–like introductions, and unlimited substitution. There is scoring and nonstop action, and indoor soccer crowds are outdrawing hockey and basketball in St. Louis, Kansas City, Cleveland, and other cities. The teams play mostly Americans. But all the hoopla, all the skydivers, the marching bands, and the Frisbee-catching dogs that have been employed by professional soccer teams will not create a truly American, internationally recognized professional league until communities adopt professional soccer

teams and until young Americans see professional soccer as a career option just as they do other pro sports.

Media Coverage and Public Misunderstanding

As indicated before, the media, print and video, have sorely shortchanged
soccer. Marv Albert, NBC sportscaster, is unimpressed with soccer: "My
kids play soccer, but as a spectator sport, it has minimal meaning here.
Its stats and players have no significance" (Fischler, 1984, p. 133). The
same article quotes the *New York Times* saying it would like to cover soccer,
"but we don't have the space."

The media have had an opportunity to educate the American public
on the "world's sport," yet they have failed to grasp the essence, the
nuances of the game. Prejudiced by the rules, language, and principles
of other professional sports, and imbued with a false sense that what
Americans want in their sports is violence, statistics, and scoring, the
sportscasters have tended to deride soccer as boring, unimaginative, slow,
and unexciting. It is like going to a bullfight and looking only for the kill,
the final act, and missing the *paseillo* and all that follows. Or going to a
ballet and waiting for a spectacular *grande jeté* rather than enjoying the
preceding movements.

Let me offer some graphic examples. Whereas *Newsweek* described the
1982 World Cup by the number of journalists (8,000), the English hooli-
gans, and the Brazilians' four Samba orchestras, Giovanni Arpino (1982)
described the 1982 World Cup as "lung-consuming, heartbreaking, with a
great inner strength and . . . a few geo-political quarrels," and the Italian
players as "slippery like Rossi," "elegant and ironmade like Scirea," or
"unyielding like Zoff" (p. 1). Norman Fox (1978) of the *London Times*
described the setting of the 1978 World Cup this way: "The giant tiered
ground steeply terraced in typically South American style, was bathed
in delicate blue, a cascade of streamers, spilling over the balconies."
Fox talked of "fierce, physical pressure" by Holland (Argentina played
Holland in the final), of Poortvliet and Haan "making reckless, ominous
tackles," of "forceful interceptions by the Dutch that cut deep into Argentina's essential speed." And "none of the players stood back from the
toil and speed for long enough to assess the possible alternatives to sheer
speed." On the winning goal by Argentina, he wrote the following:

> Bertoni desperately tried to find him from the left side of the penalty area.
> In a furious scramble with defenders scurrying to regain possession, Kempes
> managed artfully to keep the ball and push it in off the Dutchmen around
> him. (p. 8)

When we learn to report soccer in this loving, poetic, dramatic fashion,
professional soccer will come alive here also. Instead, describing a goal
in a highly charged 1982 World Cup semifinal match between Italy and
Poland, an American sportswriter said, "In the 22nd minute, the Italians

staged one of their patented counterattacks that led to a Polish foul. Then: Antognoni to Cabrini to Rossi in front of the goal and a 1-0 lead for Italy" (Vecsey, 1982, p. 16). Or in reference to an indoor game, "Dipede . . . has logged 365 minutes, a record in the MISL . . . and has a 13-9 record with a 4.70 goals against average" (Covitz, 1984, p. 9). We are looking for stats when we should be looking for style and flair—which of these descriptions would most attract you to the sport?

Lacking an understanding of the flow of play in soccer, we tend to describe scoring opportunities, blatant fouls, and sideline behavior. We call low-scoring soccer games dull, yet a 1 to 0 baseball game is an exquisite pitching/fielding duel. We deride the lack of scoring in soccer, yet a healthy 21 to 14 football score is in reality a 3 to 1 average soccer score. A 135 to 134 professional basketball game is truly boring until the last 5 minutes, or unless you know what to look for in the players' moves.

Soccer has never made it on commercial television, although ABC has broadcast the Soccer Bowl and the 1982 World Cup final, and NBC is broadcasting seven of the World Cup games from Mexico. Even so, because of interruptions for commercials, most of us watched the World Cup final last year between Italy and West Germany on SIN from Mexico, where commercials came at the beginning, halftime, end, and overlayed without interfering with the flow of play. As one ABC official commented at the time on ABC's use of two 30-second spots for soccer, "ABC rarely missed a goal." But a soccer match is not just goals, as Lawrie Mifflin (1982) pointed out on the eve of the 1982 World Cup final:

> A soccer match is like theater, with a main story that also embraces smaller, personal dramas between players facing each other man-to-man, and with a step-by-step denouement. Missing part of the dialogue in a play is not like missing anything "major," either, but it's still missing essential ingredients of the story. (p. 15)

That's our problem—because of ignorance of the game, our sportscasters continue to look for the wrong thing in soccer. Even television cameramen, in contrast to foreign telecasts of soccer, don't know what to look for in a match, missing most of the subtle movements "off the ball," as we say. They focus on either goals or scoring opportunities, and then they deride the sport as dull. I don't believe the media's misunderstanding of soccer is fundamentally malicious, but it does relate to ignorance of the sport's artistry and style.

Entrenchment of Existing Sports

Baseball, football, and basketball still dominate the American professional and amateur sport scene. All are "American" sports, or in the case of baseball and football, derivations of English forerunners. Recall that soccer has not flourished in Canada, with its hockey and Canadian football, or in Australia with its "Australian rules football," or in India with its field hockey. Similarly, soccer is bucking powerful sport traditions in our country.

From my own coaching, soccer is not competing with basketball for the kids' time or for indoor facilities (except where indoor youth soccer is taking hold), nor is it competing with high school and college basketball. It is slightly competitive with youth baseball, but only when spring seasons overlap. Besides, baseball and soccer are qualitatively different. Soccer does tend, however, to go head-to-head with football and seems to be pulling ahead dramatically at the youth level. There is obviously no competition at the professional level, although college soccer is replacing football at many smaller, budget-conscious colleges.

My question is, what happens to a sport when its base of good athletes and parental participation dries up? Soccer today resembles a pyramid, with most of the good players still in the youth ranks. Football resembles an inverted pyramid, with the best players in high school, college, or the professional ranks. On Long Island, one recreation director responded to a community's request to turn a football field over to the soccer program with, "But soccer is not an American sport." The threat is obvious and strong.

More and more, as kids face a conflict in deciding on team sports to pursue, parents are encouraging soccer over football, at times over baseball. And for girls, soccer has opened up a new team sport option where, in many leagues, they compete on mixed teams until their teens.

Overcoaching, Overparenting, Overbearing in a Low-Keyed Sport

This is a sensitive subject. Lee Stern, owner of the Chicago Sting in the NASL, recently observed that "I don't know what it feels like to kick a soccer ball, but I know how it feels to hit a baseball or shoot a basketball or throw a football. And I probably represent 99% of the male population over 35 in this country" (Mifflin, 1983, p. 12). Few men and almost no women over 35 have ever played soccer, many have never seen top-class competition, yet they are the parents of the budding soccer players. Surprisingly, they are also flocking to "over 35" soccer leagues for their own recreation and fitness goals.

A kid sees a recreation department notice or hears of a team forming, or parents seek out an alternative to football or consider soccer as a team sport for their girls, or a kid is bored with standing in the outfield in baseball but is too small for basketball or football, and soccer has become the option. This has created a problem in coaching and officiating; soccer's growth has far exceeded the availability of coaches and officials knowledgeable about the game, and uninformed but well-meaning parents have jumped in to fill the void. The fathers tend to apply principles from other, more familiar sports (one football father told me that the three principles of soccer are "run, release, and receive"). The mothers (a phenomenon in itself when one considers that fully 25% to 40% of all youth soccer coaches, administrators, and officials are women), with few prior team sport hang-ups, read a few books and take over teams, leagues, and refereeing. So we face a nation of enthusiastic kids, mothers who transport and coach them, and fathers who still harbor thoughts of their kids executing the pivot at second base or running a buttonhook pattern for a forward pass. What are the implications?

Overcoaching. Some of my fellow junior coaches buy clipboards and stopwatches before they step on a practice field. They read a book and proceed to apply a 4-3-3 or a 3-3-4 with a "sweeper" before they assess the youngsters' talents. For example, I've heard coaches yell, "Kick it harder," which has no meaning in soccer; or always play the same kid in goal, denying him or her field experience and experimentation with ball control skills at an early age; or bring only one ball to practice, lining up 15 players for shots on goal and letting the rest stand with their hands in their pockets. Each kid on my team has a ball, and I encourage them to fool around, hotdog, show off—after all, soccer brings out individual, personal expression with the ball. Pele's basic ball control skills were honed on the streets of his village, Três Coraçóes, in the state of Minas Gerais, on his local "barefoot team."

In almost all our American team sports, coaches are highly visible and at times dominate play. In contrast, once a soccer game starts, a coach should be invisible to let the players dominate (coaching from the sidelines warrants a "yellow card," a warning in international play). What a difficult concept for American parents, especially fathers used to taking orders from football coaches or being instructed to steal second base in their playing days.

Overcoaching, too much emphasis on systems, predictable and repetitive moves, physical attributes, or conservative play can conflict with individual development and the free flow of soccer, with creativity, and with the need for each player to assert his or her "soccer personality." "Play with impudence," as one of my old coaches used to say. Tim Sheldon (1983), writer for *Soccer America*, recently pointed out the following:

> I'm convinced that youngsters develop the highest level of skill just by horsing around with a ball by themselves or with friends in the yard or driveway, or sometimes—I shouldn't say it—in the street.

> Without adult interference, they can do, literally, anything they want with the ball. They develop a truly personal relationship with the ball. It becomes part of themselves. Later, in organized games, their movements will be second nature.

Overbearing coaches get even worse higher up the ladder. I have watched high school and college coaches maintain meaningless statistics and miss the flow of the game; test how high a player can jump and forget that heading the ball, an unusual weapon unique to soccer, is all timing; or so lock their players into set positions that all interchangeability of positions—a characteristic of a good soccer team—is lost.

American-authored books on soccer are starting to appear. Most deal with techniques, not with the artistry of the sport. *Go for Goal: Winning Drills and Exercises for Soccer* (Ford & Kane, 1984) is a recent addition to my sport library, advertising that it can "improve player performance and increase chances of victory with 120 proven drills with 100 variations." Think of the matrix a new coach faces as he or she tries to get a 10-year-old to kick with the outstep. There are even 22 drills to learn the soccer laws, yet there are only 17 laws!

Through our overcoaching, through our books, we are trying our best to make a simple game complex, to turn an art form into a science. We are trying to apply coaching controls and authority in a sport that by its nature rewards creativity and individuality, to measure the unmeasurable, and to emphasize technique over feeling.

Overparenting. Parents new to soccer do not know how to watch the sport. It is a game that brings out emotions, especially when our own children are playing. Spectators around the world get passionate about their teams—witness the moats in South American stadiums, the World Cup fervor, the intense loyalities of *afficionados* documented so ably by Janet Lever (1983) in *Soccer Madness*. But children are impressionable, and parents tend to be intense, aggressive, overinvolved, even overprotective in a sport for children that they don't understand. "My kid plays center field," admitted one father at one of my games, and another so coached his son in goal that the player's foot got tangled in the net as the other team advanced.

Our culturally acquired "win-at-any-cost" mentality gets in our way with soccer and puts undue pressure on kids out for fun, with parents at times berating their youngsters, insulting referees, and contradicting coaches. In Montgomery County, outside Washington, DC, a cardiologist-parent of a 10-year-old player abused the referee unmercifully, approached him on the field during the game, and was subsequently slugged by the official. He sued the official and the judge gave the referee 24 hours of community service. The incident resulted in a code of conduct for parents drawn up by the league.

Soccer has attracted parents who are middle- and upper-middle-class professionals, highly competitive, hard-driving, and who want desperately for their kids to succeed. The problem is endemic and leagues are now taking steps to curb parent overreaction to the sport, advising teams of forfeits unless parents are controlled. Maybe soccer will have a civilizing influence on parents, once they come to understand the subtleties of the sport.

A White Middle-Class Sport

Soccer is still a white, suburban, small town or white ethnic, urban sport, with smatterings of Hispanic teams in Spanish-speaking communities. Black communities and black kids around the country, especially in our urban areas, have not yet adopted soccer in a manner similar to their suburban neighbors. There is no expectation of payoff, as there is with basketball or football, so black kids are not hungry for soccer.

Few black parents know the game. Fields are scarce in inner-city neighborhoods, in contrast to basketball hoops found in every playground, driveway, and alley. And no one has attempted to concentrate resources for the development of soccer leagues, clinics, and administrators for the black community.

Yet the potential is there. An American Pele or Eusebio is yet to be discovered, but in working with black youngsters in soccer clinics and on my team, I am convinced that someday black kids will discover soccer, will excel, will be the "Magic Johnsons" and "Dr. Js" of soccer, and will contribute to our development as a truly competitive soccer nation.

Factors Fueling Soccer's Growth

Soccer has arrived, at least at the youth-community level, and it may be useful to speculate on some of the factors that are contributing to its acceptance in such a short time span.

Soccer's Inherent Characteristics

Soccer and individual expression.   Soccer is a game for the player, not for the coaches, and this makes it unusually difficult for both coaches and parents who have grown up with other, coach-dominated sports. Manfred Schellscheidt (1983), former U.S. Olympic coach, put it this way:

> I encourage them to express themselves because it is a game of expression, . . . of personality, . . . of character. Once a player has the tools, once he has the physical skill, he must express his personality. . . . It's not something you can program, . . . that you can predict. . . . It's an instant reaction, the initiative of the player and his reaction to things as they happen. We must encourage the player to take chances, do the unexpected, have courage to take people on and go forward as well as have the discipline that counts . . . when we are in defense.

Team sports can often be frustrating for youngsters; some never even touch the ball. Yet touching the ball is what sports for kids should be all about. And it is in this regard that soccer, as a team sport, has an advantage over baseball, where the only offensive player is the pitcher and everyone else reacts to his or her moves; and football, where linemen can go through a career without touching the ball. In soccer, each player touches the ball between 20 and 30 times a game, giving each youngster an opportunity to develop his or her own relationship and skills with the ball. For Desmond Morris, a good player "is possessed of spontaneous inventiveness that sets the game alight and wins matches" (Morris, 1981, p. 85). The inventiveness comes in the use of the ball—passing, dribbling, shooting, intercepting—the magic is indeed in the ball.

Soccer's appeal as a game.   As Clay Berling, editor of *Soccer America*, continually points out, there are two conflicting elements in any sport, its "artistry" and its "competition." The artistry makes it worth playing and watching, the competition makes it a sport. People seem drawn to soccer because of the artistry in the context of competition. Soccer has been compared to ballet and other forms of dance, and in some countries leading coaches and players actually teach ballet.

Another appealing aspect of soccer is the simplicity of its rules. There are only 17 laws in soccer, relatively unchanged for over 100 years, and immediately intelligible to diverse nations and cultures around the world. Communication in matches between teams of different languages, with the officials speaking a third language, is done through a series of internationally recognized hand signals, a "soccer semaphore."

Given its simplicity, its artistic nuances, the head-to-head combativeness, and the impossibility of delay (the ball is the focus and always in play), the game moves fast with few frills. Recall the 1982 World Cup Final—10 minutes warm-up, two teams and three officials walk on, two national anthems are played, and then 90 minutes of action. No cheerleaders, no marching bands, no television time-outs, no huddles—just constant action.

In its simplicity as a game, soccer may be at a disadvantage in a society that prides itself on mastering complexity, on having a clear beginning, middle, and resolution (when will we come to realize that a draw is an honorable result, rather than imposing a false victory with an aberration like the "shootout"?). Consider that 11 of the 28 NFL teams now use computers to call plays and set defenses with increasing sophistication and predictability, in direct contrast to soccer's individual inventiveness and unpredictability.

Physical attributes.   Both football and basketball tend to emphasize size and weight, with linemen too big to play tailback and tailbacks too small to play line, with guards too small to play center, and centers too awkward to be point guards. In contrast, soccer does not punish normal-sized people, but rewards skill, balance, intelligence, and stamina, not brute strength or unusual height. The differences in physical size are not pronounced in youngsters playing football and basketball; they become critical as players move on to high school, college, and the pro ranks. Physical size just does not enter into the soccer equation; I've seen players a foot shorter than me outjump me for a head ball. There are no indefensible "slam dunks"—spectacular as they are, they are ruining basketball. As Morris (1981) points out, physical aspects take a back seat to the two essential ingredients of the good soccer player: *skill*, which makes the player an acrobat with the ball, and *fitness*, which gives the player an athlete's body and the stamina for a full match. Add in *experience* for the understanding of strategy and tactics and a *positive mental state* for motivation and confidence in him- or herself.

Great physical effort is obviously needed in soccer, with severe demands on muscles, lungs, and the heart. Only a few sports demand more, and all are individual sports (decathlon, handball, marathon, pentathlon, Tour de France, and wrestling). But if soccer succeeds in our country, it will be due as much to the "thinking power" it permits each player as to the players' physical prowess.

Soccer costs. Growing up in Philadelphia, with no money for shin guards, we used *Popular Mechanics* magazine to cover our shins. A used, tattered ball and a garage door, and we had a game. Years later I recall alighting from our team bus on a street corner in a small Brazilian town to stretch our legs before a match. A dozen scruffy neighborhood urchins came up and proceeded to take their socks off to stuff them in another sock for a makeshift ball, and to do things with this sock-ball on a stony lot that we hadn't mastered in all our years of playing.

Costs are already influencing police athletic leagues, Little Leagues, the YMCA, and other community-based organizations to adopt soccer because of its low expense/high participation ratio. Many high schools and colleges, hard-pressed financially, are turning to soccer as an alternative sport program. We can outfit a young soccer player for less than $20, whereas football equipment can run to $250 per player. The inexpensiveness of soccer is not its major attraction for players, but it is for a cost-conscious administrator seeking an alternative to more highly priced athletic programs.

Violence and the fear of serious injury in football. Violence may be as American as apple pie, as H. Rap Brown once said, but parental concern and apprehension about severe injury to young football players is a factor in the turn to soccer. I have broken both legs in soccer and suffered some 40 to 50 stitches from crashing of heads, along with numerous sprains and muscle pulls, in my 20-year active career. I can still, however, throw and kick a ball, run, play tennis, and ride a bicycle, in contrast to some football-playing friends who will never do these activities because of injured shoulders, knees, and backs.

Over one half of football injuries are to the knee, ankle, or shoulder, and 21.3% of these injuries are fractures. In soccer, most injuries are to the foot or lower leg, and few result in fractures (Southmayd & Hoffman, 1981). Players don't get killed in soccer, but 13 high school football players died in 1984, 4 from directly related football injuries. Many football players are encouraged to "play to hurt" in the heat of competition as a mark of character, but it is almost impossible in soccer because of the nonstop pace and the openness of the game.

With strength and weight coordinators, with bigger, more conditioned, faster players, we are going to see increased football injuries in spite of the excellent advances in equipment. For example, the weekly NFL injury report contains 300 names with 400 injuries, with the most common injury a concussion (defined as a blow to the head), followed by knee injuries. Compare this state with the case of Diego Maradona, formerly of Barcelona's soccer team, the world's highest priced player, who suffered severely torn ligaments in his ankle from a vicious tackle by a Bilbao player a few years ago. It was reported that the Barcelona spectators "each died a small death," the Barcelona papers screamed "The Crime" the next day, with pictures of Maradona on a stretcher, and the offender became known as "the Butcher of Bilbao." He was suspended for 18 games. Can you imagine the outcry if the NFL took similar action?

We may get some vicarious charge from watching the Sunday afternoon football mayhem, but we sure don't want our kids playing it. There are signs that the public is starting to react to role-model football players talking about "breaking faces," or the Raiders' owner saying, "We take what we want," or the Washington Federals' ad, "Wanna Fight?" which teaches both bad grammar and violence. Television ratings for the NFL are down 6 to 20% per game, the colleges down 11% since 1977. One features writer for the *Christian Science Monitor* observed that "the moments of action to moments between" ratio in football is 1:20 in favor of "still life" and that "a sport that lives on the borderline between boredom and violence has some explaining to do" (Maddocks, 1983, p. 21).

Football coaches are now concerned about the loss of better athletes to soccer, which I heard one describe as "an imported, un-American menace to our youth." Where soccer is played year-round, it is also cutting into baseball, which has, as one of my young players put it, "the striking out, the sitting on the bench, and the standing around which doesn't happen in soccer." The "tidal wave" of young soccer players will eventually have an effect on all our sport programs, with implications for our culture that we cannot even begin to foresee.

Coed soccer and the family context.   My two girls, aged 12 and 14, played on my predominantly boys team and held their own. The youngest continues to play and leads our male-dominated team in scoring. The mother of another girl player recalled that she had no team sport options while growing up, other than as a cheerleader or pompon girl, and welcomed the opportunity soccer gave for girls to compete on an equal basis with boys. Up to puberty, girls are often taller, more agile, sometimes faster, and perhaps a little less intensely competitive than boys—all characteristics allowing them to compete in a game that encourages coolness, thinking, body coordination, and stamina rather than size and strength. The implications of this massive entry of girls directly into male team sport have yet to be examined, but it is an area ripe for research.

Concomitantly, soccer has generated family involvement. When a coach is needed, nets have to be put up, or a schedule of team play arranged, mothers have jumped in, read a few books, and carried substantial weight in the sport around the country. When asked about the role of girls playing and mothers participating and the effect on the male ego, I reply that if a person is competent, enthusiastic, and willing to work hard at perfecting soccer skills, then he or she will be accepted regardless of sex. That also applies to life, and the coed soccer revolution may in the long run be a contributing factor to a more accepting, equalitarian society.

The international pressure.   America made a serious bid in 1983 to host the 1986 World Cup and had extensive support in countries that want to see our nation take its place among the world's soccer-playing nations. More and more Americans see soccer in their travels, full World Cup competition from beginning to end will be broadcast quadrennially to the United States, and cultural exchanges will bring glamorous foreign teams to our shores. Hundreds of youth teams now go abroad every year to participate in tournaments and "friendlies." We are a global village, as Marshall McLuhan observed, and the village plays soccer. Given the growth of the sport here, we will not be far behind. Consider the more than one million spectators who attended the 1984 Olympic soccer matches, even though the U.S. was eliminated early.

Soccer's Potential for Influencing American Culture

If sports are a metaphor for life, a means for society to inculcate and civilize its young by developing character traits and values society desires, and if soccer is a rising phenomenon, a tidal wave of youngsters and teams, it might be useful to speculate on the potential of soccer to influence our culture and our lives. At least we can raise some issues for discussion and research.

Soccer and Family Life

Heretofore, the father was the dominant sports role model in most families, especially with his influence on his sons and team sports. Now, over 25% of all youngsters playing soccer are girls, many on coed teams, and women equal men in leadership positions in the sport. If girls and women can compete successfully in these previously male-dominated sporting roles, and they obviously can in soccer, what will be the effect on role differentiations in the family and on male/female relationships as kids grow up? I can only think it will be healthy—with mutual respect for competitiveness, skill, and enthusiasm wherever found, unless the male egos are so fragile that such competition is threatening. I don't believe it is.

In how many team sports can girls compete on a par with boys, before puberty? And if women are assuming increasing roles in society outside the home, will soccer aid this revolution? *Time* magazine ("Comes the Revolution," 1978) reported several years ago on women in sports, observing that "the revolution in women's athletics is a full, running tide, bringing with it a sea change—not just in activities, but in attitudes as well" (p. 59).

"Sweating girls are becoming socially acceptable," as one parent put it, and the traditional male characteristics from sports are being experienced by females—aggressiveness, working cooperatively to achieve goals, persistence in skill development, courage, competitiveness, and knowing that success isn't final and failure isn't fatal—all healthy psychological traits. Again, we are sure of one thing: Soccer isn't going to detract from the development of these important character traits; it may even help.

Redirection of Community/Organizational Resources

Soccer is already competing for limited outdoor facilities with football and baseball; it is now starting to compete for indoor space as teams play through the winter. Resistance from athletic directors and recreational center heads has been strong, but community pressures and the sheer numbers of young players have brought pressure for change. We've already examined some of the factors contributing to its growth, and it is my experience that public officials, once they understand soccer's appeal, low costs, mass participation, and encouragement of family and community involvement, quickly become supporters, recognizing the declining base for youth and eventually high school and college football.

Preparation for Life

Sociologists and psychologists commonly agree that sports have a role in preparing young people for adult life. *Time* ("Comes the Revolution," 1978) cited sociologist David Riesman, who said, " 'The road to the board room leads through the locker room.' He explains that American business has been 'socialized' by sport. 'Teamwork provides us with a kind of social cement: loyalty, brotherhood, persistence' " (p. 55).

What traits do we most desire in our young people? In an article in the *Village Voice*, Tom Carson (1984, p. 61) talks about football's "maniacally singleminded reduction of all relations to power relations. . . . Football is the American reality principle at its hairiest—and the conquistadorial spirit is only made more pernicious for being sanitized into the kick-ass whimsy of a harmless good time. . . . It has achieved national pastime status because it really does embody certain basic themes in American life."

Congressman Jack Kemp went further when, in considering America's bid for the 1986 World Cup and the possible expense, he railed on the floor of the House that American "football" is the only *real* football, the epitome of democratic capitalism, whereas soccer, or "European football," is a manifestation of European socialism. I am not sure of his interpretation, but if we listen to the experts writing about corporate America in the years ahead, we are moving toward corporate executives who have "independent, creative minds," who are "visionary," seeing and taking advantage of opportunities, who are "wary of authority" and sensitive to others, and who are nimble and fast, "good at changing positions in fast moving markets" (Wayne, 1984, p. 12). Wayne could have been describing a good soccer player!

The Professionals and International Cooperation

Indoor soccer is here, attracting sell-out crowds, although the purists mumble about its deviation from the traditional outdoor game. But the game proves fans will come out for professional soccer. An eventual full-fledged professional league, representing the best of American youth and bringing identity to cities (as football, baseball, and basketball now do), is the sine qua non for full acceptance of soccer in our country. We may be a decade away, but it will come when the tidal wave hits the beach.

Judging by the outpouring of good will for the United States Olympic Hockey Team in 1980, a truly competitive national soccer team would be therapeutic, even though undue "sports nationalism" has its negative side also. Participation in the World Cup and in international tournaments on a competitive basis would expose the sham of a "World Series" or "World Football Champions" by permitting us to compete in a real "world" championship. James Michener (1976), a former youth soccer player, believes World Cup soccer competition

> offers a new dimension in sport, better in some ways than the comparable Olympics, for the overall level of performance is higher, and I will personally applaud the day when the sport becomes part of the American scene, with or without the sanction of TV. (p. 374)

We have been unduly nationalistic and ethnocentric about our professional sports, looking down with some condescension on other cultures that do not play, or come up to our levels, in football, basketball, or baseball. But they, in turn, perceive us as less than civilized because we can't play soccer with them or even discuss it intelligently. I believe our youth are showing the way, competing successfully and as good sportsmen in international tournaments. They are staying with local families, increasing understanding between cultures, and overcoming language and cultural barriers with their feet and their good will.

I heard a story recently about a visiting Danish youth team playing against a Long Island junior side. An American boy was injured in the game, and a Danish player immediately kicked the ball out-of-bounds to stop the game and enable the player to get medical attention. When the game was restarted with a throw-in several moments later, the American player who took the throw-in sent the ball directly to his Danish opponent as a gesture of appreciation. Winning isn't really everything.

Let me end with my junior team, the Rangers (after the famed Glascow Rangers, my father's team), and the joy on my daughter's face when she scored her first goal. I think of my sense of pride as my kids discover that working together as a team is far more effective than doing it alone. I think of the warm feeling of sportsmanship as our kids line up and shake hands after kicking each other for an hour. I think of our parents who thank me for encouraging their kid to get more out of himself or herself. And I think of the kid who comes up and wants to know when we will be signing up for next season. I couldn't have said it 10 years ago, but soccer is here and none of us will ever be the same again.

References

Arpino, G. (1982, November). After the World Cup. *Notzie Dall'Italia* [News from Italy], 1-4.

Carson, T. (1984, February 7). The offensive line. *Village Voice*, p. 61.

Comes the revolution. (1978, June 26). *Time*, 54-59.

Covitz, R. (1984, February 23). Comets finally remember how to win. *Soccer America*, p. 9.

Fischler, S. (1984, January 31). Indoor soccer. *Village Voice*, 133-134.

Ford, G., & Kane, J. (1984). *Go for goal: Winning drills and exercises for soccer*. Rockleigh, NJ: Allyn & Bacon.

Fox, N. (1978, June 26). Argentina keep a date with destiny by scoring dramatically in extra time. *London Times*, p. 8.

Hoge, W. (1982, June 24). At soccer cup time, Brazil gets the biggest kick. *New York Times*, p. A-2.

Lever, J. (1983). *Soccer madness*. Chicago: University of Chicago Press.

Maddocks, M. (1983, October 7). Trying to like football. *Christian Science Monitor*, p. 21.

Michener, J.A. (1976). *Sports in America*. Greenwich, CT: Faucett.

Mifflin, L. (1982, July 5). Prestige is ABC goal in Cup TV. *New York Times*, p. 15.

Mifflin, L. (1983, November 13). Why N.A.S.L. is in trouble. *New York Times*, pp. 1, 12.

Morris, D. (1981). *The soccer tribe*. London: Jonathan Cape.

Schellscheidt, M. (1983, July 14). *Soccer America*.

Sheldon, T. (1983, September 22). *Soccer America*.

Southmayd, W., & Hoffman, M. (1981). *Sports health: The complete book of athletic injuries*. New York: Quick Fox.

Vecsey, G. (1982, July 9). Now U.S. may get a turn. *New York Times*, pp. A-1, 16.

Wayne, L. (1984, March 25). A pioneer spirit sweeps business. *New York Times*, pp. 1, 12.

CHAPTER 19

1984: Perversions of the Play-Impulse

James H. Weatherly
Mississippi State University
Joan Weatherly
Memphis State University

Just as the 18th century was coming to a close—its optimism first fanned, then dimmed by the French Revolution—the German poet Schiller (1793/1967) described mankind's inherent sense of aesthetic freedom in terms of play. What later came to be known as "the play-impulse" (*spieltrieb*) springs, he thought, from excess energy. This energy can be channelled into creativity that, spontaneously produced by his imagination, completes the creator's existence, leading to activities neither subserving the necessity of nature nor fulfilling any moral duty, yet balancing both. But, he warned, the creative impulse that can make man playing "truly man" can also be perverted in two general ways. Deprived of the proper exercise of the play-impulse, man becomes enslaved by gross materialism or by the moral sense restraining him from within. Schiller's theory is summarized in the *Lincoln Library* as follows: "Yielding to his appetites," one "lapses into a hopeless, passive state" (slave type) and "opposing them, he becomes a stern, vigilant guardian of the law, understanding no password save duty" (dictator type) ("The Play Impulse," p. 1503). The spirit is satiated in the too-passive state and starved in the too-watchful attitude, the individual in either case lacking the ability to reconcile these opposite states (Schiller, 1793/1967).

Just as the 19th century was coming to a close, Thomas Hardy, the English novelist and poet, informed by Darwin and Spencer, wrote a powerful, pessimistic novel, *Jude the Obscure* (1895/1972), summing up the 19th century and looking forward to 20th-century existentialism. In this strange book, literature's strangest child, Little Father Time, murders a brother and a sister and kills himself, thus symbolically wiping out the century's optimistic faith in progress. Halfway through the 20th century, George Orwell wrote *1984* (1949/1961), a novel depicting the postwar world and warning of what might come to pass before the end of the century in a totalitarian world. One of the most horrifying aspects of that nightmare novel is the brutality of the dictatorial children, illustrative of Schiller's dictator type. Recently, on the very eve of 1984, Neil Postman (1982) has warned that childhood is disappearing, a phenomenon already prophesied by Hardy in 1895. Lurking in the background of all of these views of play and children is the machine on which a new vision of the universe was modeled, but which by 1950, according to Orwell and Postman, had degenerated into the telescreen from which Big Brother watches to ensure that even the very thought of creativity or the play-impulse will be trampled under the iron heel of power, forever perverted along with Oldspeak (*culture*, to use Schiller's term).

In his recent book *The Disappearance of Childhood* (1982), Neil Postman argues that "the period between 1850 and 1950 represents the high-watermark of childhood" and that "the establishment of television by 1950 completed the Beginning of the End" of childhood, for television is equally accessible to child and adult, requiring no special skills (pp. 67, 79). According to Postman, childhood began with the development of the printing press in the early Renaissance and the need for children to develop communication skills (word imagery) to read and understand printed material. This gave rise to the crucial import of secrecy in distinguishing children from adults and led to the reinvention of schools to teach the "secret" mysteries of adulthood. The possession of secrets gives adults the authority to determine appropriate and shameful behavior for children—shame being, says Postman, "the mechanism by which barbarism is held at bay" (pp. 80-86). By the turn of the century, says Postman, "Childhood came to be defined as a biological category, not a product of culture," and ironically "the symbolic environment that gave life to childhood began to be disassembled, slowly, and inconspicuously" (pp. 67-68).

The crucial implication of the invention of the telegraph (1844) is that unlike Darwin's ideas, which were "embodied in language," "Morse offered us ideas embodied in a technology, which is to say, they were hidden from view and therefore never argued" (p. 69). At the time of its invention, almost everyone seems to have thought that the telegraph was "a neutral conveyance" that implied no ideas (p. 70). But ultimately the telegraph "moved history into the background and amplified the instant and simultaneous present." And "most important, *the telegraph began the process of making information uncontrollable*" (p. 71).

Several of Postman's insights seem to clarify certain aspects of Jude, particularly the strange, never-well-explained title of Hardy's novel, *Jude the Obscure*, and its even stranger child's name, "Little Father Time." According to Postman (1982), "electric speed was not an extension of human senses, but a denial of them," and Little Father Time, who is first seen coming to Jude and Sue all alone in a railway car, is associated with machinery; in one stroke, says Postman, the telegraph eliminated "both time and space as dimensions of human communication, and therefore disembodied information to an extent that far surpassed both the written and printed word and eliminated personality" (p. 70). In *Jude the Obscure*, which summarizes 19th-century culture, Hardy dramatizes much of what Postman says in *The Disappearance of Childhood*.

Hardy's strange, brooding Little Father Time cannot be dismissed merely as mentally deranged when he murders his brother and sister, hangs himself, leaves a note saying, "Done because we are too menny," and becomes the "nodal point of all the accidents, mistakes, fears, and errors of his parents" (p. 363). When Little Father Time's stepmother insists afterward that she caused his actions, the boy's father Jude answers as follows:

> It was in his nature to do it. The doctor says there are such boys springing up amongst us—boys of a sort unknown in the last generation—the outcome of new views of life. They seem to see all of its terrors before they are old enough to have staying power to resist them. He says it is the beginning of the coming universal wish not to live. (p. 364)

Sue Bridehead insists, however, that she is to blame for the deaths:

> Ah, but it was I who incited him really, though I didn't know I was doing it! I talked to the child as one should only talk to people of mature age. I said the world was against us, that it was better to be out of life than in it at this price; and he took it literally. And I told him I was going to have another child. It upset him. O how bitterly he upbraided me! (p. 365)

When Jude asks why she told him these things, Sue can only say, " 'I can't tell. It was that I wanted to be truthful. I couldn't bear deceiving him as to the facts of life. And yet I wasn't truthful, for with a false delicacy I told him too obscurely' " (pp. 365-366). Her want of self-control, she says, kept her from telling him "pleasant untruths," rather than "half realities" (p. 366). Postman would argue that secrecy that should be maintained as a factor of childhood has been violated, thus causing the tragedy.

Throughout the novel, Hardy is concerned with the encroachment of the machine into the garden, depicting as in no other of his 15 novels (written between 1870-1895) the results of rapid changes, especially in transportation. Jude and Sue are often seen parting from each other at railway platforms. One of the novel's poignant scenes finds Little Father Time on his railway ride to join his father and stepmother, who at the time of his arrival still have some of their sense of play and try without any success to cheer him up by taking him to the Agricultural Show and Fair. But Father Time's brooding, morbid spirit cannot be touched by either Jude, Sue, or the younger children. Without yielding to any gross appetites, Father Time, nevertheless, lapses into the hopeless, passive state that, according to Schiller, characterizes the slave type. His father, Jude, for all his own brooding, half-cynical tendency, manages to retain his sense of play—potentially creative but stifled—and even in his piteous dying hour possesses a sense of irony.

In George Orwell's 1984 (1949/1961), childhood, like every aspect of humanism, has almost totally disappeared. That humanism depends on Oldspeak—history, language, and memory—is made clear as Winston Smith, the protagonist, a physical weakling who loathes the regularly televised, mandatory exercises (Physical Jerks), tries to recall his own childhood during which he had been torn from his parents: "But it was no use, he could not remember: nothing remained of his childhood except a series of bright-lit tableaux, occurring against no background and almost unintelligible'' (p. 7). Finally, at the end of the novel, having achieved what analytical psychology would call healthy individuation, Winston, duped by O'Brien and the Party and their seeming humanism, does not realize that he is submerging the *healthy* gestalt of his mother.

The reader does, however, get a good picture of the children in Oceania—which includes England, Western Europe, and America—from Winston's neighbor children, the Parsons, a boy of 9 and a girl of 7. Even their mother, who keeps looking nervously at them, is afraid of these monstrous children; in fact, ''what most struck Winston was the look of helpless fright on the woman's grayish face'' when the boy rudely ''bellows'' after him (p. 23). Mrs. Parsons tries to apologize for their noisiness, saying, '' 'They're disappointed because they couldn't go see the hanging, that's what it is.' '' The boy roars ''in his huge voice,'' '' 'Why can't we go and see the hanging?' '' and the little girl capers about chanting, '' 'Want to see the hanging! Want to see the hanging!' '' (p. 23). Winston remembers that ''some Eurasian prisoners, guilty of war crimes, were to be hanged in the Park that evening. This happened about once a month, and was a popular spectacle. Children always clamored to see it'' (p. 23).

It is clear that the play-impulse is not dead, but perverted, in the ''boy'' and ''girl'' (one aspect of their problem and times being reflected in the fact that they are not mentioned by name): One of them tries ''to keep tune with the military music from the telescreen'' on a comb, and they especially love playing ''Hate Song,'' which is popular during Hate Week. Evidently the children, or at least the boy, play at physical sports, for Winston sees strewn about the room—in which ''everything had a battered, trampled-on look, as though the place had just been visited by some large violent animal'' (p. 21)—games equipment. There were ''hockey sticks, boxing gloves, a burst football, a pair of sweat shorts turned inside out'' (p. 21), though some of these could belong to the elder Parsons. They attend some sort of school, for there are some exercise books, the only books of any sort in sight. The children blast into the room with a trampling of boots and ''another blast of the comb'':

> Up with your hands! yelled a savage voice. A handsome, tough-looking boy of nine had popped up from behind the table and was menacing him with a toy automatic pistol, while his small sister, about two years younger, made the same gesture with a fragment of wood. Both of them were dressed in the blue shorts, gray shirts, and red neckerchiefs which were the uniform of the Spies. Winston raised his hands above his head, but with an uneasy feeling, so vicious was the boy's demeanor, that it was not altogether a game.

> You're a traitor! yelled the boy. You're a thought-criminal! You're a Eurasian spy! I'll shoot you, I'll vaporize you, I'll send you to the salt mines! (pp. 22-23)

The hardened viciousness of the children, so like that often seen in movies depicting Nazi children, illustrates what Schiller calls the dictator type of perversion of the play-impulse. These children are spirit-starved and have become "stern, vigilant guardians of the law, understanding no password save duty" ("The Play Impulse," p. 1503). Indeed, hardly a week passes without at least one *Times* report of a "child hero" turning in his parents. The Parsons children would just as soon turn in their parents as Winston or anyone else to get Spy points. Later the girl reports her father, the most loyal Party member, for yelling "Down with Big Brother" in his sleep. As they jump about, shouting "Thought-Criminal," they are frightening, "like the gamboling of tiger cubs which will soon grow up into man-eaters." Winston sees "a sort of calculating ferocity in the boy's eye, a quite evident desire to hit or kick" him "and a consciousness of being very nearly big enough to do so," and thinks, "It was a good job it was not a real pistol he was holding" (p. 23). Later their father tells Winston that he has threatened to take the boy's catapult away, but he brags about their constant lookout for spies, reporting that his little girl helped capture a foreign spy and again that they both burned a suspicious-seeming old lady to death (p. 55).

In the speech he imagines for Big Brother, Winston creates Comrade Ogilvy, who at the age of 3 "had refused all toys except a drum, a sub-machine gun, and a model helicopter" and who at six, "a year early, by a special relaxation of the rules" had

> joined the Spies; at nine he had been a troop leader. At eleven he had denounced his uncle to the Thought Police after overhearing a conversation which appeared to him to have criminal tendencies. At seventeen he had been a district organizer of the Junior Anti-Sex League. At nineteen he had designed a hand grenade which had been adopted by the Ministry of Peace and which, at its first trial, had killed thirty-one Eurasian prisoners in one burst. At twenty-three he had perished in action. (p. 42)

Big Brother's further comments "on the purity and singlemindedness" of Comrade Ogilvy's life reveal that Oceania's ideal hero would be a dictator type as described by Schiller:

> He was a total abstainer and a nonsmoker, had no recreations except a daily hour in the gymnasium, and had taken a vow of celibacy, believing marriage and the care of a family to be incompatible with a twenty-four-hour-a-day devotion to duty. He had no subjects of conversation except the principles of Ingsoc, and no aim in life except the defeat of the Eurasian enemy and the hunting-down of spies, saboteurs, thought-criminals, and traitors generally. (p. 42)

Winston's reflections on the typical "horrible" children of Oceania echo those in the Ogilvie speech he wrote for Big Brother:

> What was worst of all was that by means of such organizations as the Spies they were systematically turned into ungovernable little savages, and yet this produced in them no tendency whatever to rebel against the discipline

of the Party. On the contrary, they adored the Party and everything connected with it. The songs, the processions, the banners, the hiking, the drilling with dummy rifles, the yelling of slogans, the worship of Big Brother—it was all a sort of glorious game to them. All their ferocity was turned outwards, against the enemies of the State, against foreigners, traitors, saboteurs, thought-criminals. (p. 24)

Hence these children, constantly fed a diet of propaganda on the telescreen and in the youth organizations, and totally deprived of all the child-creating secrets, require no Hate Week activities to arouse their hate of the enemy of the state. Clearly they exemplify Schiller's dictator type.

Including George Orwell among those who would say no to the question, "Can a culture preserve human values and create new ones by allowing modern technology the fullest possible authority to control its destiny?" Postman argues that childhood "must, in the long run, be a victim of what is happening. . . . Electricity makes nonsense of the kind of information environment that gives rise to and nurtures childhood" (pp. 145-147). Pictures, according to Postman, call upon our emotions, not our reason, "making us feel, not think" and virtually putting our minds to sleep (p. 73). In *1984*, Orwell suggests that the image of Big Brother is crucial because totalitarianism depends on emotion and the slightly mysterious, *seemingly* loving Big Brother makes the Party *appear* benevolent and humanistic. Certainly Orwell was mainly describing postwar England and the western world in 1948 (the numbers of which he reversed to make 1984) and not making predictions about 1984, but Postman hits precisely on the main problem of electrical technology as described by Orwell. Indeed, much of what Postman says about the disappearance of childhood brought on by the "Total Disclosure Medium" is anticipated in *1984* with the effects of electric surveillance. The essence of Orwell's Appendix, "Principles of Newspeak," is that the Party's official language is a clipped, telegraphic, totally utilitarian language that annihilates man's ability to think and to make comparisons between the abstract and the concrete, the very essence of humanism, language, and literacy. Finally, all spirit of the play-impulse is gone for Winston—the "last man in Europe," as Orwell thought of calling the book—as are all his abilities to reconcile opposites sexually or linguistically.

As in Orwell's *1984*, the world of today is filled with many perversions of the play-impulse. Sports today are played with serious intent and as a test of our national virtue. Orwell (1945/1968) notes the following in "The Sporting Spirit," a 1945 essay about sports in the West:

> You play to win, and the game has little meaning unless you do your utmost to win. On the village green, where you pick up sides and no feeling of local patriotism is involved, it is possible to play simply for the fun and exercise; but as soon as the question of prestige arises, as soon as you feel that you and some larger unit will be disgraced if you lose, the most savage combative instincts are aroused. (p. 41)

Concrete examples of this ferocity have been seen in international sporting contests that lead to orgies of hatred (as seen in the 1936 Olympic games in Berlin and in the 1980 games in Russia), with politics and nationalism more important (as seen in the 1984 games in the U.S.) than play. Serious sport, writes Orwell, is laced with hatred, jealousy, boastfulness, disregard of all rules, and sadistic pleasure in witnessing violence, or "war minus the shooting" (p. 42). In *1984*, children take their war games literally; so today in Lebanon, Iran, and other countries, children aged 9 to 13 are engaged in war and hate games, as children are called upon to perform adult tasks. Though maimed and captured, the children are still motivated to live and die for the Ayatollah just as the children in *1984* are taught to give allegiance to Big Brother. In *1984*, Orwell predicted the huge hordes of intensely emotional, loyal Eurasians ready to die irrationally for their leader.

Today there appears to be a growing confusion between what is child's play and what is adult work, which is according to Postman a symptom of the disappearance of childhood. Recently, a quarterback received $40 million for a 43-year contract to play a child's game, and a 19-year-old (still eligible to play high school ball) was given a $6-million contract to play professionally with adults. The confusion is compounded when a 4-year scholarship that provides educational and tutorial benefits, room, board, and laundry is defined as mere compensation for play; however, a football jersey given as a memento is defined as pay for work. Another obvious symptom of the merging of childhood and adult values can be seen in Little League baseball and peewee football. As with most youth sports, the games "have become increasingly official, mock-professional and extremely serious" (Postman, 1982, p. 129). There is no spontaneous making up of rules or fooling around. Children play their games without spontaneity and under careful supervision, with pep rallies and crowd behavior similar to Orwell's "Two-Minute Hate" sessions. As Postman notes and Orwell dramatizes, "For adults, play is serious business. As childhood disappears, so does the child's view of play" (Postman, 1982, p. 121). With this intense competition among youth, we are seeing the entry of more children into professional and world-class amateur sports, but fewer and fewer children are playing the traditional childhood games just for fun.

Even crime is no longer an exclusively adult behavior, with younger and younger children being charged with violent crimes. The frequency of serious childhood crimes has pushed the courts to try many children in adult courts. The trial of one Florida youth, who claimed television inspired him to murder an elderly neighbor, was itself televised. Not unlike Hardy's Little Father Time, this child seems to be a slave type, a slave to the "telescreen." Moreover, Hardy's prediction that children would come "to will not to live" is currently reflected in the alarming suicide rates of children and teenagers. Children are again being viewed as miniature adults, with an attendant increase in teenage pregnancies and venereal disease. Child alcoholism and drug addiction, prime examples of Schiller's slave type, are also increasing. Not only do little girls have beauty contests, but they as well as boys are used for commercial advertising, pornography, and sexual exploitation. Bizarre stories of literally enslaved children turn up all too frequently on the "telescreen."

It must of course be admitted that although electricity does "make nonsense of child nurturing information" (Postman, 1982, pp. 146-147), it nevertheless has given rise to a new form of play that reasserts, or can reassert, the validity of Schiller's theory of the play-impulse—video games. These games can result in any of the three types Schiller named: the dictator, the slave, or the creator. It is probably not too soon to say that video games will help produce some of the first category, millions of the second, and precious few of the third. On the other hand, the phenomenon of video games reflects the truth of another of Postman's ideas—that childhood and adult games are becoming more and more alike. Games have become, according to Edmonds (1982), symbolically and literally a religion, with the underlying metaphysic of sport equivalent to overcoming the fear of death. Video games, such as Pac-Man, are, says McFarland (1982), "based on the Christian understanding of life" (p. 956). As play becomes enmeshed with ritual, ceremony, and mysticism, it becomes a serious, consuming task that appears to stifle the play-impulse.

Orwell's *1984* was—as has already been said hundreds of times—a warning. Postman says that his own work is a warning, but he does not offer much hope that it will be heeded. Hardy was obviously sending a warning to the 20th century. Schiller's theory, too, was a warning, but even though it offers the positive alternative of creativity that we always complain about not getting, the destructive types seem to emerge with greater and greater frequency (the pun on *frequency* is intentional). Perhaps now is a good time to reconsider Schiller's Platonic idea of aesthetic education and to at least consider Morse's famous message: "What hath God wrought?"

References

Edmonds, A.O. (1982). Sports, ritual and myth. In D.W. Hoover & J.T.A. Koumoulides (Eds.), *Conspectus of history* (Vol. I, No. 8, pp. 27-42). Muncie, IN: Ball State University.

Hardy, T. (1972). *Jude the obscure* (F.R. Southerington, Ed.). New York: Bobbs-Merrill. (Original work published 1895)

McFarland, J.R. (1982). The theology of Pac-Man. *Christian Century*, **99**, 956-958.

Orwell, G. (1961). *1984*. New York: NAL. (Original work published 1949)

Orwell, G. (1968). The sporting spirit. In S. Orwell & I. Angus (Eds.), *The collected essays, journalism and letters of George Orwell* (Vol. 4, pp. 40-44). New York: Harcourt, Brace & World.

The Play Impulse. (1937). In *Fine arts, Lincoln library of essential information* (p. 1503). New York: Frontier Press.

Postman, N. (1982). *The disappearance of childhood*. New York: Delacorte Press.

Schiller, F. (1967). *On the aesthetic education of man* (E.A. Wilkinson & L.A. Willoughby, Eds. and Trans.). Oxford, England: Clarendon. (Original work published 1793)